ONWARD

PETER LANG
New York • Washington, D.C./Baltimore
Bern • Frankfurt am Main • Berlin • Vienna • Paris

Peter Baker, editor

ONWARD

CONTEMPORARY
POETRY AND POETICS

PETER LANG
New York • Washington, D.C./Baltimore
Bern • Frankfurt am Main • Berlin • Vienna • Paris

Library of Congress Cataloging-in-Publication Data

Onward: contemporary poetry and poetics/
Peter Nicholas Baker, editor.
p. cm.
Includes bibliographical references.
1. American poetry—20th century—History and criticism—Theory, etc.
2. Experimental poetry, American—History and criticism. 3. Poets,
American—20th century—Interviews. 4. Language and languages in
literature. 5. American poetry—20th century. 6. Poetry—Authorship.
7. Poetics—Poetry. 8. Poetics. I. Baker, Peter.
PS325.069   811'.5409—dc20   96-8308
ISBN 0-8204-3032-3 (Pbk.)

Die Deutsche Bibliothek-CIP-Einheitsaufnahme

Onward: contemporary poetry and poetics/
Peter Nicholas Baker, ed.
– New York; Washington, D.C./Baltimore; Bern;
Frankfurt am Main; Berlin; Vienna; Paris: Lang.
ISBN 0-8204-3032-3 (Pbk.)
NE: GT

Cover design by James F. Brisson.

The paper in this book meets the guidelines for permanence and durability
of the Committee on Production Guidelines for Book Longevity
of the Council of Library Resources.

Printed in the United States of America.

Acknowledgments

Grateful acknowledgment is made to reprint previously published works:

Writings and poems by Bernadette Mayer previously published in various small magazines reprinted by permission of the author.

"Rejection of Closure" by Lyn Hejinian previously published in *Poetics Journal* 4 (1984), reprinted by permission of the author. Lyn Hejinian, *The Cell* (Los Angeles: Sun & Moon Press, 1992), pp. 8, 9-10, 20-21, 33, 55-56, 57-58, 132, 161-162, 163. ©1992 by Lyn Hejinian. Reprinted by permission of the publisher.

"A Defence of Poetry," by Charles Bernstein, is a reply to "Making (non)sense of postmodernist poetry" by Brian McHale, published in *Language, Text and Context*, ed. Michael Toolan (London and New York: Routledge, 1992); it originally appeared in *Aerial*. Section two is adapted from an interview which originally appeared in Manuel Brito's *A Suite of Poetic Voices* (1994). "Pinky Swear" and "Rivulets of the Dead" originally appeared in *Turbulence*. Section 5 originally appeared in "Frame Lock" in *College Literature*. Section 7 is from an ongoing interview with Tom Beckett and originally appeared in *The Iowa Review*. "The Inevitable Flow of Material Things through the Pores of the Years" originally appeared in *Sulfur*. All reprinted here by permission of the author.

"Inserting the Mirror," by Rosmarie Waldrop, was published in *The Reproduction of Profiles* (New York: New Directions, 1987). Copyright © 1987 by Rosmarie Waldrop.

A French version of "Dormouse Poem," by Harry Mathews, appeared in the first issue of *Revue de la littérature générale* (Paris: Éditions P.O.L., 1995).

Previously published poems by David Bergman reprinted by permission of the author.

"Were You: Notes & A Poem for Michael Palmer," by John Taggart, from *Loop* (Los Angeles: Sun & Moon Press, 1991), pp. 79-102. © 1991 by John Taggart. Reprinted by permission of the publisher.

"On Drafts: A Memorandum of Understanding," by Rachel Blau DuPlessis, is a revision—both an expansion and a cutting—of a statement under the same title published in *TO: A Journal of Poetry, Prose + the Visual Arts* 1, 1 (1992): 72-77. With thanks to the editors Seth Frechie and Andrew Mossin. "Draft 11:

Schwa," published in *Drafts 3-14* (Elmwood, Conn.: Potes & Poets Press, 1991). © 1991 by Rachel Blau DuPlessis, all rights reserved. With thanks to the editor Peter Ganick.

"Floating Trees," "Flame," "Like Rocks," "Like Peaches," "The Shepherd of Resumed Desire," "Like Someone Driving to Texas by Herself," "OP-ED," and "Provisional Remarks/ On Being/ A Poet/ Of Arkansas," by C. D. Wright, originally appeared in *Chelsea, Field, Torque, The Colorado Review, Phoebe, Caliban,* and *The Southern Review,* respectively. Reprinted by permission of the author. "The box this comes in," from *String Light* (Athens: University of Georgia Press, 1991), pp. 59-62, reprinted by permission of the publisher.

Poems by Albert Cook from the volumes, *Affability Blues, Delayed Answers, Modulars* and *Modes* (Lewiston, NY: Mellen Press), reprinted by permission of the author.

"Was That a Real Poem Or Did You Just Make It Up Yourself," by Robert Creeley, from *Collected Essays of Robert Creeley,* reprinted by permission of Regents of the University of California and the University of California Press. "Nothing New," originally appeared in *Kiosk* (1995). "Four Days in Vermont," first appeared in *Conjunctions* 24 (1995); reprinted by permission of the editor.

"Closure," by Stephen Rodefer, originally was published in *Emergency Measures* (Great Barrington, Mass.: The Figures, 1987); "Preface," "Codex," and "Index," originally published in *Four Lectures* (Great Barrington, Mass.: The Figures, 1982); "Prologue to Language Doubling" originally appeared in *Jimmy and Lucy's House of K*; "Enclosure of Elk" originally was published in *Passing Duration* (Providence: Burning Deck, 1991); "The Library of Label" originally appeared in *Contact II*; "Statement for Reading the Prioresse's Room" originally appeared in *Angel Exhaust* (U.K.); "Brief to Butterick" was first published in *The Scope of Words: In Honor of Albert S. Cook* (New York: Peter Lang, 1991); all reprinted here by permission of the author.

"Our," by Clark Coolidge, was originally published in *Space* (1970); "[from] A Letter to Paul Metcalf," originally appeared in *In the American Tree* (Orono, Maine: National Poetry Foundation, 1986); Section XIII of *Mine* (Great Barrington, Mass.: The Figures, 1982); "A Sex of Lists," from *Mesh* (Detroit: In Camera, 1982); "From Notebooks (1976-1982)" was published in *Code of Signals* (Berkeley: North Atlantic, 1983); "[from] Regarding Morton Feldman's Music and Wherever It All Now Goes" originally appeared in *Sulfur*; "XI: Letters" and "XLII: Last" from *The Book of During* (Great Barrington, Mass.: The Figures, 1991); all reprinted by permission of the author.

Contents

ix

Poetics (Introduction)

Poetics is a vital, vast, ancient, yet strangely neglected field. Except, of course, by poets. And yet many if not most poets would probably assent to the proposition that a poetics is best discerned from the poem itself. Any statement on poetics presents immediate difficulties for such an aesthetic, because the statement risks being seen as ancillary to the poem, and may actually misrepresent the *implicit poetics* in the poet's work. Given these risks, many poets choose reticence as their primary mode—one limit of such reticence being silence—which is then sometimes accompanied by an active disdain for the subject.

One way to approach the idea of *implicit poetics* is in terms of an immanentist theory of language, or the idea that words bear direct relation to what they represent, even carrying a little bit of the essence of the thing in the word. Such immanentist theories deriving from the religious tradition ("and the word was with God and the word was God") drove William of Occam, in the fourteenth century, to counterpose the complete separation of word and referent, in his philosophy of nominalism. Jacques Derrida is often accused of representing such a nominalist stance in his philosophy of deconstruction (as I discuss in *Deconstruction and the Ethical Turn*). Ezra Pound's language theory is explicitly immanentist, as when he instructs his Italian translator of *The Cantos*: "Don't worry about the meaning of the poem. Translate accurately line by line. The meaning is inherent in the material." Pound's poetics in *The Cantos* thus demonstrates what I call (in *Obdurate Brilliance*) the "myth of transparency," or the ideology of direct apprehension of the surrounding context from the text of the poem. The opposite error—that the meaning of a text can be established through saturating the text with its contexts—currently goes under the name of the new historicism.

Without worrying too much (right now) about the accuracy of labels, much of what is called mainstream poetry today operates either knowingly or unknowingly out of the transparency model of language. Anthologies of poetics by mainstream poets are thus usually concerned with craft and technique—how the poem is put together—when the poet is not discussing where he or she went on his/her last vacation or MacArthur grant to gather material. The poem's meaning is either inherent in the material (themes) or what it represents (nature). This view of poetics as purely *practical* and *personal* both derives from and sustains the contemporary poetic practice variously termed workshop or MFA verse, and can be found exemplified in nearly every issue of the *AWP Chronicle*.

In the past twenty-five or so years vibrant alternatives in the theory and practice of poetry have risen out of the movement known as Language poetry. Following the "radical modernism" of Stein, Zukofsky and others, in Charles Bernstein's appellation, or what Marjorie Perloff has called "the other tradition," this practice has as one explicit goal (among others), citing Zukofsky, "to stop the gaze on words as things." By now, Language poetry has been around long enough that, like deconstruction or Mt. Pinatubo, it no longer exists, but its practitioners, many of them represented here, are still very active and its effects, as John Ashbery indicates in his interview, may be even more interesting than the initial productions of those associated with the movement. Literary history (which H. R. Jauss terms "conceivably the worst medium through which to display the historicity of literature") is already at work deriving a genealogy to explain the transition between the radical modernism of Stein, Zukofsky and others, and the Language poets. Materials for such a genealogy are generously represented here in the selections by John Ashbery and Robert Creeley, as well as those of Clark Coolidge and Bernadette Mayer.

There is no raw material.

So Harry Mathews begins his contribution. Mathews, a member of the *Ourvoir de littérature potentielle*, or OULIPO group, brings impeccable credentials to his theorizing, or non-theorizing, of the production of the poem. As with Lyn Hejinian's already-classic essay, "Against Closure" (revised and expanded for publication here), Mathews' statement is manifesto-like, and thus reminiscent of the radical

2

modernism of André Breton and early surrealism. Manifestos are less concerned with explanation than with demonstration; they attempt not to analyze, but rather to make manifest artistic practices and attitudes. Looking at the materials assembled here, it has impressed me that there are two clear poles, or limits, or borders, to their expressive strategies. If the manifesto is one such border, the other is collage. Some of these collage assemblages, such as those of Charles Bernstein and Nicole Brossard, were created or at least shaped explicitly for this collection. Others are the results of collaborations between the poets and/or the editor and/or the editor's friends, notably Rod Smith, Lee Ann Brown, and Peter Gizzi. In addition to the indefatigable efforts of Rod Smith, the preparation of this volume has been aided considerably by Jennifer Ashton, Pete Hill, and Michael Ruby.

The relation of poetics to poetry always to some extent resists explanation. Yet we are drawn to explore this relation as part of a life commitment to poetry, a commitment those in the present volume recognize under the sign of necessity, Samuel Beckett's "all that I can, more than I could." Each poet's approach necessarily involves questions of individual history and practice while grounding the work in communities of poets and artists actively exploring the creative imagination. This volume emerges from these communities and hopefully will serve as a resource for those already involved in the work and those yet to come.

Or, as Bernadette Mayer likes to say, "Onward."

Peter Baker
Washington D.C., 1996

3

20 Questions about Form or New Forms:

1. Does anyone know what the form of a poem is?
2. What is the form of a past poem we agree to admire?
3. What is the form of a modern poem we agree has changed the world?
4. What is the form most indigenous to contemporary poetry?
5. What poet has written most newly?
6. What do you want to find out?
7. What do you know? Who knows it?
8. Who knows what you do not know?
9. Who can say the things you know most well?
10. Who knows things you don't know and says them?
11. Who says them beautifully and well?
12. Is poetry exact?
13. How can we find out in writing the answers to questions that occur in sleep?
14. What past form (sonnet, etc.) is most full of knowledge, relevance to the moment now?
15. What form reflects thought and its conclusions best? For the past? For now?
16. If we could find the form that reflects the mind's actual workings, would we win the Nobel prize?
17. What is sweet tea?
18. Do new forms become sort of in the authorship of sleep?
19. What do you learn of form when you begin to speak or write?
20. How does form become right next to the side of the mind?
21. Still we haven't gotten to new forms, have we?
22. A form implies that something is done, besides a beginning it seems to have an end like the the indirect and ending paper on which we want to write now?
23. So what for form, it is just a known.
24. Is there enough paper so you can sleep beside the new forms?

Experimental Writing, or, Writing the Long Work

1. "The writer does not yet know what words are. He deals only with abstractions from the source point of words. The painter's ability to touch & handle his medium led to montage techniques 60 years ago. It is to be hoped that the extension of cut-up techniques will lead to more precise verbal experiments closing this gap & giving a whole new dimension to writing, put (the writer) in tactile communication with his medium. This in turn could lead to a precise science of words & show how certain word combinations produce certain effects on the human nervous system."

2. The workshop will involve language experiments to lead to, or, while you are in the process of, a long work. For the time being this long work could be described as keeping a journal, & for the time being keeping a journal is simply writing IT all in one book AS IF it is one work it is.

3. Writers: & scientists: Whitman, Burroughs, Coolidge, Poe, Gertrude Stein, Einstein, Wittgenstein, Ashbery, Dada, Surrealist, Chomsky, Lilly, Lacan, Kerouac, Zukofsky, Joyce &tc.

4. Starting November the workshop will have an extra night every week for readings performances lectures etc. by people in the workshop & others whose work connects with ours. (This is a long term writing project with no end at all (see #7)).

5. "...things dont happen in logical sequence & people dont think in logical sequence. Any writer who hopes to approximate what actually occurs in the mind & body of his characters cannot confine himself to such an arbitrary structure as 'logical' sequence. Joyce was accused of being unintelligible & he was presenting only one level of cerebral events: conscious sub-vocal speech. I think it is possible to create

multilevel events & characters that a reader could comprehend with his entire organic being."

6. Dream experiments: investigate the dreaming mechanism as it relates to writing; see if the dream can produce poem, song &tc., viable works in our culture; dream as a state of consciousness, dream as problem-solving or problem-setting technique in art; working with the dream as a group of writers, and

7. Dream's an analogy to re-processing in process, so rewrite it, it's changed, but it's a memory according to how you record it now & as it could go on forever, this could, dream's a memory kept in process kept in present & as it could go on forever, this could, & so if you are interested in a writing project that has any end at all, the workshop can provide you with false ending in publishing.

8. Most of the experiments & investigations, then, center around writing as a state of consciousness: we write, read it & study the act of writing. Craft & technique are analyzed only in the light of the revelation of tricks, in the traditional sense. Plagiarism is encouraged and all tricks are shared.

9. We are not interested in the poem as precious object on the page, with alot of white space all around, but only in the poem or writing as part of long-term process & as lead-in to more experiments & investigations in whatever tradition to achieve things you think could not be achieved in words, to liberate words, to escape from the image-prison &

10. to find what more is communicable, or, what is communicable now

11. in reading & writing.

12. "...& Finnegans Wake rather represents a trap into which experimental writing can fall when it becomes purely experimental. I would go so far with any given experiment & then come back; that is, I am coming back now to write purely conventional straightforward narrative. But applying what I have learned from the cut-up & other techniques to the problem of conventional writing. It's simply if you go too far in one direction, you can never get back & you're out there in complete isolation, like this anthropologist who spent the last 20 years of his life on the sweet potato controversy (which way it floated)..."

13. List of experiments, lists of magazines to publish in, reading list: available on request. Also, anthology of dream material.

14. All quotes from William Burroughs, *The Job*.

Thoughts on a Course .

what are experiments I would do now?
> write gibberish
> write in a form
> work with dreams
> find the structure already in a piece
> outside-inside

what do I know now, what would I read now?

> poetry is everyday
> what is rhyme
> what are dictionaries

> what is song
> hearing & color — synesthesia

to teach about

> music in the ear, instinct
> visuals — pictures, objects, window, room, outdoors

a structure for a lecture as there is structure in the room
> — hermetic ideals — as there is structure in the words
> ——leads to memory

> memory is everyday, ways of living
> what is concentration
> ——leads to consciousness & dreaming

what is specific

methods, the mirror, the son, what is listened to,
what is created as pure imagination (Hawthorne)

books & influences: scientific texts, what Graham
Greene said about the orindary man looking orindary
writing novels, the poet not; what Neal Cassady said
about words torturing him

writing slow and writing fast

to teach about

imitating, stealing, writing to pictures and writing
to sounds

what is new, I don't know

should I explain Clark, Dadaists, Shakespeare,

grammar & the sentence

the rest is history

what is humanism, idealism, liberalism
skip that
what is order, skip that too

what can I teach

rip pages out of books at random & study them
what are random methods, old age like the incorporation
of that, what John Cage says about mushrooms & being radical

You hear with your eyes & you see with your ears — G. Stein
        was able to do everything & nothing

what is mystical — the song & the knowledge in it
        when you meditate, when you take a word or sound,
        Jackson Mac Low, Abraham Abulafia, lists, lists are
        forms, hermetic memory, control of the universe

what is given, language is inherent, who is speaking,
        who am I speaking to, memory is better before language,
        psychology a prod, science an invention

what enters in — ideas, food, friends, knowledge, events
        better skip that

back to what is new
        what is secret, what is shared, what language to
        what extent is shared (private language)

tricks: beginning & ending, formulas, rhythms, using other
        writing, tape recording, intimacy (wrong category),
        waiting to see what is shared

what is studying, inside & out

what is American, the Latinate sentence from England, the
        word from Williams, the closed door on imagery,
        the short sentence, the Anglo-Saxon thud, the busy
        memory, the psychology, the myriad attitude (stance),

what is unavoidable, the audience, the proliferation

untitled what's thought of as a boundless...

untitled what's thought of as a boundless, continuous expanse extending in all directions or in three dimensions within which all material things are contained at this moment as a sign of the infinitive the matter at hand compared to one of two things compared to one of two places compared to more than one of two things no more than what's thought of as a boundless continuous expanse extending in all directions or in three dimensions within which all material things are contained in addition never existing before but known for the first time in addition putting as much as possible into from a point outside to one inside the one that's nearby furthest from the first a place sort of slang putting as much as possible into from a point outside to one inside my presence here to express the future and imply intention in addition to express the future and imply intention my presence here sound by ringing more than one of two things in that place compared to more than one of two things and the other of them compared to more than one of two things and the first one of them no more than not good-looking in addition having been around for a long time moving along toward the east when I face north the one that's nearby the side of the less-used hand taking longer than usual a wide stretch of open space put as much as possible into every one or two or more piece of a whole happens to have come into sight not any places where something was rubbed, scraped or wiped out no more than being a single thing in addition being one more than one toward the east when I face north my name every one of two or more open space for passing happens to have spaces in between a plot not any test of skill in-volving rules likable to the same extent that it can be introducing any of the choices to tell exactly which how much or how totalling one less than four in this place or at this point the one between two and four people

12

carrying communications back and forth make completely full what're thought of as boundless continuous expanses extending in all directions or in three dimensions within which all material things are contained not any sounds of the voice or movements of the features or the body that express joy the red fluid circulating in the heart arteries and veins of people and animals spelled phonetically in addition in the direction of the one that's nearby the side which is west when you face north in a position above but in contact with the one that's nearby totalling one more than four of the device for measuring time totalling one more than six according to the device for measuring time one of the four equal parts of something in the direction of totalling one less than nine according to the device for measuring time of France people carrying communications back and forth the state of living together as husband and wife spelled phonetically drawing out to a certain point in the direction of distant in space or time a position or space beside the one that is central what one of them divisions of the whole happens in this place or at this moment being a single thing the ones mentioned before happen in the direction in addition alongside of one more than one the ones mentioned before happen what ones of the things mentioned in a course leading to the other side to the same degree distant in space or time contained by any one turned in the opposite direction one less than four the ones mentioned before happen for what reason one less than five the ones mentioned before happen to be bringing about the ones which causing to come with you in the direction of the one that's nearby an open space for passing moving along they happened to be bringing about the one which instead of the ones mentioned before by means of guides for arranging things in addition the fronts of heads from the tops of foreheads to the bottoms of chins, and from ears to ears the ones my presence here

Collaborative list of familiar words (made with 8th & 9th Graders)

What's in a name? that which we call a rose
By any other name would smell as sweet (WS)
a rose is a rose is a rose (G. Stein) is a rose
raisin in the sun (Langston Hughes)
The king was in the counting house counting out the money....
I sing the body electric....these United States....(Whitman)
A thing of beauty is a joy forever (Keats)
(I summon up) remembrance of things past (WS)
Ask not for whom the bell tolls / it tolls for thee (Donne)
no man is an island (entire of it self) (Donne)
something there is that doesnt love a wall (Frost)
Abide with me (fast falls the eventide) (Henry Lyte)
Look homeward Angel (Milton)
For fools rush in where angels fear to tread (Pope, Essay on Man)
O little town of Bethlehem (Philips Brooks)
all's well that ends well (WS)
God is love (First epistle of John, bible)
To everything there is a season, & a time to every purpose under
heaven......(Ecclesiastes)
Smiling through her tears (Homer)
Turn a deaf ear (Swift)
(The) sight (of you is good) for sore eyes (Swift)
Keep a stiff upper lip (Phoebe Cary, 19th c.)
I saw the best minds of my generation......(A. Ginsberg)
I think therefore I am (Descartes)
It was the best of times.... (Dickens)
O brave new world that has such people in it (WS, Tempest)

Shall we gather at the river......
We shall meet on that beautiful shore (Ira David Sankey)
Promises and pie-crust are made to be broken (Swift)
Winter of our discontent, etc. (WS)
First in war, first in peace, first in the hearts of his
fellow citizens (Henry Lee on Washington)
I hate and I love (odi et amo) (Catullus)
                    it is a tale
told by an idiot, full of sound & fury
signifying nothing (WS, Macbeth)
Water water everywhere
Nor any drop to drink (Coleridge)
When in disgrace with fortune & men's eyes (WS)
This is the way to kill a wife with kindness (WS)
Dance by the light of the moon (Ed. Lear)
Curioser & curioser (Lewis Carroll)

                            etc.

                    children of the future age
                    reading this indignant page
                    know that in a former time
                    love, sweet love, was thought a crime
                                (Wm. Blake)

The Presentation of Fruitstands in January

so-called inauguration 1981
proposal of love from an inept suitor
pity poor instinctual America love all
wrong greedy mismatched middle class mates
is all doesn't need to be said at Liberty meanwhile
on the streets powerless in the funny light
a man named "I cant remember anything" said "I'm not
doing bad I've got only a homeopathic alcoholism"
but otherwise he turned with Rastafarian braids
or sets of hair to the crowds behind shouting
"Hey! Narrative! I'm crossing, I'm waiting!"
Then I shot behind a single man thinking to make
things safe for me by crossing the street behind him,
he, the typical wayfaring dentist-type, jaywalked south
as I was going north. An inaugural woman in the xerox
place turned as I was nearly leaning on her stuff and
I saw she was white pale like she is with her bright
red lipstick, I was shocked as if I was watching a Herzog
movie no Fassbinder, in fact I'd been thinking of having
my manuscript put in a binding for Clark, I met Gerard.
I shot into the grocer's wondering if they thought I buy
too much beer there, I got the apple from the fruit market
the one where the Korean woman articulates "twenty cents"
so beautifully, once I bought a clementine there,
the same place where they have the best red potatoes,
very small ones. In Maria's near Marie's school they
do not have as much variety as good cheap ripeness,
Italian pasta and olive oil, and once they had purple

cauliflower which I'd never seen before. Maria or Sally
adds up the prices in Italian, quattrocento, millecento,
abracadabra felice navidad I am madly in love.
At the fruitstand next to hers, which is another Korean one,
there they have everything, it's like entering the fucking World
Trade Center, the entire business center of the world
of fruits and vegetables — leeks, broccoli rape, bibb lettuce,
red lettuce, sprouts, the accustomed luxury of watercress,
big red potatoes, fennel, giant peculiar-looking strawberries
from Florida, real loose spinach, it's winter, carrots with tops,
beets with greens and all the things the Korean markets can seem
to have that other places dont. Further down the street is a
perfunctory market that sometimes seems to have the cheapest apples
not only Cortland but also Macintosh and Delicious though I dont know
why the Delicious are always more expensive since they dont taste good.
Beyond is the famous 7th Street market which is open all night,
there you can obtain cheap baskets of aging fruits, cheap lettuce,
cheap broccoli and nuts but if you're not on your guard
you'll wind up buying 2 grapefruits for a dollar forty-nine.
Across the street before that, if you can cross the street,
is another of the famous Korean markets which has everything all
that is both precious and mundane but the carrots are expensive there.
Nearest our house is a tiny alleyway of a fruit market at which
the people are so slow to weigh what you buy that you'd best not
have to stop there if in a hurry, however oranges and grapefruits
are cheap and they have olives and figs. Behind that place hidden on
4th street is another place that also sells flowers. This place is so
expensive you can never go there, I don't understand how they manage
    it
somebody told me they sell nickel bags there & once we bought flowers

and the woman was as if out of Dickens so you could see having an
    irrational
devotion to her, the flowers are the only ones nearby. I forgot to mention
the new semi-religious health food place on 9th street, that, when it's not
too cold, sells fruits & vegetables outdoors. They began to sell them very
cheap but now everything is expensive again. All the markets have to put
some or most things inside when it gets to be zero or below, or they
    cover
the oranges and stuff with plastic. In the morning it's nice to watch
the markets opening up and imagine running one, you could write on a
    crate.
At one of the Korean ones there's always a child running around.

On this inauguration day of the most hateful ideals
I like to think nostalgically of fruits and vegetables
because the sight of them gives pleasure
and the fruits and vegetables, their weight and measure, are
transient enough that there is stuff to give away or sell
at reduced costs to those whose exigencies are more primary,
though we are all feebly observably ready to marry
with our most ideal love a grief at the most sorry most
sublime state of being human among the ages of the people
I see this January on First and Second Avenues between 4th Street
and 12th Street (this is not the half of it), I wish I could meet
a man or woman who would say to me today looks this way dont worry
& if each color passes by you like a lover so lent to the streets
a bright presence like a person then the sadness of a person's desire
doesnt matter, to reflect like the transient vegetables this joy
as if an object was the way people say it's a girl or boy!
Sentient apple, quite fat, did love my stealing it.

Happiest tree-like broccoli was endeavoring to seduce me.
Enticing fancy leek enabled me to be meek (poor man's
asparagus), so I saw everything & was able to calm down
by stopping to look and see if the famous comice pears were
almost ripe enough for us to have the patience to wait to eat them.
It may sound opulent to mention so much stuff
but actually all this this and that—dont be fooled—
is as it should be and thus I pray is as it would be
if only you, impatient sullen mushroom, would love me.

The Complete Introductory Lectures on Poetry

To Ted Berrigan

It was when the words on the covers of books,
titles as true as false leaves led me to believe
in inviting the ultimate speculation of love —
that I could learn *all* of the subject —
that I first began to entertain what is sublime

Like a moth I thought by reading *Jokes and
Their Relation to the Unconscious* or *Beyond
the Pleasure Principle* or *Eat the Weeds* or
The Origin of the Species or even a book on
Coup d'Etats or *The Problem of Anxiety* I
could accomplish all the knowledge the titles implied

Science that there is often more
in the notes on the back of a discarded envelope,
grammar in the shadows slanted on the wall
of the too bright night to verify the city light

and then awakening, babies, to turn and make notes
on the dream's public epigrams and one's own
weaknesses, self that's prone to epigrammatic ridicule

and to meditate on fears of all the animal dangers
plus memories of reptilian appellations for all
our stages of learning to swim at a past day camp

It is to think this or that might include all
or enough to entertain all those who already know

20

that in this century of private apartments
though knowledge might be coveted hardly anything
is shared except penurious poetry, she or he
who still tends to titles as if all of us
are reading a new book called *THE NEW LIFE*.

Hardship

I'm all screwed up
I'm afraid of the
electric socket
at last we talked
after all that
about how we were
both all screwed up
but you loved us
anyway that once
as if our mother
had pulled back all
the hair and skin
protecting me hardly
& pressed your teeth
into me gently
& as intensely
& maybe habitually
as if I'd know
as I've ever known
with secret techniques
how to give women
women's pleasures
(another person speaks
other words
about all of this)
then all of a sudden
you stopped
everything else

kept going on
many other things
were happening
I cant remember
though I'm obsessed
to remember to have
the same feeling again
I did then
it's September
& I'm sure
I'll see you around

A Marriage of Cut Flowers

I could hit your penis
it's a room in a hotel
this has no mr. meaning at all
there must be new forms
& new songs all the time
the promiscuous lilacs,
the too-sweet tuberose,
some sweet williams and
and a pink delphinium dolphin
fill this room with something
sweetness cold and the smell of
a fire plus an outrageous desire
to fuck everyone as in the millenium
it might be a great pleasure then
to seduce and slap at the smells
like these occasionally wild flowers
misplaced in a room where someone
who sees them says this place must
be a funeral parlor a field or a whoreouse
and all that it is
my complaining darling

Untitled

I must admit I love a man who is not living
I find myself mating with him in all my sleeping
I meet him here & there, he takes different shapes
often I just see him off in the distance looking
& I always notice his eye and mine catch each other
in an awkward way but I've no idea who is he

I think of him every night when I go to bed
I'm sure this has to do with catholic adolescent sex

He's a lunatic I think but he turns me on
All the time I see him & I think of him
He sits on me because he's dead or living
He is not unscrupulous as I am unforgiving
I think sometimes he's my old aunt who was too simple
She had a regimen of chocolate and oranges to eat
But often I can make her more attractive than that
especially when no one else is awake in the house

My this lover I think made me commit murder
Because of all the beauty in the world but when
he didnt do that he made me replete in my own arms
and that is the most unfortunate part which is why
I can never tell anybody about any of this or else
I'm going to go to someplace worse than American jail
I know I belong there because I like solitude
and besides I am nobody with this awful other
Who I turn all the time into another like maybe you

You cant hate me for writing this down can you?
I could say anything I wanted couldnt I?
Besides this man has beautiful curly black hair
And I love to put my hands into it & make him
Kiss me all the way down till we are forgetting
the heads and feet of the bed we are in.

Lyn Hejinian

The Rejection of Closure (1984)

> Whether we like it or not, our eyes gobble squares, circles, and all manner of fabricated forms, wires on poles, triangles on poles, circles on levers, cylinders, balls, domes, tubes, more or less distinct or in elaborate relationships. The eye consumes these things and conveys them to some stomach that is tough or delicate. People who eat anything and everything do seem to have the advantage of their magnificent stomachs.
>
> — *Paul Klee*

In writing, an essential situation, both formal and open, is created by the interplay between two areas of fruitful conflict or struggle. One of these arises from a natural impulse toward the boundedness of closure, whether defensive or comprehensive, and an equal impulse toward a necessarily open-ended and continuous response to what's perceived as the "world," unfinished and incomplete. Another, simultaneous struggle is the continually developing one between literary form, or the "constructive principle," and the ever-regenerating plenitude of writing's materials. The first involves the poet with his or her subjective position; the second objectifies the poem in the context of ideas and of language itself.

These two areas of opposition are not neatly parallel. Form cannot be equated with closure, nor can raw materiality be equated with the open. I want to say this at the outset and most emphatically, in order to prevent any misunderstanding. Indeed, the conjunction of *form* with radical *openness* may provide a version of the "paradise" for which the poem yearns—a flowering focus on a distinct infinity.

For the sake of clarity, I will offer a tentative characterization of the terms *open* and *closed*. We can say that a "closed text" is one in which all the elements of the work are directed toward a single reading of it. Each element confirms that reading and delivers the text from any lurking ambiguity. In the "open text," meanwhile, all the elements of the work are maximally excited; here it is because ideas and things exceed (without deserting) argument that they have been taken into the dimension of the work.

It is not hard to discover devices—structural devices—that may serve to "open" a poetic text, depending on other elements in the work and by all means on the intention of the writer. One set of such devices has to do with arrangement and, particularly, with rearrangement within a work. The "open text," by definition, is open to the world and particularly to the reader. It invites participation, rejects the authority of the writer over the reader and thus, by analogy, the authority implicit in other (social, economic, cultural) hierarchies. It speaks for writing that is generative rather than directive. The writer relinquishes total control and challenges authority as a principle and control as a motive. The "open text" often emphasizes or foregrounds process, either the process of the original composition or of subsequent compositions by readers, and thus resists the cultural tendencies that seek to identify and fix material, turn it into a product; that is, it resists reduction.

> It is really a question of another economy which diverts the linearity of a project, undermines the target-object of a desire, explodes the polarization of desire on only one pleasure, and disconcerts fidelity to only one discourse. (Luce Irigaray, 104)

"Field work," where words and lines are distributed irregularly on the page, such as Robert Grenier's poster/map entitled "Cambridge M'ass" and Bruce Andrews's "Love Song 41" (also originally published as a poster), are obvious examples of works in which the order of the reading is not imposed in advance. Any reading of these works is an improvisation; one moves through the work not in straight lines but in curves, swirls, and across intersections, to words that catch the eye or attract attention repeatedly.

Repetition, conventionally used to unify a text or harmonize its parts, as if returning melody to the tonic, instead, in these works, and somewhat differently in a work like my *My Life*, challenges our inclination to isolate, identify, and limit the burden of meaning given to an event (the sentence or line). Here, where certain phrases recur in the work, recontextualized and with new emphasis, repetition disrupts the initial apparent meaning scheme. The initial reading is adjusted; meaning is set in motion, emended and extended, and the rewriting that repetition becomes postpones completion of the thought indefinitely.

But there are more complex forms of juxtaposition. The mind, said Keats, should be "a thoroughfare for all thoughts." My intention (I don't mean to suggest I succeeded) in a later work, "Resistance" (now subsumed into "The Green"), was to write a lyric poem in a long form—that is, to achieve maximum vertical intensity (the single moment into which the idea rushes) and maximum horizontal extensivity (ideas cross the landscape and become the horizon and weather). To myself I proposed the paragraph as a unit representing a single moment of time, a single moment in the mind, its content all the thoughts, thought particles, impressions, impulses—all the diverse, particular, and contradictory elements that are included in an active and emotional mind at any given instant. For the moment, as a writer, the poem *is* a mind.

To prevent the work from disintegrating into its separate parts—scattering sentence-rubble haphazardly on the waste heap—I used various syntactic devices to foreground or create the conjunction between ideas. Statements become interconnected by being grammatically congruent; unlike things, made alike grammatically, become meaningful in common and jointly. "Resistance" begins:

> Patience is laid out on my papers. Its visuals are gainful and equably square. Two dozen jets take off into the night. Outdoors a car goes uphill in a genial low gear. The flow of thoughts—impossible! These are the defamiliarization techniques with which we are so familiar.

There are six sentences here, three of which, beginning with the first, are constructed similarly: subject—verb—prepositional phrase. The three prepositions are *on*, *into*, and *in*, which in isolation seem similar but used here have very different meanings. *On* is locational: "on my papers." *Into* is metaphorical and atmospheric: "into the night." *In* is atmospheric and qualitative: "in a genial low gear." There are a pair of inversions in effect here: the unlike are made similar (syntactically) and the like are sundered (semantically). Patience, which might be a quality of a virtuous character attendant to work ("it is laid out on my papers") might also be "solitaire," a card game played by the unvirtuous character who is avoiding attention to work. Two dozen jets can only take off together in formations; they are "laid out" on the night sky. A car goes uphill; its movement upward parallels that of the jets, but whereas their formation is martial, the single car is somewhat domestic, genial and innocuous. The image in the first pair of sentences is horizontal. The upward movement of the next two sentences describes a vertical plane, upended on or intersecting the horizontal one. The "flow of thoughts" runs down the vertical and comes to rest—"impossible!" (there is a similar alternation between horizontal and vertical landscapes in other sections of "The Green.")

One of the results of this compositional technique, building a work out of discrete intact units (in fact, I would like each sentence itself to be as nearly a complete poem as possible), is the creation of sizeable gaps between the units. The reader (and I can say also the writer) must overleap the end stop, the period, and cover the distance to the next sentence. "Do not the lovers of poetry," asks Keats, "like to have a little Region to wander in where they may pick and choose, and in which the images are so numerous that many are forgotten and found new in a second reading... Do not they like this better than what they can read through before Mrs. Williams comes down stairs?" Meanwhile, what stays in the gaps, so to speak, remains crucial and informative. Part of the reading occurs as the recovery of that information (looking behind) and the discovery of newly structured ideas (stepping forward).

In both *My Life* and "The Green," the form (grossly, the paragraph) represents time. Conversely, in Bernadette Mayer's *Midwinter Day*, time is the form—imposed, exoskeletal. The work was written according to a predetermined temporal framework; it begins when the "stopwatch" was turned on (early morning, December 22, 1978) and ends when time ran out (late night of the same date).

> It's true I have always loved projects of all sorts, including say sorting
> leaves or whatever projects turn out to be, and in poetry I most
> especially love having time be the structure which always seems to me
> to save structure or form from itself because then nothing really has to
> begin or end. (Bernadette Mayer, personal letter)

Whether the form is dictated by temporal rules or by numerical rules—by
a prior decision that the work will contain, say, x number of sentences,
paragraphs, stanzas, or lines, etc.—it seems that the work begins and
ends arbitrarily and not because there is a necessary point of departure
or terminus. The implication (correct) is that the words and the ideas
(thoughts, perceptions, etc.—the material) continue beyond the work.
One has simply stopped because one has run out of fingers, beds, or
minutes, and not because a conclusion has been reached or "everything"
said.

The relationship of form, or the "constructive principle," to the
"materials" of the work (its ideas, the conceptual mass, but also the
words themselves) is the initial problem for the "open text," one that
faces each writing anew. Can form make the primary chaos (i.e. raw
material, unorganized impulse and information, uncertainty, incompleteness, vastness) articulate without depriving it of its capacious vitality, its
generative power? Can form go even further than that and actually
generate that potency, opening uncertainty to curiosity, incompleteness
to speculation, and turning vastness into plenitude? In my opinion, the
answer is yes; that is, in fact, the function of form in art. Form is not a
fixture but an activity.

In an essay entitled "Rhythm as the Constructive Factor of
Verse," the Russian Formalist writer Yurii Tynianov writes:

> We have only recently outgrown the well-known analogy: form is to
> content as a glass is to wine.... I would venture to say that in nine out
> of ten instances the word 'composition' covertly implies a treatment of
> form as a static item. The concept of 'poetic line' or 'stanza' is

imperceptibly removed from the dynamic category. Repetition ceases to be considered as a fact of varying strength in various situations of frequency and quantity. The dangerous concept of the 'symmetry of compositional facts' arises, dangerous because we cannot speak of symmetry where we find intensification. (127-28)

(Compare this with Gertrude Stein's comment in "Portraits and Repetitions": "A thing that seems to be exactly the same thing may seem to be a repetition but is it.... Is there repetition or is there insistence. I am inclined to believe there is no such thing as repetition. And really how can there be.... Expressing any thing there can be no repetition because the essence of that expression is insistence, and if you insist you must each time use emphasis and if you use emphasis it is not possible while anybody is alive that they should use exactly the same emphasis" 104). Tynianov continues:

The unity of a work is not a closed symmetrical whole, but an unfolding dynamic integrity.... The sensation of form in such a situation is always the sensation of flow (and therefore of change).... Art exists by means of this interaction or struggle.

Language discovers what one might know, which in turn is always less than what language might say. We encounter some limitations of this relationship early, as children. Anything with limits can be imagined (correctly or incorrectly) as an object, by analogy with other objects—balls and rivers. Children objectify language when they render it their plaything, in jokes, puns, and riddles, or in glossolaliac chants and rhymes. They discover that words are not equal to the world, that a shift, analogous to parallax in photography, occurs between things (events, ideas, objects) and the words for them—a displacement that leaves a gap. Among the most prevalent and persistent categories of jokes is that which identifies and makes use of the fallacious comparison of words to world and delights in the ambiguity resulting from the discrepancy:

—Why did the moron eat hay?
—To feed his hoarse voice.

—How do you get down from an elephant?
—You don't, you get down from a goose.

—Did you wake up grumpy this morning?
—No, I let him sleep.

Because we have language we find ourselves in a special and peculiar relationship to the objects, events, and situations which constitute what we imagine of the world. Language generates its own characteristics in the human psychological and spiritual conditions. Indeed, it near *is* our psychological condition. This psychology is generated by the struggle between language and that which it claims to depict or express, by our overwhelming experience of the vastness and uncertainty of the world, and by what often seems to be the inadequacy of the imagination that longs to know it—and, furthermore, for the poet, the even greater inadequacy of the language that appears to describe, discuss, or disclose it. This psychology situates desire in the poem itself, or, more specifically, in poetic language, to which then we may attribute the motive for the poem.

Language is one of the principal forms our curiosity takes. It makes us restless. As Francis Ponge puts it, "Man is a curious body whose center of gravity is not in himself" (47). Instead it seems to be located in language, by virtue of which we negotiate our mentalities and the world; off-balance, heavy at the mouth, we are pulled forward.

> She is lying on her stomach with one eye closed, driving a toy truck along the road she has cleared with her fingers. Then the tantrum broke out, blue, without a breath of air.... You could increase the height by making lateral additions and building over them a sequence of steps, leaving tunnels, or windows, between the blocks, and I did. I made signs to them to be as quiet as possible. But a word is a bottomless pit. It became magically pregnant and one day split open, giving birth to a stone egg, about as big as a football. (*My Life*)

Language itself is never in a state of rest. Its syntax can be as complex as thought. And the experience of using it, which includes the experience of understanding it, either as speech or as writing, is inevitably active—both intellectually and emotionally. The progress of a line or sentence, or a series of lines or sentences, has spatial properties as well as temporal properties. The meaning of a word in its place derives both from the word's lateral reach, its contacts with its neighbors in a statement, and from its reach through and out of the text into the outer world, the matrix of its contemporary and historical reference. The very idea of reference is spatial: over here is word, over there is thing at which the word is shooting amiable love-arrows. Getting from the beginning to the end of a statement is simple movement; following the connotative by-ways (on what Umberto Eco calls "inferential walks") is complex or compound movement.

> To identify these frames the reader has to 'walk,' so to speak, outside the text, in order to gather intertextual support (a quest for analogous 'topoi,' themes or motives). I call these interpretative moves inferential walks: they are not mere whimsical initiatives on the part of the reader, but are elicited by discursive structures and foreseen by the whole textual strategy as indispensable components of the construction. (Eco 32)

Language is productive of activity in another sense with which anyone is familiar who experiences words as attractive, magnetic to meaning. This is one of the first things one notices, for example, in works constructed from arbitrary vocabularies generated by random or chance operations (e.g., some works by Jackson Mac Low) or from a vocabulary limited according to some other criteria unrelated to meaning (for example, Alan Davies's *a an av es*, a long poem excluding any words containing letters with ascenders or descenders, what the French call "the prisoner's convention," either because the bars are removed or because it saves paper). It is impossible to discover any string or bundle of words that is entirely free of possible narrative or psychological content. Moreover, though the "story" and "tone" of such works may be interpreted differently by different readers, nonetheless the readings differ within definite limits. While word strings are permissive, they do not license a free-for-all.

Writing develops subjects that mean the words we have for them.

Even words in storage, in the dictionary, seem frenetic with activity, as each individual entry attracts to itself other words as definition, example, and amplification. Thus, to open the dictionary at random, *mastoid* attracts *nipplelike, temporal, bone, ear*, and *behind*. Turning to *temporal* we find that the definition includes *time, space, life, world, transitory*, and *near the temples*, but, significantly, not *mastoid*. There is no entry for *nipplelike*, but the definition for *nipple* brings over *protuberance, breast, udder, the female, milk, discharge, mouthpiece*, and *nursing bottle*, but again not *mastoid*, nor *temporal*, nor *time, bone, ear, space*, or *word*. It is relevant that the exchanges are incompletely reciprocal.

> and how did this happen like an excerpt
>   beginning in a square white boat abob on a gray sea
>   tootling of another message by the hacking lark
> as a child to the rescue and its spring
>   many comedies emerge and in particular a group of girls
>   in a great lock of letters
>   like knock look
> a restless storage of a thousand blastings
>   but cow dull bulge clump
>   slippage thinks random patterns
>   through wishes
>   I intend greed as I intend pride
>   patterns of roll extend over the wish
>   (*Writing Is an Aid to Memory*)

The "rage to know" is one expression of the restlessness engendered by language. "As long as man keeps hearing words/ He's sure that there's a meaning somewhere," says Mephistopheles in Goethe's *Faust*.

It's in the nature of language to encourage, and in part to justify, such Faustian longings. The notion that language is the means and medium for attaining knowledge, and, concomitantly, power, is, of course, old. The knowledge toward which we seem to be driven by language, or which language seems to promise, is inherently sacred as well as secular, redemptive as well as satisfying. The *nomina sint numina* position (that there is an essential identity between name and thing, that the real nature of a thing is immanent and present in its name, that nouns are numenous) suggests that it is possible to find a language which will meet its object with perfect identity. If this were the case, we could, in speaking or in writing, achieve the "at oneness" with the universe, at least in its particulars, that is the condition of complete and perfect knowing.

But if in the Edenic scenario we acquired knowledge of the animals by naming them, it was not by virtue of any numenous immanence in the name but because Adam was a taxonomist. He distinguished the individual animals, discovered the concept of categories, and then organized the various species according to their different functions and relationships in a system.

What the "naming" provides is structure, not individual words.

As Benjamin Lee Whorf has pointed out, "Every language is a vast pattern-system, different from others, in which are culturally ordained the forms and categories by which the personality not only communicates, but also analyses nature, notices or neglects types of relationship and phenomena, channels his reasoning, and builds the house of his consciousness" (252). In this same essay, apparently his last (written in 1941), entitled "Language, Mind, Reality," Whorf goes on to express what seem to be stirrings of a religious motivation: "What I have called patterns are basic in a really cosmic sense." There is a "PREMONITION IN LANGUAGE of the unknown vaster world." The idea

is too drastic to be penned up in a catch phrase. I would rather leave it unnamed. It is the view that a noumenal world—a world of hyperspace, of higher dimensions—awaits discovery by all the sciences [linguistics being one of them] which it will unite and unify, awaits discovery under its first aspect of a realm of PATTERNED RELATIONS, inconceivably manifold and yet bearing a recognizable affinity to the rich and systematic organization of LANGUAGE. (247-48)

It is as if what I've been calling, from Faust, the "rage to know," which is in some respects a libidinous drive, seeks also a redemptive value from language. Both are appropriate to the Faustian legend.

Coming in part out of Freudian psychoanalytic theory, especially in France, is a body of feminist thought that is even more explicit in its identification of language with power and knowledge—a power and knowledge that is political, psychological, and aesthetic—and that is identified specifically with desire. The project for these French feminist writers is to direct their attention to "language and the unconscious, not as separate entities, but language as a passageway, and the only one, to the unconscious, to that which has been repressed and which would, if allowed to rise, disrupt the established symbolic order, what Jacques Lacan has dubbed the Law of the Father" (Marks 835).

If the established symbolic order is the "Law of the Father," and it is discovered to be not only repressive but false, distorted by the illogicality of bias, then the new symbolic order is to be a "woman's language," corresponding to a woman's desire. So Luce Irigaray writes:

> But woman has sex organs just about everywhere. She experiences pleasure almost everywhere. Even without speaking of the hysterization of her entire body, one can say that the geography of her pleasure is much more diversified, more multiple in its differences, more complex, more subtle, than is imagined.... "She" is indefinitely other in herself. That is undoubtedly the reason she is called temperamental, incomprehensible, perturbed, capricious—not to mention her language in which "she" goes off in all directions. (103)

"A feminine textual body is recognized by the fact that it is always endless, without ending," says Helene Cixous: "There's no closure, it doesn't stop" (53).

The narrow definition of desire, the identification of desire solely with sexuality, and the literalness of the genital model for a woman's language that some of these writers insist on may be problematic. The desire that is stirred by language is located most interestingly within language itself—as a desire to say, a desire to create the subject by saying, and as a pervasive doubt very like jealousy that springs from the impossibility of satisfying these yearnings. This desire resembles Wordsworth's "underthirst / Of vigor seldom utterly allayed."

> When I'm eating this I want food.... The I expands. The individual is caught in a devouring machine, but she shines like the lone star on the horizon when we enter her thoughts, when she expounds on the immensity of her condition, the subject of the problem which interests nature. (Carla Harryman, "Realism")

If language induces a yearning for comprehension, for perfect and complete expression, it also guards against it. Thus Faust complains: "It is written: 'In the beginning was the Word!' / Already I have to stop! Who'll help me on? / It is impossible to put such trust in the Word!" Such is a recurrent element in the argument of the lyric: "alack, what poverty my Muse brings forth..."; "Those lines that I before have writ do lie..."; "for we / Have eyes to wonder but lack tongues to praise...." (Lines from Shakespeare's sonnets 102, 115, and 106).

In the gap between what one wants to say (or what one perceives there is to say) and what one can say (what is sayable), words provide for a collaboration and a desertion. We delight in our sensuous involvement with the materials of language, we long to join words to the world —to close the gap between ourselves and things—and we suffer from doubt and anxiety because of our inability to do so.

Yet the incapacity of language to match the world permits us to distinguish our ideas and ourselves from the world and things in it from each other. The undifferentiated is one mass, the differentiated is multiple. The (unimaginable) complete text, the text that contains everything, would in fact be a closed text. It would be insufferable.

A central activity of poetic language is formal. In being formal, in making form distinct, it opens—makes variousness and multiplicity and possibility articulate and clear. While failing in the attempt to match the world, we discover structure, distinction, the integrity and separateness of things. As Bob Perelman writes:

At the sound of my voice
I spoke and, egged on
By the discrepancy, wrote
The rest out as poetry
　　　　("My One Voice")

Works Cited

Andrews, Bruce. *Love Songs*. Baltimore: Pod Books, 1982.

Cixous, Hélène. "Castration or Decapitation?" *Signs* 7:1 (1981).

Davies, Alan. *a an av es*. Elmwood, Conn.: Potes & Poets, 1981.

Eco, Umberto. *The Role of the Reader*. Bloomington: Indiana University Press, 1979.

Goethe, Johann Wolfgang von. *Faust*. Randall Jarrell (tr.), New York: Farrar, Straus & Giroux, 1976.

Grenier, Bob. *Cambridge M'ass*. Berkeley: Tuumba Press, 1982.

Harryman, Carla. "Realism," in *Animal Instincts*. Berkeley: Tuumba Press, 1982.

Hejinian, Lyn. "The Green," *The Cold of Poetry*. Los Angeles: Sun & Moon, 1994.

_____. *My Life*. Los Angeles: Sun & Moon, 1987.

_____. *Writing Is An Aid To Memory*. Berkeley: The Figures, 1978.

Irigaray, Luce. "This sex which is not one, " in *New French Feminisms*. Amherst: University of Massachusetts Press, 1980.

Keats, John. Letter to Benjamin Bailey, October 8, 1817.

Klee, Paul. *The Thinking Eye*. New York: Wittenborn, 1961.

Marks, Elaine. "Women and Literature in France," *Signs* 3.4 (1978).

Mayer, Bernadette. *Midwinter Day*. Berkeley: Turtle Island, 1982.

Perelman, Bob. "My One Voice," *Primer*. Berkeley: This Press, 1981.

Ponge, Francis. *The Power of Language*. Serge Gavronsky (tr.), Berkeley: University of California Press, 1979.

Stein, Gertrude. "Portraits and Repetitions," in *Writings and Lectures,* Patricia Meyerowitz (ed.), Baltimore: Penguin, 1971.

Tynianov, Yurii. "Rhythm as the Constructive Factor of Verse," in Matejka and Pomorska (eds.), *Readings in Russian Poetics.* Ann Arbor: Michigan Slavic Contributions, 1978.

Whorf, Benjamin Lee. *Language, Thought, and Reality.* Cambridge: MIT Press, 1956.

Poems from *The Cell*

There are boulders allowed among
      the cows
Clouds under the thought that
      proved to be too short
Just as one rests an
      hypotenuse there is the feeling
      of hopelessness
The line is not continuous
A stroke in sight and
      blinking
Scale, scale, and flower
In theory there's observation or
      there's prediction to justify
Specificity scooping under the trees
      and red spots immediately absorbed
As well as skeletons cooling
Between mutually exclusive descriptions but
      with difficulty a person might
      decide
So many persons, who cannot
      greet
The sentence is complete and
      separate like a hedgehog, like
      a charcoal, or a rock
The soft world is between
      rocks
The person of which I
      speak is between clocks

October 8, 1986

Exploration takes extra words
Words qua sentience and thinking
These are spread over a
  position—being long and pointed
  over
They anticipate an immoderate time
  and place
Reality moves around making objects
  appear as if they belong
  where they are
Then it shifts, say, up
  and down, with the sunlight's
  yellow interstitial coloring matter
The sun here is an
  exceeding stricture
I've yet...I keep thinking...
  all open daylit areas carry
  to peripheries their yellow floating
  ovoid motes
Eggs go out of optical
  range, but only ellipsing
The particular attraction empties in
Blown convincing field, it rattles
  with brown grass turning
I'm looking, prematurely, for a
  particular point of view—that
  of one who has already
  achieved objectivity
Objectivities and metonymies
But one can't die
Sex sexes scale and flies
  faithful to the ground
       October 11, 1986

Solid harbor, thick liquid town,
     where women bump around skillfully
     and with ardor
With boundaries—they are said
     to have a problem with
     boundaries
Without bodies
The progress of domestic time
     can be made—with docks
     coming right up into it
It has a certain necessity
     for winds, cups, or zinnias
Sustaining orientation
For haste
The many retentive sequences, sentences
But the person with bodily
     exercises identifies with its city
So a person is compensating
     letting others in front
It seems to have made
     now a model of incommensurability
In it a person isn't
     satisfied when queried except walking
     expressly
A model of momentum
It is a small amount
     of time in a place
     known as an extent of
     experience
Unknown
Its sincerity is unofficial

Not an absolute but a
          continuum
It darkens and unregenerate darkens

                    October 29, 1986

In the dark sky there
          are constellations, all of them
          erotic and they break open
          the streets
The streets exceed the house
On occasion the body exceeds
          the self
Everyday someone replaces someone and
          someone's mother is sad so
          as to exceed
The bed is a popular
          enclosure from which to depart
Outside the stars are stunning
          —touching
It is a question of
          scale
It is erotic when parts
          exceed their scale

                    November 15, 1986

You patrol? outside the
          self? around a body and
          the follicle in which it
          stands?

Or cell?
Request?
Have you reverted?
All memory of having looked
        is loose
It is so cold parallels
        wobble in the chamber whose
        grain drifts
A sign on the fire
        door says silence
A sign on the floor
        says come in
Patrol (but there are no
        opposites) is narrowing
But I was not moving
        anywhere on my feet
Within such fear of death
        if it is a thrill
        to cease
But in the succeeding request
        I ask decease to be
        stable, not diffused or decreased
The cell of description of
        anything (and virtually uninterrupted)
Her death in a beginning
It is in a prolonged,
        ruthless, unguarded kinesis
The cell in shifts
Cells in drifts
So we're feeling a loss
        but not a conclusion
The smallest unit of imagination
        in time, a retrospection

A unit of space so
        small it seems to be
        going backwards

                January 14, 1987

If reality is simply that
        which is accessible to reason
        when it folds over and
        it sticks up
Then sexuality is very optimistic—
        a very optimistic interest
It is a cyclops with
        a sharp eye for the
        apparent position and the actual
        position
And a working eye
Until we have a whole
        landscape of undivided situations
Although beauty is divided somewhat
        freely
The boundaries between me and
        the rosey cobblestones and leaves
        are nowhere parallel
But slide who are insatiable,
        genuine, solemn, looming
The ghost is only the
        poor attempt of nature to
        present herself as me in
        the language of inquiry

The naked breasts we call
      night and day or me
      and not-me
Inseparable from exposure, inspiration is
      what the ghost contained or
      could supply
Qualified praises—flesh rises to
      an emotion
The reasonable outlook, knowledge
It is based on acknowledgment
      in the end
Provocations
Justice, joy—if a cyclops
      pertains squinting and springing coincidentally
      upright until partially blinded
Of anything that is, there
      might be more

January 16, 1987

On *what* do the eyes
      finally come to rest
Sentences that hang the face
The eyes winching their things
Quietly to *what*
The body is bent to
      speak of thoughts changing into
      new forms
Many thoughts are of no
      things

November 15, 1987

47

This is my sense of
        name and pleasure
So to speculate—what is
        the same as what
Lathered with existence after exercise
        a person is elite
It's pink and yellow
Science, duty, golden justice, and
        flame
Etc.
The bugs are whirligigging in
        the breezes of cooked fish,
        their sour milk, of putrid
        rinds of something, gristle, juice
Some of that rhythmic circulation,
        but without much horizon, is
        in the nature of the
        job (work)
At work, when I know
        what to say, I think
        it
Ours is a planet, but
        I've never seen it
Then alone, at home, in
        the kitchen where the food
        is concealed in aromas of
        salt water the pelicans crash
Arise
There is solitude throughout the
        history of literature
And someone in it

February 17, 1988

We've lived our years at
              various rates
Some are inappropriate and therefore
              we have gender
A person is time not
              speed
A person (I will call
              it you) and the low
              warm ochre color of my
              pencil
The person more pointed than
              the pen
We are very pleased
Little feet, long head—but
              well-designed—shapely and with sequels
I took with me a
              large crate of potatoes
A bank
There are many symmetries yet
              to be distributed
We got our money in
              the middle
Veering, and then subsiding
We did experience an irresistible
              normal crumble—the sex organs
              being variously funnels
And funny—substances hyphenated amid
              our experiences
Music, croak, and resumption
Substantives are not evocations but
              convections—time is drawn into
              the self

It is swimming after the
       smallest rates and sticks

                              June 11, 1988

We move roughly from sex
       to uncertainty
My meditation is a silica

Sands abob in the waters
       between inevitability
Or they are tuna with
       spiders astride

Writing in mobs
Soaking

And isn't this itself the
       endless triangulation: water, thing, and
       nearing
It seems the only backlit
       method

Then going back to the
       sex forgotten, the one directly
       ahead
Smaller than gravel, more coarse
       than silt

The future is dying
But tomorrow is that to
       which the future is unequal

                              June 13, 1988

Charles Bernstein

The Parts Are Greater than the Sum of the Whole

1.

A Defence of Poetry

for Brian McHale

My problem with deploying a term liek
nonelen
in these cases is acutually similar to
your
cirtique of the term ideopigical
unamlsing as a too-broad unanuajce
interprestive proacdeure.
You say too musch lie a steamroller when
we need dental (I;d say jeweller's)
tools.
(I thin youy misinterpret the natuer of
some of the poltical claims go; not
themaic
interpretatiomn of evey
evey detail in every peim
but an oeitnetation towatd a kind of
texutal practice
that you prefer to call "nknsense" but
for *poltical* purpses I prepfer to call
ideological!
, say Hupty Dumpty)
Taht is, nonesene see,msm to reduce a
vareity of fieefernt

prosdodic, thematic and discusrive
enactcemnts into a zeroo degree of
sense. What we have is a vareity of
valences. Nin-sene.sense is too binary
andoppostioin, too much oall or nithing
account with ninesense seeming by its
very meaing to equl no sense at all. We
have preshpas a blurrig of sense, whih
means not relying on convnetionally
methods of *conveying* sense but whih may
aloow for dar greater sense-smakinh than
specisi9usforms of doinat disoucrse that
makes no sense at all by irute of thier
hyperconventionality (Bush's speeches,
calssically). Indeed you say that
nonsenese shed leds on its "antithesis"
sense making: but teally the antithsisi
of these poems you call nonselnse is not
sense-making itslef but perhps, in some
cases, the simulation of sense-making:
decitfullness, manifpulation, the
media-ization of language, etc.
I don't agree with Stewart that "the
more exptreme the disontinuities...the
more nonsisincial" : I hear sense
beginning to made in this sinstances.
Te probelm though is the definaitonof
sense. What you mean by nomsense is

soething like a-rational, but ratio (and
this goes back to Blake not to meanion
the pre-Socaratics) DOES NOT EQUAL
sense! This realtioes to the sort of
oscillation udnertood as rhytmic or
prosidci, that I disusccio in Artiofice.
Crucialy, the duck/rabitt exmaple is one
of the ambiguity of *aspects* and clearly
not a bprobelm of noneselnse: tjere are
two competing, completely sensible,
readings, not even any blurring; the
issue is context-depednece)otr
apsrevcyt blindness as Witegenstein
Nonesesen is too static. Deosnt't
Prdunne even say int e eoem "sense occurs
"at the contre-coup:: in the process of
oscillatio itself.
b6y the waylines 9-10 are based on an
aphorism by Karl Kraus: *the closer we
look at a word the greater the distance
from which it stares back.*

2.

Which means I try to derail trains of thoughts as much as follow them; what you get, in my poems, is a mix of different types of language pieced together as in a mosaic—very "poetic" diction next to something that sounds overheard, intimate address next to philosophical imperatives, plus a mix of would-be proverbs, slogans, jingles, nursery rhymes, songs. I love to transform idioms as much as traditional metrics because I'm looking to say things I can only say in poems; I'm driven by that necessity. Sometimes there's a gap between sentences, sometimes the sound or sentiment carries over that gap: these shifting, modulated transitions express my philosophy as much as my prosody.

For the destination is always staring just out-of-view and all the signs are flashing "access denied." I make meaning of the failure to arrive, for so often it is a breaking down of the chain of sense that lets me find my way. A way away from the scanning over and over what went wrong—the failure of community that may, in flits and faults, give way to conversation. I start with the senselessness of the world and try to make some sense with it, as if words were visceral and thoughts could be tolls. It's the loss, I want to say, I don't know *of what*—but not to find either (neither voice nor truth: voicings, trusts).

For me poetry and poetics are not so much a matter of how I can make words mean something I want to say but rather letting language find ways of meaning through me. Form is never more than an extension of sound and syntax: the music of poetry is the sound of sense coming to be in the world.

I've never been much for balance, but there's clear advantage to staying on your feet or not falling off the bed. I was a slow learner (which I suppose may be why I like to teach): I found it difficult to reproduce socially prized models of balance, symmetry and grace; no doubt I grew to resent these things, more often conventions than the immutable principals they purported to be. It seemed to me I kept my balance in some mighty awkward ways: it may be my aesthetic now, but it was largely given to me by disadvantage. Disadvantage, that is, puts you in mind of your particular vantage and that enables some sort of eco-balance: balance within a complex, multilevel system—where posture, say, or grammar, is not the only factor. Within a poem, the more active questions of eco-balance are one of proportion and judgement. I think what may make my work seem difficult is that I am always testing my judgments, throwing them off-balance so that I can see where they land: and this testing, this interrogation, of judgment and senses of proportion constitute the aesthetic process for me.

On balance, I am reminded of a remark made by Wittgenstein to his sister, Hermine: "You remind me of somebody who is looking out through a closed window and cannot explain to himself the strange movements of a passerby. He cannot tell what sort of storm is raging out there or that this person might only be managing with difficulty to stay on his feet." When the reader is sealed off from the world of the poem, it may well seem strange and demanding; it is only when you get a sense for this world, and not just the words, that the poem can begin to make sense.

In one of my earlier works, *Veil*, I overtyped the same page a number of times with a continuously running text that became increasing illegible to me as I proceeded to write, thus creating a visual image of opacity—what much of my work may achieve through other means. The sense of stain, as in soiling, and its associated sadness, is crucial; but also, as in biochemistry, the stain allowing you to identify otherwise invisible substances. In this sense, my poetry is an acoustic staining. That's why I'm inclined to dwell on (in) forms of damage, maladjustment, dislocation. This is not an aesthetic theory so much as an experiential dynamic—call it the everyday: that we have our misalignments more in common than our adjustment to the socially correct norms. Normalcy is the enemy of poetry—my poetry, "our" poetry.

When a recent *New York Times* (8/19/92) runs a piece on "out-of-sync" kids and how "we" can help them fit in, I see my poetics (and their debt to Hawthorne, Thoreau, and Emerson) spelled out in reverse.

"We've all known children like this," Jane Brody begins, "they stand too close or they touch us in annoying ways; they laugh too loud or at the wrong times; they make 'stupid' or embarrassing remarks,...they mistake friendly actions for hostile ones,...they move too slowly, or too fast, for everyone else; their facial expressions don't jibe with what they or others are saying, or their experience is seriously out of step with current fashions." While I both identify and try to attend to such differences, peculiarities and idiosyncracies of perception, the article predictably prescribes the psychological orthodontics of correction and behavioral modification to obliterate the dis-ease, which is given the high-fallutin' name of dyssemia (flawed signal reception), a suitable companion discipline to my own poetic preoccupation, dysraphism.

My work *Veil* has an epigraph from Hawthorne's "The Minister's Black Veil." The minister who veils his face in the story gives this explanation for his veil: "There is an hour to come when all of us shall cast aside our veils. Take it not amiss, beloved friend, if I wear this piece of crape till then." Our bodies veil us from transparency (say, assimilation) and the veil acknowledges that: that we can't communicate as if we had no veils or bodies or histories separating us, that whatever communication we can manage must be in terms of our opacities and particularities, our resistances and impermeabilities—call it our mutual translucency to each other. Our language is our veil, but one that too often is made invisible. Yet, hiding the veil of language, its wordness, its textures, its obstinate physicality, only makes matters worse. Perhaps such veils will be cast aside in the Messianic moment, that utopian point in which history vanishes. On this side of the veil, which is our life on earth, we live within and among the particulars of a here (hear) and now (words that speak of and to our condition of everydayness).

3.

Pinky Swear
(A Nude Formalist Sonnet)

Such mortal slurp to strain this sprawl went droopy
Gadzooks it seems would bend these slopes in girth
None trailing failed to hear the ship looks loopey
Who's seen it nailed uptight right at its bearth
There's been a luring and a ladling lately
That swills the pitch and hiccups fates gone dim
With gumption and such buckle-bursting hurt
Allies with pomp paraded, permed and soapy
You'd guess the call was made by that same twerp
Destroyed the rig and left you almost dopey
  Let daze frequent a thought that's soft and gloopy
  Fluttering like a drill 'een here and earth
  Then spin a phrase or spill a toast in verse
  Such swivel cups the sail of tusked whoopee

4.

The Revenge of the Poet-Critic

What is a poet-critic, or critic-poet, or professor-poet-critic?; which comes first and how can you tell?; do the administrative and adjudicative roles of a professor mark the sell-out of the poet?; does critical thinking mar creativity, as so many of the articles in the Associated Writing Program newsletter insist? Can poets and scholars share responsibilities for teaching literature and cultural studies or must poets continue to be relegated to, or is it protected by, creative writing workshops, where, alone in the postmodern university, the expressive self survives?

  Of course I must agree, I confide to the prize-winning poet, all this stuff about poetry groups and movements is a publicity stunt for poets without the imaginative capacity to assert their unique individuality in forms and voices utterly indistinguishable from the other prize-winning poets who vote these awards to each other on panels and juries that systematically rule out any trace of individuality expressed by particularity of tone, diction, syntax or form. Indeed, you force me to concede the point, I tell the politically committed academic, this poetry excludes most of the people in the world (who haven't yet learned English!); it's turned its back on the ordinary reader by making no effort to reach out to him or her. And, yes, indeed, Professor, I also must admit, even though it seems to go against your last point, that all this poetics stuff is just an attempt to attract readers, making the work just one more commodity being peddled. Of course you're right, I tell the few friends I have left, now that I am poet-professor at the University at Buffalo, I have retreated to an Ivory Tower, removed from the daily contact I used to have, as a poet-office worker in Manhattan, with the broad masses of the American people...the ones that I used to meet at downtown poetry readings and art openings.

And surely it is a scandal, I tell my students, how Americans are afflicted with attention deficit disorder, just like they say in *Time* magazine, which after all should know, being one of the major sites of infection for the disease it laments, with its "you can never simplify too much" approach to prose and its relentless promotion of exclusively predigested cultural product. And since we all know students can't follow a linear and symbolic argument of a conventional poem, how can you possibly expect them to read the even-more-difficult poems you seem bent on promoting, interjects a concerned younger member of the faculty, eager, in his own classes, to present the ideological cracks in the surface of popular culture? You want to take things that appear accessible and linear, I reply, and show how they are complex and inaccessibly nonlinear; I want to take things that appear complex and nonlinear and show how this complexity is what makes them accessible in the sense of audible (auditable). And, I continue, waving my arms and upping the tempo as my colleague's eyes begin to spin in orbits, isn't the non-linearity of much so-called disjunctive poetry indeed a point of contact with the everyday cultural experiences of most North Americans, where overlays of competing discourses are an inevitable product of the radio dial, cable television, the telephone, advertizing, or indeed, at different level of spatialization, cities? But isn't advertizing and the commercialization of culture a bad thing, interrupts the future public intellectual, isn't that what poetry should be trying to resist; and isn't the sort of poetry you promote just a capitalization to the alienated fragmented discourse of postmodern capitalism? If you say so, I reply in the manner of Eeyore, as if I had found myself caught in a Gap ad (Robert Frost Wore Khakis: "the gap I mean"). But you can't quite have it both ways: the form of much of the most innovative modernist and postwar poetry may not be the obstacle you imagine it to be, so don't use that fact as a way of dismissing the activity as esoteric. Neither hypotaxis nor parataxis has an intrinsic relation to poetry, cultural resistance, or accessibility: the mistake is to demonize radically paratactic approaches as both the unreflected product of the worst of the culture and at the same time as esoteric, though I would suggest this particular double bind is a very effective tool for the stringent enforcement of cultural hegemony within a multicultural environment. And do beware the role of public intellectual, my friend, for when *The New York Times* starts talking about either the death or rebirth of public intellectuals, they can only remind us that intellectuality as a form of linguistically investigative activity has been banned for a long time from its pages and that public intellectuals unwilling to clip their tongues the better to induce in readers thinking-deficit disorder have not gone away, they have been barred from this and other standard bearers of the culture.

So no, I tell my colleagues, I don't ever give exams since my aim is not to evaluate the undergraduate students but to profess poetry to them, who have mostly hardly read a poem by a living poet, never gone to a poetry reading, never heard a tape of a poet reading her or his work, never had a poet come to a class to talk about writing. You see, I go on, I want to teach first and foremost how to become immersed in the experience of poetry; I teach from the point of view of writing poetry rather than analyzing it; recognizing the forms and structures and processes of making a poem more than assigning a fixed meaning to these forms and processes. I call this method a reading workshop, an immersion course in poetry as a second language, or PSL—people in solidarity with language.

For the ideolectical poetry of which I speak is fundamentally performative. It is in a mutlilectal social space, with its multiple overlays of colliding languages—slang and professional, advertising and technical, personal and bureaucratic, machinic and infant—that this work finds its context. By performative, I mean to emphasize the acoustic dimension of this poetry, a soundscape that cannot be accounted for by recourse to traditional ideas of prosody or measure. A new poetry demands a new prosody as much as a new poetics.

In creating an aural poetry, I think it's possible to have the resonant presence of language without hypostatizing a single speaker as the source of the language. Writing, that is, can become answerable to itself in ways that do not advance upon orality but are co-present with it. To do this, however, writing cannot revert to the conditions of orality, nostalgically imagining itself as secondary, as transcript of the voice, but rather must acknowledge its own materiality and acoustic density/destiny, its visible aurality.

But it must also acknowledge its performativity, which means that teaching and writing about twentieth-century poetry needs to take account of the phonotext and much as the visual inscription, the performance and much as the publication.

5.

I've only just begun to contradict myself. But I contain no multitudes; I can't even contain myself.

Nor am I interested in proving anything. —Except to you, sir: to you I want to prove a thing or two, I'll tell you that.

6.

Rivulets of the Dead Jew

Fill my plate with *boudin noir*
Boudin noir, boudin noir
Fill my plate with a hi-heh-ho
& rumble I will go

Don't dance with me
'till I cut my tie
Cut my tie, cut my tie
Don't fancy me till
The rivers run dry
& a heh & a hi & a ho

I've got a date with a
Bumble bee, bumble bee
I've got a date with a
wee bonnie wee
& ahurtling we will go

7.

We interrupt this entry in *ONWARD: Contemporary Poetry and Poetics*
to bring you the following public service announcement:

You say *ironic* I say comic, you say *alienated*
I say *disaffected*—besides I'm no alien, I'm from New York!
You've got to make the bridge before you can (double)
cross it. Give me a place to stand and I will look for
a place to sit. A poem should be at least as funny as

watching paint dry in the Cenozoic moonlight.
It's only a joke but then it's only a poem.
As Amberian has written:
In one-liners, there truth dwells in its [lowest] tracings"
[lit. most base, close to the ground].
What was it Freud said about jokes, it slips my mind?
In the great historic project of undermining the hegemony
of men's authoritative discourse, humor finds it hard
to keep a straight face. Is verse lite slighted?
Or is it one of those urban versus—
what do you call it now?—nonurban? issues,
in that much of the distrust of the comic extends a pastoral
and lyric tradition, a poetics of sincerity,
that the hyperironic (including the panironic, postironic,
malironic, cataironic, and parairionic), what you call radically ironic
poetry, actually
works to erode. But then, if you don't distrust the comic
what *are* you going to distrust? Just let me take off this
truss! To quote Amberian again
Sincerity is closest to deception
which no doubt echoes the well-known proverb,
"Beware a sincere man selling fish,"
which means, roughly, judge a *man* by what he says
not by his force of conviction or tone of veracity.
Can we talk?
Sincerity is the last refuge of scoundrels,
profundity an ingredient in every devil's potion,
&, hey, you!, don't tell me about love when you're
turning your back on me as if to talk to some
Higher Authority. The only Higher Authority I know
about is my landlord and I already paid her this month.
Against High Seriousness as such!
I'm for a men's poetry that questions the importance

of earnest anguish, of new-found sensitivity,
of subjective acumen as market "tool," that wants
to make fun of much that men hold dear. Surely
there be that delight in giddiness, in which the ecstatic
refuses to valorize itself. The raucous, the silly,
the foolish render the viscosity of the world's
vicissitudes. *The shortest distance from transcendence
to immanence is hilarity.*

Let there be one, two, many languaging poetries! (There always
have been.) Let readers coproduce meanings and let meanings
coproduce readers! Let alienation be encountered so that
alienation can be countered! Let counters be mixers and
mixers be movers and movers put up big tents for lots of
acts. And let disaffection melt away in the sounds of
laughter so that grief may compose itself in the space
between the laughs.

8.
The Inevitable Flow of Material Things through the Pores of the Years

Bleached
to the point of
subordination
blasted
stochastically
in the increase
of manners taken to
calling
COMMENCED BLAZON
surreptitiously trips
resolute

tourniquet
guiding the lackadaisical
flurry
(improvisatory hindsight)
chugging
bean-bag apocalypse
interlineated upon
systematic
(or did she say systemwide?)
malfeasance
gumping up the
animation emulator
not a minute before
toking on toxic
thought detectors
tossed together with
targeted segments
of remorse, the
motive for infinitesimally
orgasmic
liquid labors, clutched
ordinances dancing on
head of a
whining for
Mercurial acrobatics, phonocentric
disquisition. *I*
mend the tense
so the lore may
open,
fiddle with keys
to find cues
or is
deputation

allergic to
elation, mirroring
churl on its way
to stippled
evisceration.

After
the crash
the
closest
we get
is
still too
far
&
words &
speeches
don't amount
to
a hill
of cream,
dreaming
an end to
scores,
a land below
the
flakes.

By my clock
it's ten to
& the minutes
burn a hole
in my

socket, the
seconds scar
a moment after
gone
but wayward
knows no way
than toil's
triumphalist
deflation, tailoring
tokens to
abutments, tug
to tissue.
The lowliest
incursions
are marbled in
fume of
doing's dated
demotion (demolition)
crawling
toward the
crossed souls
of delay and
infusion.
Millions more
proclaim
all that they
defame—defining
polis by
madness,
common fact
by its
disdain. Once
there was

a plate, a hat
I gave it to my love
with spins & claps
but quick she
put it
far away
now
neither can we
find
to put them
on a
tray.

Less light, less light
So we may lurking go
& go atumbling to the glen
& come astumbling home again
For Felix & Emma & Jane
Have scarcely had time for blame
The march, long march to history
Has cast its shadow too far to see
& we in the haze go foundering
As far as dusk is deep
We in the glaze go floundering
& foundering sound the leaks

Waiting in line
at square restaurant
with round tables
oval windows
sky keeling
turvy topsy
yearning dissuasively

for the violas in
plaintive view
as society turns them
(everyone)
into monikers of not-sure-
what-to-do-next, certain
enjambment, virtual
expiation. "I don't
know what you
mean" "Never heard
of the pie" "Close
the closet" "Bring your
anti-dousing lip gear".
Solo flight to
expectation, illuviation
ill-illumined
quagmire.

You be the monster
I'll be
bountifully unresplendent in my
taffy-boy alligators
or
lull-me-with-a-bazooka
mint concatenations.
You be
cyclic necessity
before I take off to
overblown barrage, cuddly
tutelage, encephalic
twisters. Torched
but never
touched, saddled

with torque
(torso) of
history's elephantine
grunge (grudge). Toot
toot! No
telos—no
turkeyshoot, bombastic
(emblematic)
erasures, strip
pining. Gurgle against
dusk, put a
flume in the
goggling
apparatus—hazelnut
boom in micturating
cadavers of
mottled obliquity and
fractal
obeisance. Foam
let me foam
among the crumpled
locks of dismay's
store—the shellack
of diligence (dissidence), the
garage without entrance.
Such spray as might
bilk a mannikin,
tangle with a
dweeb. Crucify my
makeshift allowance, derogate
the hole in this
rustic avalanche of
unadulterated

charm. Beside the bottle
is the periwinkle
in sync with
blinding arbitration's
two-bit architectonics.
Betray the doily
and sunder the
swift limp of
interpolation's bogus
village. Jillions for jihads
but not one
red fence for
occipital
invagination, hydroponic
telekinesis.

Can something be
sort of
or does it have to be
yes or no
highly or discombobulated
bilious or acridly
ripe for fulmination.
If the circumstance allows
she'll recalibrate her
orbit and pass within
nanoseconds of our
outer utterance, the one
with the wigged
obelisks and shard-skin
bona-fides. Ugh! the tolling
of the turbans, the bluster
of the warps. Oops! the syncopation

of the doldrums, the
cantillation of inordinate
inherence. Yippi yi eh
yippie ey oh! frisked the
earls and made them
brisket on rye. Forty
cents, forty cents
& not a second more.
I'll be there in
blink o' inch
soon's the ink's
a sigh—soon as
the ink's a sigh
my friend, & the rain
has a pocket to
put it in.
Then I'll come
jagged & I'll come
jigged
into the higgletty piggletty
rig!
*
Yes, forty
dents, forty dents
& not a minute more.
I'll be there in a
squint & a pinch
soon's the link's
a sigh—soon as
the link's up high
my friend, & the pain
has a locket to
put it in.

71

Then I'll come
ragged and I'll come
wigged
into the piggletty higgletty
jig!

Rosmarie Waldrop

Thinking of Follows

I. Composition as Explanation

In the beginning there is Gertrude Stein: "Everything is the same except composition and as the composition is different and always going to be different everything is not the same."

This is also to say, in the beginning is Aristotle: "by myth I mean the arrangement of the incidents."

FRAMEWORK:

a) LINGUISTIC:

Every speech act (every use of signs) consists of selection and combination (Saussure, Jakobson). This means words always have a double reference: to the code and to the context. The code gives us a vertical axis with substitution sets where the elements are linked by similarity. We choose from them whether to say the man, the guy, the fellow, whether to say walked, ran, ambled, sauntered, etc. Then we combine the selected words on a horizontal axis to say: "the man ran around the corner." We put them in a relation by syntax, by contiguity.

Literary language tends to divide according to an emphasis on one axis or the other. Some are more concerned with *le mot juste*, with *the* perfect metaphor, others, with what "happens between" the words (Charles Olson).

b) HISTORICAL:

For the long stretch from Romanticism through Modernism (and on?), poetry has been more or less identified with the axis of selection, relation by similarity, metaphor. This has large implications:

that the "world" is given, but can be "represented," "pictured" in language; (Baudelaire: "Man walks through a forest of symbols");

that the poem is an epiphany inside the poet's mind and then "expressed" by choosing the right words;

that content (and "meaning") is primary and determines its ("organic") form; (Creeley / Olson: "Form is never more than an extension of content");

finally, that the vertical tendency of metaphor (Olson: "the suck of symbol") is our hotline to transcendence, to divine meaning, hence the poet as priest and prophet.

"SHALL WE ESCAPE ANALOGY" (Claude Royet-Journoud), or, COMPOSITION AS PROCESS:

Nothing is given. Everything remains to be constructed. (Robert Creeley: "a world that's constantly coming into being")

I do not know beforehand what the poem is going to say, where the poem is going to take me. The poem is not "expression," but a cognitive process that, to some extent, changes me.

John Cage: "Poetry is having nothing to say and saying it: we possess nothing."

As I begin working, far from having an "epiphany" to express, I have only a vague nucleus of energy running to words. As soon as I start *listening* to the words, they reveal their own vectors and affinities, pull the poem into their own field of force, often in unforeseen directions, away from the semantic charge of the original impulse. What matters is not so much the "thing," not "the right word," but what "happens...between" (Olson).

Paul Valéry: "When the poet enters the forest of language it is with the express purpose of getting lost."

Barbara Guest: "The poem enters its own rhythmical waters."

Edmond Jabès: "The pages of the book are doors. Words go through them, driven by their impatience to regroup.... Light is in these lovers' strength of desire."

George Oppen: "When the man writing is frightened by a word, that's when he's getting started."

PALIMPSEST:

But it is not true that "nothing is given": Language comes not only with an infinite potential for new combinations, but with a long history contained in it.

The blank page is not blank. No text has one single author. Whether we are conscious of it or not, we always write on top of a palimpsest (cf. Duncan's "grand collage").

This is not a question of linear "influence," but of writing as dialog with a whole net of previous and concurrent texts, tradition, with the culture and language we breathe and move in, which conditions us even while we help to construct it.

Many of us have foregrounded this awareness as technique, using, collaging, transforming, "translating" parts of other works.

I, A WOMAN:

This fact clearly shapes my writing: thematically, in attitude, in awareness of social conditioning, marginality—but does not determine it exclusively.

Lacan is preposterous in imposing his phallic cult on the signifier—and in bad faith when he claims gender neutrality.

Conversely, I don't see much point in labeling certain forms as "feminine." (Even though I like some of the suggestions, e.g. Joan Retallack's & Luce Irigaray's, that the feminine is "plural," comprising all forms that conspire against monolithic, monotonal, monolinear *uni*verses.)

I don't really see "female language," "female style or technique." Because the writer, male or female, is only one partner in the process of writing. Language, in its full range, is the other. And it is not a language women have to "steal back" (Ostriker). The language a poet enters into belongs as much to the mothers as to the fathers.

COMMUNICATION:

In crossing the Atlantic my phonemes settled somewhere between German and English. I speak either language with an accent. This has saved me the illusion of being the master of language. I enter it at a skewed angle, through the fissures, the slight difference.

I do not "use" the language. I interact with it. I do not communicate *via* language, but *with* it.

What will find resonance is out of my hands. If the poem works (and gets the chance to be read) it will set off vibrations in the reader, an experience with language–with the way it defines us as human beings.

Walter Benjamin: "Art posits man's physical and spiritual existence, but in none of its works is it concerned with his response. No poem is intended for the reader, no picture for the beholder, no symphony for the listener."

MEANING, especially DEEPER:

All I am saying here is on the surface, which is all we can work on. I like the image in *Don Quixote* that compares translation to working on a tapestry: you sit behind it, with a mess of threads and a pattern for each color, but have no idea of the image that will appear on the other side.

This holds for writing as well. I work on technical aspects, on the craft. I try to make a pattern that works, coheres. My obsessions and preoccupations find their way into it.

But what the poem will "mean" is a different matter. I can only hope that it will give a glimpse of that unreachable goal (which, paradoxically, is also its matrix), the concentration, the stillness of those moments when it seems we're taken out of ourselves and out of time.

II. Practice

"I don't even have thoughts, I have methods that make language think, take over and me by the hand. Into sense or offense, syntax stretched across rules, relations of force, fluid the dip of the plumb line, the pull of eyes..."

(A Form/ Of Taking/ It All)

1. EXPLORING THE SENTENCE:

The tension of line and sentence. But especially the sentences. Erosion of their borders. Sliding them together, towards a larger (total?) connectedness.

Both in *The Aggressive Ways of the Casual Stranger* and in *The Road Is Everywhere or Stop This Body* I worked on making the object of one phrase flip over into being the subject of the next phrase without being repeated:

> Exaggerations of a curve
> exchanges time and again
> beside you in the car pieces the road together
> with night moisture
> the force of would-be-sleep
> beats through our bodies
> denied their liquid depth
> toward the always dangerous next
> dawn bleeds its sequence
> of ready signs

The target was strictly grammatical. Consciously I was pushing at the boundaries of the sentence. I was interested in having a flow of a quasi-unending sentence play against the short lines that determine the rhythm. So, on one level, I was simply exacerbating the tension between sentence and line that is there in all verse. And since the thematic field was cars and other circulation systems (blood, breath, sex, economics, language, a set of metaphors never stated, but made structural) I liked the effect of hurtling down main clause highway at breakneck speed.

It was only later, that I realized that this challenge to a rigid subject-object relation has feminist implications. Woman in our culture has been treated as object par excellence, to be looked at rather than looking, to be done to rather than doing. Instead, these poems propose a grammar in which subject and object function are not fixed, but reversible roles, where there is no hierarchy of main and subordinate clauses, but a fluid and constant alternation.

After a while, though, I began to long for subordinate clauses, complex sentences. So I turned to writing prose poems. I became fascinated by Wittgenstein and by the form of the proposition because of its extreme closure. This was a challenge because my previous poems had mostly worked toward opening the boundaries of the sentence, either by sliding sentences together or by fragmentation. I tried to work with this challenge, accept the complete sentence (most of the time) and try to subvert its closure and logic from the inside, by constantly sliding between frames of reference. I especially brought the female body in and set into play the old gender archetypes of logic and mind being "male," whereas "female" designates the illogical: emotion, body, matter. Again, I hope that the constant sliding challenges these categories.

"You took my temperature which I had meant to save for a more difficult day." (*The Reproduction of Profiles*)

2. FRAGMENTS:

"Isogrammatical lines connecting the mean incidence of comparable parts of speech map the discourses of the world, I say. Against their average, extremes of sense and absence create the pleasure of fragments. Break the silence and pick up the pieces to find a cluster of shards which catches light on the cut and the next day too." (*A Form/ Of Taking/ It All*)

This glint of light on the cut, this spark given off by the edges is what I am after. Juxtaposing, rather than isolating, minimal units of meaning.

And the break of linearity. When the smooth horizontal travel of eye/mind is impeded, when the connection is broken, there is a kind of orchestral meaning that comes about in the break, a vertical dimension made up of the energy field between the two lines (or phrases or sentences). A meaning that both connects and illuminates the gap, so that the shadow zone of silence between the elements gains weight, becomes an element of the structure.

> puberty: he
> and I know I
>
> puff of smoke
> insults
> the future
> *
> centers unlimited
> mirrors
> a not yet open door
> precisely: an occasion

Jabès, like the German Romantics, holds that the fragment is our only access to the infinite. I tend to think it is our way of apprehending anything. Our inclusive views are mosaics.

3. COLLAGE or THE SPLICE OF LIFE:

I turned to collage early, to get away from writing poems about my overwhelming mother. I felt I needed to do something "objective" that would get me out of myself. I took books off the shelf, selected maybe one word from every page or a phrase every tenth page, and tried to work these into structures. Some worked, some didn't. But when I looked at them a while later: they were still about my mother. (As Tristan Tzara would have predicted. His recipe for making a Dadaist

79

poem by cutting up a newspaper article ends with: "The poem will resemble you.")

This was a revelation—and a liberation. I realized that subject matter is not something to worry about. Your concerns and obsessions will surface no matter what you do. This frees you to work on form, which is all one can work on consciously. For the rest, all you can do is try to keep your mind alive, your curiosity and ability to see.

Even more important was the second revelation: that any constraint stretches the imagination, pulls you into semantic fields different from the one you started with. For though the poems were still about my mother, something else was also beginning to happen.

Georges Braque: "You must always have two ideas, one to destroy the other. The painting is finished when the concept is obliterated."

(Barbara Guest would qualify that the constraints must be such that they stretch the imagination without disabling it.)

Collage, like fragmentation, allows you to frustrate the expectation of continuity, of step-by-step linearity. And if the fields you juxtapose are different enough there are sparks from the edges. Here is a paragraph from *A Key Into the Language of America* that tries to get at the clash of Indian and European cultures by juxtaposing phrases from Roger Williams's 1743 treatise with contemporary elements from anywhere in my Western heritage.

OF MARRIAGE

Flesh, considered as cognitive region, as opposed to undifferentiated warmth, is called woman or wife. **The number not stinted, yet the Narragansett (generally) have but one.** While diminutives are coined with reckless freedom, the deep structure of the marriage bed is universally esteemed even in translation. **If the woman be false** to bedlock, **the offended husband will be solemnly avenged**, arid and eroded. He may remove her clothes at any angle between horizontal planes.

4. "TRANSLATION":

By this I mean taking some one aspect of an existing work and translating it into something else. For instance, *When They Have Senses* uses the grammatical structure of Anne-Marie Albiach's E*tat* as a matrix, much in the way poets used to use a metrical scheme. It was an additional challenge that E*tat* is in French, so that the grammatical patterns did not work very well in English and thus had a built-in push beyond themselves.

An example closer to home is *Differences for Four Hands*. This sequence began with following the sentence structure of Lyn Hejinian's prose poem *Gesualdo* and "translating" it into a kind of invocation of Clara and Robert Schumann.

In the finished version this is not all that easy to trace any more. Hejinian's sentence is much more quirky than what I ended up with, because I needed something closer to the tension between fluidity and stillness that's characteristic of Schumann's music. And a sentence about the increasing number of children: "Run. Three children through the house." "Run. Five children through the house." became a kind of refrain or ostinato which changes the structural feel. But here is a passage which has remained quite close:

Hejinian, *Gesualdo*:
Two are extremes. You place on noble souls. The most important was an extraordinary degree. What has been chosen from this, but a regular process of communication, shortly implored for long life and forgiveness. You are a target of my persuasion. I am overlooking the city. At times I am most devout and at others most serene, and both pleasure and displeasure haunt me. My heart is not above the rooftops.

Differences for Four Hands:
Any two are opposite. You walk on sound. The coldest wind blows from the edges of fear. Which has been written down. Passion's not natural. But body and soul are bruised by melancholy, fruit of dry, twisted riverbeds. Loss discolors the skin. At times you devour apples, at others bite into your hand.

5. RHYTHM:

Rhythm is the elusive quality without which there is no poem, without which the most interesting words remain mere words on paper, remain verse. "Upper limit music, lower limit speech" said Zukofsky. Rhythm, I mean, not meter. It is hard to talk about, impossible to pin down. It is the truly physical essence of the poem, determined by the rhythms of my body, my breath, my pulse. But it is also the alternation of sense and absence, sound and silence. It articulates the between, the difference in repetition.

6. REVISIONS:

I think on paper, revise endlessly. I am envious of a poet like Duncan who has such absolute confidence that anything that comes to him is right. "Speaking in the God-Voice" I heard him call it. "Of course," he added, "if you speak in the God-Voice you say an awful lot of stupid things!" More important to me: he considered new poems his revisions of the old ones—this is beautiful.

But I feel closer to what John Ashbery said in conversation with Kenneth Koch, that he feels any line could have been written some other way, that it doesn't necessarily have to sound as it does.

I am slow and need to think about things a long time, need to hold on to the trace on paper. Thinking is adventure. Does adventure need to be speedy? Perhaps revising is a way of refusing closure? Not wanting to come to rest?

Inserting the Mirror

1

To explore the nature of rain I opened the door because inside the workings of language clear vision is impossible. You think you see, but are only running your finger through pubic hair. The rain was heavy enough to fall into this narrow street and pull shreds of cloud down with it. I expected the drops to strike my skin like a keyboard. But I only got wet. When there is no resonance, are you more likely to catch a cold? Maybe it was the uniform appearance of the drops which made their application to philosophy so difficult even though the street was full of reflection. In the same way, fainting can, as it approaches, slow the Yankee Doodle to a near loss of pitch. I watched the outline of the tower grow dim until it was only a word in my brain. That language can suggest a body where there is none. Or does a body always contain its own absence? The rain, I thought, ought to protect me against such arid speculations.

2

The body is useful. I can send it on errands while I stay in bed and pull the blue blanket up to my neck. Once I coaxed it to get married. It trembled and cried on the way to the altar, but then gently pushed the groom down to the floor and sat on him while the family crowded closer to get in on the excitement. The black and white flagstones seemed to be rocking, though more slowly than people could see, which made their gestures uncertain. Many of them slipped and lay down. Because they closed their eyes in the hope of opening their bodies I rekindled the attentions of love. High-tension wires very different from propensity and yet again from mirror images. Even if we could not remember the color of heat the dominant fuel would still consume us.

3

Androgynous instinct is one kind of complexity, another is, for example, a group of men crowding into a bar while their umbrellas protect them against the neon light falling. How bent their backs are, I thought. They know it is useless to look up—as if the dusk could balance both a glass and a horizon—or to wonder if the verb 'to sleep' is active or passive. When a name has detached itself, its object, ungraspable like everyday life, spills over. A solution not ready to be taken home, splashing heat through our bodies and decimal points.

4

I tried to understand the mystery of names by staring into the mirror and repeating mine over and over. Or the word 'me.' As if one could come into language as into a room. Lost in the blank, my obsessive detachment spiraled out into the unusable space of infinity, indifferent nakedness. I sat down in it. No balcony for clearer view, but I could focus on the silvered lack of substance or the syllables that correspond to it because all resonance grows from consent to emptiness. But maybe, in my craving for hinges, I confused identity with someone else.

5

Way down the deserted street, I thought I saw a bus which, with luck, might get me out of this sentence which might go on forever, knotting phrase onto phrase with fire hydrants and parking meters, and still not take me to my language waiting, surely, around some corner. Though I am not certain what to expect. This time it might be Narragansett. Or black. A sidewalk is a narrow location in history, and no bright remarks can hold back the dark. In the same way, when a child throws her ball there is no winning or losing unless she can't remember her name because, although the street lamp has blushed on pink the dark sits on top of it like a tower and allows no more than a narrow cone of family resemblance.

6

I learned about communication by twisting my legs around yours as, in spinning a thought, we twist fiber on fiber. The strength of language does not reside in the fact that some one desire runs its whole length, but in the overlapping of many generations. Relationships form before they are written down just as grass bends before the wind, and now it is impossible to know which of us went toward the other, naked, unsteady, but, once lit, the unprepared fused with its afterimage like twenty stories of glass and steel on fire. Our lord of the mirror. I closed my eyes, afraid to resemble.

7

Is it possible to know where a word ends and my use of it begins? Or to locate the ledge of your promises to lean my head on? Even if I built a boundary out of five pounds of definition, it could not be called the shock of a wall. Nor the pain that follows. Dusk cast the houses in shadow, flattening their projections. Blurred edges, like memory or soul, an event you turn away from. Yet I also believe that a sharp picture is not always preferable. Even when people come in pairs, their private odds should be made the most of. You went in search of more restful altitudes, of ideally clear language. But the bridge that spans the mind-body gap enjoys gazing downstream. All this time I was holding my umbrella open.

8

I wondered if it was enough to reverse subject and object, or does it matter if the bow moves up or down the string. Blind possibility, say hunger, thickened. How high the sea of language runs. Its white sails, sexual, inviting to apply the picture, or black, mourning decline in navigation. I know, but cannot say, what a violin sounds like. Driftwood migrates toward the margin, the words gather momentum, wash back over their own sheets of insomnia. No harbor. No haul of silence.

Harry Mathews

Dormouse Poem

There is no raw material

Late one spring, I caught a dormouse that must have recently become a mother: while visiting the attic of our farmhouse the next day, I heard a small cheeping sound that led me to two hairless pink baby dormice that had emerged from their hidden nest to wriggle blindly across the floor in quest of the sustenance that only their mother could provide.

Let's take a photograph. The babies are dead and gone. The image looks like nothing imaginable and is clearly pretextual.

I encountered my first dormouse when I saw it perched on a hot-water pipe running under the ceiling of the stable that I had made into a living-room in my house in **Lans-en-Vercors**. The pipe formed one end of a dormouse run that led from the entrance to the room on the south side to a wall, perpendicular to the north side, that separated the stable from a cold-storage room; the wall doubtless concealed a **rodent stairway**, or perhaps elevator, to the upper floor and beyond that to the attic. In the living-room, the visible dormouse route included the hot-water pipe (south), the top of the **wooden manger** (folklorically left in place), the books on the top shelf of a narrow bookcase, and a plastic wiring tube (east), finally another hot-water pipe leading into the **perpendicular wall** (north).

resistants battle in a coal-mining region

row dents: tear weight

wouldn't main chirr?

tissue like late Gothic archi- tecture

Siamese
l'ébrécheur de
merles
sans son, aide à
lilas
bol y va

The shelf of books on this dormouse highway held nothing but opera librettos. Not long after their first appearance, the dormice began eating—nibbling, really—a number of librettos, taking extreme care in their selection. Paperbound and slim, the librettos were packed tightly together in chronological order without any consideration of nationality, so that I was surprised to see that the dormice had managed to extract *Thaïs, Les Pêcheurs de Perles, Samson et Dalilah,* and *Bolivar* for their exclusive nourishment. Their adroitness as well as their altogether sympathetic patriotism easily persuaded me to tolerate their misdemeanors.

the prank and
the Pope
si mon bock a
l'nez gras

The day nevertheless came when, having found the edges of *Dido and Aeneas* and *Simon Boccanegra* showing familiar mutilations, I knew that the dormice must go. I caught one with a rat trap. I found it, not dead, with its skull cracked and its right eye half out of its socket and left it in the trap for half an hour in a sinkful of water before throwing it on its back in the

composite hip

compost heap. Three hours later the dormouse had righted itself and was breathing in hurried gasps. I put it out of its misery, swearing I would never again inflict such suffering on so courageous a creature.

the greatest
flax

I then acquired two cats, Basta and **Max**. Basta, a talented mouser, proved useless in catching dormice. They continued to look down on us from the hot-water pipe and Basta would look back, his body elongated towards them like a rubber band stretched to

the inspired
actress-
detective

the limit, or **Saint Teresa in her ecstacy**, the image of absolute yearning. I meanwhile fell madly in love with the cats, the first I'd ever had.

Having learned of **Have-A-Heart** traps, I cheering drums decided to try one out: a rectangular wire box with with a narrowing entrance at one end that led into a kind of antechamber from which the quarry was then supposed to nose his way under a horizontally hinged lid that closed behind him as he reached the bait (for dormice, **a piece of fruit**). It struck me that even a Apis of root curious beast would need the instructions sheet to penetrate all the way to the heart of this contraption. And why would he ever go near it in the first place?

I felt that I could at least mitigate the latter problem; so after baiting the trap with a slice of apple and setting it behind the upright board that crowned the bookcase against the perpendicular wall (the northern hot-water pipe passed through it), I surrounded the drinking Violetta's health cage on every side with broken pieces of **Melba toast**, which for some reason I felt would appeal to dormice and conceivably draw their attention to the trap's existence.

The day passed. I was alone at the time. After dinner, I sat down at my harpsichord (directly in front of the libretto shelves, with the perpendicular wall at my back). I began sightreading the *Goldberg* a justice's deviations *Variations* and was well into the repeat of the second half of the theme when I heard behind me a rapid crunching sound. Turning round, I beheld a young dormouse, its elbows resting on the library cornice, a fragment of Melba toast in its paws, its **kohl-ringed** gold rink-dyes **eyes** staring at me, its ears cocked, its head tilted to one side in the manner of Georges Perec. I dared not move, or even stop playing, and so read on, from time to time glancing around at my ever-attentive audience, until at last its appetite for Bach or for Melba toast diminished and it disappeared. I couldn't of course tell whether it was this or another animal that I found next morning in the trap, possessed by the apparent demons **of terror and furious disbelief** that were soon to become familiar to me.

Since then I have caught hundreds of dormice, at least ten every year and one year as many as fifty-nine. The variation in numbers has less to do with **baby booms** than with the mundane fact of my presence in mid spring, when the dormice awaken from their winter slumber, and mid fall, when they arrive for the next hibernation. Once caught, they are immediately transferred to **a roomier bird cage**. The transfer demands alertness–the animals are as prehensilely agile as monkeys and fast as quail; in fact the only way I ever caught one that got away was while it flew through the air. When there are four or five dormice in the cage I drive across the valley into a forest and release them. Once they realize I am not subjecting them to yet another humiliating trick, they shoot out of the cage and across the ground to the nearest tree, whose far side they climb to a safe height before stopping to peer down at me. According to my **Swiss animal guide**, dormice are sedentary and will not travel more than **twelve hundred meters,** so there is little risk of their invading the nearest farms, and none at all of their returning to mine.

France in the 1790s: unrestrained loss of faith

bay, beep Poons!

the goal-net needed a bigger woman

swish annual guy Delft under Demeter the Apostles' cento prosodies

Sometimes after dinner on autumn nights, when Marie and I were reading in the living room, we would hear the dormice beginning to stir in their cage (they are **nocturnal creatures**), I would move the cage nocturne alters itches nearer to the couch where we sat, and we would abandon our books to watch our captives bustle about their wire walls and aggressively take turns running in the **drum-like wheel** (intended for I know not what fishbait: parmesan pet) that I had fastened to one side of the cage; its contours blurred with the speed of the whirl imparted to it. At the end of the evening, after turning out the lights, we could hear the wheel whirring in the dark late into the night, **late into our sleep**. long after our death

Textual intercourse

A. Markers:

> slice a single intuition into several simultaneous approaches
> take away writing's patent of nobility
> the myth of *raw* material
> magnetize the filings in a particular direction
> the implied stereotype and its proper name
> conversely, reread an existing stereotype literally
> originality vs/with dehierarchized leveling, plus (above all)
>   efficacy
> poetry: infrapersonal static spaces (Baudelaire's *spleen*,
>   Mallarmé's *azur,* etc.)
> how to treat Unidentified Verbal Objects with poetic precision
>   without freeze-framing them?

B. Explorations

[1. Rhymes:

dormouse	twelve hundred meters
farmhouse	nocturnal creatures
mutilations	crunching sound
Goldberg Variations	turning round

>   the variation
>   the next hibernation]

[2. Narrative elements omitted:

the young dormouse behind the bedroom wall-hanging
the stubborn young dormouse that pried its wire bars apart
the asbestos fire-gloves used to handle the dormice
the ineffectual air-pistol]

3. | dormouse | *ruse mood* |
    |---|---|
    | *door muse* | mode or us |
    | door: me, us | more do us |
    | doom ruse | muse rood |
    | doom user | moor Duse |
    | doom rues | moor-used |
    | doom suer | mouse rod |
    | Duse, Moro | ur Om-dose |
    | douse ROM | *used room* |
    | O rum dose! | sour dome |
    | O use dorm! | sour mode |
    | *our domes* | *some dour* |
    | rouse mod | sue O dorm! |

4. Identified verbal objects

Lans-en-Vercors
rodent stairway
wooden manger
perpendicular wall
Thaïs
Samson et Dalilah
Les Pêcheurs de Perles
Bolivar
Dido and Aeneas

Simon Boccanegra
compost heap
Basta and Max
Saint Teresa in her ecstacy
Have-A-Heart traps
a piece of fruit
Melba toast
Goldberg Variations
kohl-ringed eyes
terror and furious disbelief
baby booms
roomier bird cage
Swiss animal guide
twelve hundred meters
nocturnal creatures
drum-like wheel
late into our sleep

5. Use:

Experiment:

Cross two Rousselian procedures—homophony, polysemy

Example:

the verbal object "twelve hundred meters"

through homophony: Delft under Demeter

through polysemy:
The Apostles [twelve] cento [hundred] meters
    [= prosodic measures]

divide and recombine:

> For Demeter, cento meters
> Delft under the Apostles

hence:

> "   ...At a wedding the
pertinent goddess approached among prodigious pastiche
>   prosodies."

> "   ...dusty missionaries
shunted down corridors of blue-and-white tiles"

Birth [draft]

After the conclusive battle of the sounding horns,
  incense rose towards a resistance of slag heaps.
The accumulated weeping left the gaze of the onlookers absorbed
  by the destructive string of holes pierced in the rock.
Clumsily installed, big drains then buzzed in the champagne flood
  that drenched our domes and anchors. In time they dried; but
then disease afflicted us, a disease that gave outer cells the
  precedence of birth, so that buffoons came to blows over
their likeness to hammer-beam roofs. One of them was singled out,
  after the plucky judgment of some dour woman in a ruse mood:
"Germans are all Siamese." Others remained silent—the bitch,
  the strong man, the lilac—and in silence they flourished.
Next came the exquisite effacer, chipping the beaks of
  sinful Nymphenburg blackbirds, and "the Latino," throwing
his weight behind the bowl inscribed *Libertador* in the great
  tableware rebellion, and a lady who expired without notice
from the pope, who had been tricked into visiting a beloved
  aunt by some doltish Faust, his mouth black with stein foam.
We read the report of the thigh joint assembled out of odds and
  ends, the slaughter of unharvested hemp, and the lambs
still fairest at the country fair. Deluded by a prankish hussy,
  a sculptor refused to cast his favorite actress-detective
in bronze—he was the typical victim of a reverse-brainstorming
  percussion device that in cheerful mode contracted
rather than expanded mental processes; so instead he developed his great
  potato monument, which had the shape of a cuddly bull.
The usual ladies convened at Violetta's. A health was drunk
  in the digs of a young swell. Through the frozen city
islanders searched for their relative, the judge, uselessly
  tracking down his familiar deviations, beholding in passing
the watery essence under skaters' blades aglow with myriad

100

tributary wedding bands—a reminder of Paris in the '90s
in the midst of so much regularisation (the athlete struggling,

in frantic loss of faith, to pare his beloved discus
down to official dimensions; across the vast natural harbor

a plethora of boatswains piping, in hierarchical pain,
the abstractionist out to sea on a raft of spars; the

reformer's throat too sore to utter his door-muse's name;
the guttural goal keeper fined for swearing; dusty missionaries

shunted down corridors of blue-and-white tiles). There were
hopeful signals, too. Tab, an active gay and town favorite,

was named "Muslin Man of the Year." At a wedding the
pertinent goddess approached among prodigious pastiche prosodies.

A sympathetic observer who had contracted hives found relief
in the night-blooming compositions of John Field played by

a relay of select melancholics. Another citizen survived
torture—he repeated the word "Parmesan" while smothering

in a bath of live worms and grasshoppers that were
transforming him into "a loathsome coward"—to tell us, "We

pursue our lives in a used room where the thought
of 'long after' lurks in the closet grasping a red-scare scenario

of my death. But as we hear the casino wheels whirring late
into the night, late into our sleep, a pink fuse slips towards

the light (nettle root, red-onion sprout, fur-nestled bud),
towards the light, nakedness, and decisive surprise."

Key West, January 20, 1995

Birth

After the conclusive battle of the sounding horns,
     incense rose towards a resistance of slag heaps.
The accumulated weeping left the gaze of the onlookers absorbed
     by the string of hard holes dug out of the rock.
Clumsily restored, big drains then buzzed in a bubbly flood
     that drenched our domes and anchors. In time they dried; but
disease then afflicted us, a disease that gave outer cells the
     precedence of birth, so that buffoons came to blows over
their likeness to old slabs. Some remained silent—the bitch,
     the goon, the lilac—and in silence they flourished.
The exquisite effacer began chipping the beaks of sinful
     Nymphenburg blackbirds; the Unifier threw his weight behind
the bowl inscribed *Libertador* in the great tableware
     rebellion. We read of the thigh joint made of odds and ends,
the razing of unharvested hemp, the lambs
     still fairest at the country fair. A sculptor refused
to cast his favorite actress-detective in bronze and instead
     raised his great potato monument in the shape of a cuddly
bull. The usual ladies convened at Violetta's. A health was drunk
     in the digs of a young swell. Lost islanders searched for a
relative, beholding in passing the scrumble under skaters'
     blades aglow with tributary wedding bands. The desperate
athlete struggled to hammer his discus into humiliatingly
     reduced dimensions. Across the vast natural harbor,
in hierarchical grief, a plethora of boatswains piped
     out to sea an abstractionist lashed to two spars.
The reformer's throat was sore; the guttural goal keeper
     was fined for swearing; dusty missionaries were shunted down
corridors of blue-and-white tiles. There were hopeful signals,
     too. At a wedding the fitting goddess was seen to approach
among impertinent pastiche prosodies. A sympathetic observer who

had contracted hives found relief in the night-blooming
music of John Field played by relays of select
        melancholics. A citizen survived torture by repeating
the word "Parmesan" as he was smothered in a bath of live worms
        or grasshoppers that was transforming him into "a loathsome
coward." He told us, "We pursue our lives in a drab room where
        the ghost of 'long after' lurks in the closet grasping a
red-scare scenario of my death. But as we hear the casino wheels
        whirring into the night, into our sleep, pink fuses slip
towards the light—nettle root, red-onion sprout, fur-nestled
        worm—towards the light, nakedness, and decisive surprise."

Key West, March 13, 1995

David Bergman

Staying in the Lines

> Ah! love, let us be true
> To one another! for the world, which seems
> To lie before us like a land of dreams,
> So various, so beautiful, so new,
> Hath really neither joy, nor love, nor light,
> Nor certitude, nor peace, nor help for pain...

I have been teaching Victorian poetry all semester, and these famous lines of Matthew Arnold have haunted me—not with their passionate pessimism or rhetorical ripeness—but with their interpretive complexity. What am I supposed to make of the fact that Arnold calls his interlocutor "love," and then says that the world "Hath really neither love"? Is this a cunning paradox—a pre-post-modern wink to the reader—that the interlocutor is merely a literary convention, that there is no real person addressed, merely a literary fiction? Or is this a confession of her hypocrasy? You say you love me, but you don't really love? Or is this some bitterly ironic nihilistic joke—let say we love each other although there's no such thing as love? Or should I take it as the lines coventionally have been read as a form of synecdochal hyperbole—nature and institutions in general do not treat us kindly, but we as individual human beings can love and be faithful to one another?

Of course, all but the last of these readings is anachronistic, but my interest is not in historicizing interpretation (although such an enterprise is well worth undertaking for various reasons), my interest is in the poetics of the passage, its willingness to allow itself to be read in many ways in which the author did not consciously intend it to be read. I'm not speaking here of a Freudian subtext, but rather of the nature of what was once called figurative language but which we now see is to a greater or lesser extent part of all language—the way its meanings cannot be easily controlled, the profligacy of its signification.

*   *   *   *

The space that is reserved for art is the space permitted for signification to proliferate in ways that cannot be controlled. The first choral ode of *Oedipus Rex*:

> Divine Zeus and Apollo hold
> Perfect intelligence alone of all tales ever told;
> And well though this diviner works, he works in his own night;
> No man can judge that rough unknown or trust in second sight,
> For wisdom changes hands among the wise.
> Shall I believe my great lord criminal
> At a raging word that a blind old man let fall?
> I saw him, when the carrion woman faced him of old,
> Prove his heroic mind! These evil words are lies.

Dramatic irony is one of the terms we give for the proliferation of meaning intended by the author. Unreliable narration is another such term. But Sophocles knows that dramatic irony cannot be restricted to the speakers on stage or by the knowledge of the audience. "Wisdom changes hands among the wise." It is a currency whose exchange rate is always undercut by a healthy black market. Pound rails against usury, but the most precious words are those that demand scandalous interest rates and for those whose credit ratings are either most secure or dubious. Poetry is a kind of usury, demanding more in return than it seems to give. *These evil words are lies*.

*   *   *   *

A poetics that tries to comprehend itself will result in prose. The poet finds a way to be stupid with dignity—that is why Plato would not have him in The Republic. The unexamined life is not worth living, but the wholly comprehended one is shallow indeed. Keats was not the first, but perhaps the most eloquent poet, to create a poetics that would dignify a lack of understanding. *Truth is beauty, beauty truth* may well be the most successful formulation of the "evasion of philosophy," to use

106

Cornel West's phrase, that I know of. It is fitting that it is the inscription of the Grecian Urn since it is a secularization of that other rationalization of the poet's stupidity—that he is a vessel, the instrument, of divine inspiration.

* * * *

The modernist obsession with poetic technique is among many other things both a way to paper over the blindness of the poet and to facilitate that blindness, since it alone is the only means to proliferate meaning. After all, the poet should know what he's doing, not what he means. "In all important matters," Oscar Wilde tells us, "Style, not sincerity, is the essential," in part because "Only the great masters of style ever succeed in being obscure." Only by attending to the surface do we permit ourselves to uncover the obscure depths that are beyond our rationalistic control. The great stylist subverts himself as the earnest moralist can never do.

A parable: An old Jewish student of the Zohar had spent his life trying to find the true name of God, believing that with its utterance the world would be destroyed and all the spirits reunited in the Godhead. Like the infinite number of monkeys, given an infinite amount of time and typewriters to produce the complete works of Shakespeare so he from morning until night, year in and year out whispered various combinations of nonsense syllables believing that eventually he would hit the right one. One day, the townspeople found his lifeless body with a smile on his face. He had mistaken his own death for the destruction of the world, and so died happy in his ignorance. The townspeople went back to work privately delighted. They had feared that by some fluke, he might have in fact stumbled on the right name—and then where would they be?

The death of the poet is always a cause for quiet celebration.

* * * *

107

I wrote "The Window" after I broke up with my lover with whom I had lived for five years. I thought I was writing a poem about how all my attempts of being considerate turned into disaster. It was supposed to be a poem vindicating my own behavior.

The Window

All that spring I was afraid to stand
near windows for fear I'd throw myself
out of one. Twice I had found myself
flung from a chair and making a run
for it, driven by dreams of leaping
clear of the pain of his desertion:
my lover of five years who one day
in midwinter needed more distance
from a life he felt had grown too close.

Then one morning a cat was howling
in the courtyard of my building. There
he sat, a miniature tiger
in the shade of the Japanese plum.
He showed passers-by his needle-like
incisors and his bright coral tongue,
but if given a minute, he'd come
to press his flanks against your ankle,
then flip round to have his belly rubbed.

It took me no time to discover
he was defenseless as a kitten—
stripped of balls and claws, a Chippendale
sofa cut down to Shaker size. I
brought him food and water, then waited
for his owners to arrive for him.

Surely they knew he'd never survive,
denatured as he was, through the wild
predatory darkness of late May.

But at midnight he was still down there,
batting the moths at the lamppost and
ringing the ivory carillon
hung in the lilies-of-the-valley.
What else could I do but bring him up
to my fourth floor apartment? I slashed
the latest pages of the *Times*, then
filled a Macy's box with the litter,
placed box and cat on my screened-in porch,
closed the stiff French doors and went to bed.

Next morning he was gone. I could see
the corner where he butted his head
until the screen gave way and the leaf
that he left on the ledge, curled and brown
like a mouse, a gift for my concern.
I couldn't bear to look. I turned and ran
four flights down to where I'd knew he'd land—
a bank of ivy—and found—nothing—
not a dent in the thick ground cover.

I stuck to the facts not because I was trying to be honest, but to
allow the poem room to be more honest than I could ever be. Narrative
is always destabilizing because the more precise it becomes the more
self-incriminating it becomes. It is a poem such as "The Window" that
reminds me—in case I need reminding—of two lessons I have learned:
(1) you *can* know too much about a poem for your own good, or rather,
in the act of composing, it is important that you don't try to understand
what you're writing too well, and (2) that adhering to technical matters—

in this case controlling the nine-syllable line, the nine-line stanza, and the narrative pace—is important in order to distract you from the truth you're revealing about yourself and to provide the poem with a certain density of experience. "The Window" must be viewed in relation to another poem I wrote at that time in my life.

The Wrath of Medea

I know Medea's anger but can't quote
the lines she speaks, when hands about the throat
of her child, she feels his pulse beneath her thumb.
I know because I've felt that numb.

And I have smelt the stench of sweet revenge
rise up like a drunkard on a binge
to swat the snakes that coil about his brain.
Hieronymo's mad againe.

And then there comes the buzzing of the flies
swarming like pupils severed from their eyes,
roaring in the ears of pale Orestes.
I, too, have had my share of Furies

and felt the double-edge of your betrayal
perforate my heart as though in Braille
you wrote so in my blindness I could see:
By your love I was imprisoned, by your pain set free.

I wrote this poem virtually in one sitting as I waited in a little coffee shop for my psychiatrist appointment. It made me feel very good to write it—to get all that anger into disposable form. Sometimes a poem is like the glass used to store radioactive waste, a medium which won't let the toxic waste to spread and contaminate the local environment, something that will last as long as the poison within it. Poems like "The Wrath of Medea" are ways of forgetting, and forgetfulness is one of its themes. I hadn't read *Medea* for a decade, so I wasn't surprised to discover when I reread it, that the lines don't exist. It doesn't matter. I think of it as part of the madness of the poem, the fantoms of memory. As in the case of "The Window," while writing the poem I was concerned with technical matters. I've always liked the effect slant rhymes have in Emily Dickinson, and I hope in "Wrath" they give off the woozy clunkiness I was looking for. I also concentrated on both establishing a pentameter line and then violating it, of emphasizing endstops and then enjambing from one stanza to the next in a headlong dive to the end. An advantage of clearly recognizable formal properties is they so easily create expectations whose frustrations are expressive. I wanted a poem that seesawed between being mad despite its control, and controlled despite its madness. I don't think free verse would have given me the same expressive opportunities.

*   *   *   *

I am a formalist, but so are all poets. In mathematics there are no random numbers; there are only patterns of number that are more obvious than others. There are no unformal poets, but there are poets whose forms are more easily discernable than others. Discernablity, I should note, is a highly variable capacity. Many of my students cannot recognize a Shakespearean sonnet even after I have gone over its formal rules. In fact, many students have difficult recognizing rhyme. For them all poetry is strange and amorphous. Perhaps they do not look for form, because they are content with the passing sensation and resent the effort of memory which recognizing form requires—after all hearing rhyme requires keeping track of sounds. The discontinuity so prized by postmodernists and that has found its ultimate popular mode in music videos is a form of social amnesia, permission not to make connections.

* * * *

I have long ago stopped trying to justify my love of forms. I think of it as a personal peculiarity. A sonnet is not a higher mode than a free verse lyric, just a different one, with its own limitation and opportunities. Perhaps because I am a gay man, I neither hold my affections higher than other people or feel a need to justify them. I love what I love. Go figure.

* * * *

Nevertheless I have invented certain stories that help explain my love of form. Here's one: When I was three I fell off a swing and went into a coma. When I regained consciousness I had a tremor in my right hand. Thus as a child, I had more difficulty than most children staying in the lines of my coloring book, and I loved to color. I failed penmanship in grade school because—as I was repeatedly told—neatness counts. As a poet I retain the same delight I had as a child of staying within the lines. I'm not alone in this. Indeed, every poet is a child who plays the game of staying and straying within the lines. Many people think the pleasures of language should be grander than this. I don't.

* * * *

I speak "Dog" to my friend's dogs. They bark at me and I bark back at them. They howl and I howl too. Often we go up and down the tonal scale beginning with a low growl and slowly rising to a hysterical yip. Then they run to the window because they can never believe that there isn't a dog outside, and when they are satisfied that we are alone, they come back and smell my breath. Do they think I'm drunk? Finally they return to their spots three feet away from me, and bark again. We can go through this cycle sometimes three or four times before they get bored or hide anxiously beneath a table. At some level writing poetry is

112

akin to speaking "Dog." Sometimes making strange noises is pleasure enough. Indeed, the dogs through their curious ritualistic behavior have given my barking poem a form I find very satisfying.

* * * *

I have yet to write a poem in the voice of a dog—one of my favorite poems is Thomas Hardy's "Ah, Are You Digging on My Grave," in which a dog burying a bone converses with his dead mistress—but the desire to give the inarticulate speech is a very strong one, or rather I have a passion for translating ambient sound into its closest verbal equivalent, in the way the Zukofsky translated Catullus— not by rendering the *meaning* of the Latin into English, but by rendering the *sound* of Latin into English (see also Gertrude Stein's "Yet Dish").

Mozart's Canary

Purchased in the market for a song
because I sang so brightly he forgot
how dull my plumage was: the green mixed brown
and gray, the yellow paling at my throat.

He hung me in the window while the sun
drove me mad with thoughts of home, then took
my songs—desperate with joy and resignation—
took them down with a rapid, workman's stroke.

Listen to *The Magic Flute*. Tamina—
me. Papageno—me. The Queen
of the Night—yes, even she. All singing what
I poured into his ear: *free me, free me.*

He said he'd let me go when he had filled
his next commission, but then the requiem
arrived, and then.... I watched him wither and bloat,
and with the fleeting light claimed my revenge:

I simply refused to change my tune to sorrow;
each sound I made was insolent with life.
In the end he begged to have me carried off
to this back room where I have spent all winter

tilting my head up to the tainted mirror.
I watched my thin, white crown of feathers molt
like a powdered wig, then spill eighth notes like seeds
against the bars grown colder than the dead.

Ned Rorem told me that canaries don't produce eighth notes. He is right of course, but I don't know how to score for birds. What I wanted to get away from were *T* sounds. I hear a lot more *R*'s in birds and the high *E*, that I used "free me, free me." I wrote another poem soon after this one called "Mapplethorpe's Lily," which I originally set in the voice of the flower. But it seemed far too contrived. Every time I tried to imagine the voice of a lily what I heard was the buzz of a bee or a hummingbird.

* * * *

One reason it takes me so long to write poems is that their form grows out of working with the poem. If I end up writing a sonnet, it is not because I meant to write a sonnet, but rather as I worked on the poem, it headed toward the form. Each poem develops its own geometry. The stanza form of "The Window"—nine nine-syllable lines—is one that keeps emerging from narrative materials. For awhile I kept on producing two-stanza poems, each stanza six lines of seven syllables, but I never started out with that intention. The closest I come to a prearranged sense of form is if I turn up two lines that seem to me the refrain of a villanelle. But usually when I start working on poems, they turn into something very different from what I imagined they'd become. There are a number of different formal techniques I'd like to try and that I've temporarily made poems perform—but in the end, I've learned I can't force a poem to do my bidding. My job is to get out of the way of the poem, and help it along the path it seems to be heading. Sometimes I think it would be nice if I could follow Pound's advice and "make it new," but my attempts to impose technical innovations always end up in disaster. Over time I have come not just to accept, but be grateful for whatever poems are given me. I use to try to push poems along. People told me to start poems off with a bang. But this advice—which may be good for others—never worked on my poems. My poems always seem to start quietly or prosaically and build up energy as they go along. They find their way just as I find my way in them.

*   *   *   *

Because language is older, and over time a more complexly interwoven system than any one person could create, language can be wiser than any writer, do more profound things than any poet could imagine doing with it. If poetry is a space where everything counts, it is because the language we inherit has become so rich a resource that when we properly care for it, the smallest elements can be significant.

*   *   *   *

My experience that form is an integral part of the life of a poem runs counter the popular belief that the aim of formal writing is to freeze an experience, fix it, and remove it from time. Since my poems are frequently narrative and since narrative requires a sense of dynamic time (one damn thing happening after another), it might seem that bringing together fixed forms and narrative content is trying to unite antagonistic

115

elements. But in point of fact, the looseness of narrative chronology is complimented by all sorts of formal patterning. In fact, as Thom Gunn points out, the more fluid the experience, the more useful are the formal modes for conveying it. The union of formalism and narrative succeeds because it is not seamless. Formal properties make the reader more aware of the difference between the experience as lived and the poem as experienced, the fluidity of life and the rigidity of structure. In some ways Pound can champion free verse because of his belief in Confucian right reason, and it's important to note how imagism as a theory advocates both looseness of form and a virtual identity between a signifier and its signified (his ideogrammic method). Pound's poetics is more invested in a theory of mimesis than is generally acknowledged (and his racial politics has a similarly naive equation between sign and signified). For many practitioners the elimination of obvious formal devices is a way to make the poem more "natural" and to reduce the distance between it and the objects it describes.

But if formal poetry emphasizes the distance between the sign and signified by highlighting the formal properties of the sign itself, it does not remove the experience of the poem from the sense of change, flux, or temporality. Recurrence is not mere repetition. Even when lines reappear, the changing context alters their effects. It is the poor poem that merely repeats a line or a sound to fill out the requirements just as it is the poor free verse poem that is prose cut up into lines. Indeed, because of the various kinds of recurrence that appear in certain forms, they seem to me particularly successful modes for embodying the very nature of change, flux and temporality.

Days of the 1970's

The memory rises up and fades
when my youthful lover asks to know
what love was like before there was AIDS.

I could tell him about my escapades
on planes, in trains, aboard the Metro.
But the memory rises up and fades.

What of bath-house tricks? And tea room trades
with a living Michelangelo?
(Oh, how we loved before there was AIDS!)

Our militant joys marched in parades
that stretched in a line from the Pines to the Castro
as the memory rises up and fades.

Trucks and parks. Vice squad raids.
Underage boys dressed in drag for a show
whom we showered with love before they got AIDS.

In sweaters, feathers, chains and brocades,
we danced till the dawn crept sticky and slow
like a memory that conveniently fades
on what love was like before there was AIDS.

*   *   *   *

I find that my poems won't come out until they have shaped themselves formally. One summer I was going through a stack of books in the library set out because they might be of seasonal interest to the patrons, and I came across a slim volume *Bonzai for Beginners*. I thought to myself, this would make a wonderful topic for a poem. I have always been interested in bonzai and topiary. I took out the book, and my lover thinking I might want to *grow* a bonsai (as opposed to writing about them) brought back a pine seedling from the beach that he had dug up. For months I labored on this poem—the seedling died almost immediately—but the poem wouldn't come. Reluctantly I gave up

"Bonzai for Beginners."

For a different reason entirely I read a biography of Alan Turing, the mathematician, who at the end of his life was interested in the Fibonacci series in which each number is the sum of the previous two: 1, 1, 2, 3, 5, 8, 13... It seems the Fibonacci series is used to analyze organic growth. For example roots and branches are supposed to develop along the lines of the Fibonacci series. I'm not interested if this is true or not, but it occurred to me that it might make an excellent syllable count structure for the poem. I sat down, and the poem I hadn't been able to write for months came pouring out.

Bonsai for Beginners

What
the West
would achieve
by leverage, the East
would produce through scale. "Give me a
point and I will move the world," declared Archimedes.

"Make
it small
enough," said
the Zen master who
held a pebble in his hand
and fingered the continents encrusted on its shell.

Tree
that we
can only see piecemeal because
of their size can be studied whole
when reduced to the dimensions of a common bread box.

Such
wisdom
lies behind
the bonsai whose large
appeal appears undiminished
in those who feel the power of its concentration.

Here
I stand
with a pine
seedling John brought back

from the beach for me, its green quills
like eyeless darning needles jabbed into a cushion

Shall
I cut
its taproot
and plant it in some
pot no bigger than a thimble
as Mr. Morati directs in his manual?

Wrap
around
its limp trunk
and stubby branches
a bright armature of wire
so that it gleams like a maloccluded twelve year old

sent
against
his will to
the orthodontist?
Condemn it to a life of forced
confinement like the foot of a Mandarin princess?

All
beauty
is a form
of perversity,
the strange mutation
of chromosome and circumstance
than can make either a monster or a masterpiece.

But

the role
I play in
nurturing such freaks
is not beyond my frail control.
The oddities of nature may be nipped in the bud

should
I care
to nip them,
not letting my plots
be overgrown with anything
but the usual assortment of household flora.

Here
in the
U. S. A.
we have no need to
shrink the life around us and drive
it inward, introjecting its vital outward thrust

Why
stifle
what is great
within us? Such arts
have no part in modernity
and are better suited for the medieval zeitgeist

where
the whole
may be viewed
in one sitting and
inferred from any of its parts,
its locks opened by the same golden synecdoche,

where
Christ may
be revealed
in three dimensions,
his passion scene expertly carved
in a rosary no bigger than a horse chestnut.

I

want to
be weaned from
this old illusion
of completeness that brought heaven
and earth into the same compass as a grain of sand,

rid
myself
from the need
of totality
and draw my comfort from what won't
add up or by omission round to a graceful close.

John Taggart

Were You
Notes & A Poem for Michael Palmer

When I began writing some notes for a poetics essay, in response to an invitation from Michael Palmer, there was no thought of turning them into a poem. What happened, however, is that the notes proposed a new poem, one that seemed to satisfy a lack in this collection. You could say the poem meant the demise of the essay. In fact, as I became more involved in the poem's composition, the notes were increasingly taken up with "practical" considerations until they disappeared altogether. The poem ate them up. Perhaps, then, the central principle of any poetics is that it ought to result in poetry. If nothing else, this should moderate the production of poetics essays.

If of interest, the Chernoff book referred to in the notes is *African Rhythm And African Sensibility* by John Miller Chernoff. The Messiaen poem is my own "That This May Be." Caputo is John Caputo, author of *The Mystical Element In Heidegger's Thought*. Spanos is William Spanos, founding editor of *Boundary 2*; his essay is "The Errant Art of Herman Melville: A Destructive Reading of *Moby Dick*."

12.31.82
Primary: that the presumed goal of community is wrong and probably cannot be attained. The latter because individual vision challenges what has previously existed as a factor (agreed upon image) for unity. Individual vision, when first presented, must be perceived as a threat, actually as something promoting disunity. It's remarkable that Blake continues to act in this way and will no doubt do so into the future. Could a church be organized around Blake?? His vision is too various.

An instance of community is gospel singing. One has to be struck by its power, vibrant out-reaching power and possibility for total involvement.

The idea of critical detachment at a gospel service is anomalous. One either joins in or leaves; that's the choice.

The gospel service can't exist without complete prior agreement about the nature of the image/vision and its truthfulness. You can't doubt and sing with abandon. The identification, the location of the singer within the image has to be total. There is no room for the distance of irony.

The poem which establishes community will have to agree, in part, with the language of the old vision. Otherwise, the terms wouldn't be recognizable in any available, present way to an audience.

Am I thinking in terms of too simplistic an opposition in presuming the (new) poem must somehow destroy the old?

This isn't the right question.

There are things to do together and things to do by ourselves. Projects would be decided by scale. Language is not a project. By definition, it requires at least two interiors. Is anything improved when that number is increased? Perhaps the idea of one speaker and an audience of several auditors only apparently violates the nature of language as exchange.

Throw out the idea of money. The full house is still attractive. The larger the audience the more refined in the sense of simplifying the response. The larger the audience the less the possibility of involvement of individual members of the audience unless they confine themselves to the larger, single wave or direction of single mass response.

If there's to be, ultimately, destruction, then the beginning must offer the appearance of unified (recognizable) vision. How this can be done: by a fiction (several people are shown to sing together), by the use of terms that are evocative of past visions.

1.2.83

One way to have the poem fail: the audience is encouraged to be active (outloud) in its response and then is deliberately confused by the poet. The successful close of the poem is confusion. The poet has to retire in ignominy (but in secret triumph).

Poem as gospel service, poem as James Brown.

There should be some statement against performance poetry per se, that—in terms of traditional (tried, actually shared & practiced) ritual, especially by nonironic, non-white groups—it is so trivial, so merely aesthetic. The borrowing of Eno & David Byrne. These should be condemned.

What about the "spirituals" of Coltrane?

Write in the glisses, the sighs, the humming.

Artaud? Important, per Blake, that traditional terms be used. What one wants is such terms with utterly personal (private, untraditional) definitions, e.g., Jesus=the imagination.

There is a place for silence in a poetics. It's the desirable end goal.

Spanos is right to point out Melville's superiority to the Anti-Book, Anti-Scripture, the Satanism of the Romantics. The real test is whether one can stay quiet. Otherwise, each new poem is another mark of failure.

1.5.83

Yesterday, coming back from a walk with Sam, early evening, the sky divided toward the South in zones of color: bottom deep orange with outline of trees; above the orange as it starts to become pale a very light but intense violet; above that the light blue just before nightfall.

Looking back at my notes from Chernoff, I'm reminded that my assumption that a community, by definition, must be univocal isn't necessary. The community can be a "diversified assembly." The problem is how to make a separate contribution. Should it (can it) stay separate?

1.6.83
That is, separate & together.

first-phrase = (seed of) the patterned = several phrases or sentences; the standard pattern is repeated several times.

dance to come out of a trance, to join a diversified assembly with a separate contribution

music & dance: ways of posing structures and restrictions for "ethical actualization"

power of the music lies in silence of the gaps; this is where one's contribution must go & by it the music may be opened up further. The idea is to conceive the music as an arrangement or system of gaps and not as a dense pattern of sound. This rules out Xenakis. What about Riley, Glass, & Reich?

Say the rhythm before you play it. It may not be necessary to express this in nonsense syllables. Perhaps there could be such syllables which coalesce into words as the poem moves along.

1.7.83
Seed pattern: begin with a full phrase or sentence of words, then decompose it to syllables.

New poem should go in collection to break up the finale quality of the two last poems. This one needs to open the conclusion air out, make for a new kind of silence (in, within the poem vs. "stunned" audience). The opening can be combined with the idea of deliberate (designed) failure. Go beyond Eno, that sort of borrowing. James White & the Blacks.

Consider relation of the four parts to gospel song, to the "story" of the broken glass from the signal which means the train won't come on time, may collide with another train, or may not come at all. Forget the red sky, it's too pretty. The opening seed pattern has to be a song of *result*, the state of affairs after the lens has been broken.

Interpolated: put full statements by way of commentary, ie, this is the condition (landscape) that obtains *after* the destruction of the lens. The statements shouldn't be put in a section by themselves, but mixed, perhaps with the nonsense syllables.

I'll free you from demons, not capitalism!

think about it
repeats on the ends of phrases

Take end—work it out, elaborate it (into syllables, becoming more & more abstract, going toward pure gesture) and then return to extension of phrase given as words.

Ragged male voice shouting half-phrases, calm female choir *smoothly* singing whole phrases or sentences behind him

God has done great things for me (Colossians)
run jump sing & shout

drop piano, organ, bass—expose voices then slowly—fairly soft—bring them back; end comes on only slightly higher tone, which is not really close to the intensity of the middle just before the instruments drop out.

slow, restrained scream

1.8.83
The music is organized to be open to the rhythmic interpretation anyone present wishes to contribute. This organization of openness is achieved by the gaps. One makes one's contribution—a new, additional rhythm—*in* the gaps.

I may be wrong in feeling antagonistic to Peter Gabriel, reaction of the obscure against the famous. Still, I doubt if the hybrid is all that desirable. The goal still remains transformation. It's plagiarism or worse if that doesn't happen. Not to reproduce a sound, then, but to use it as a general principle to make another sound.

The train: voice, agent of the voice, the word

1.9.83
train won't deliver burning Dali baby
no Vietnamese doll baby

Opening phrase: talk about the train
time for train talk a rap??
the student said that just isn't an ordinary train
violet (why violet) did you expect blue?

rumble of the trains, vibration

the vocal tract (larynx, pharynx, mouth)=resonant chamber

voice organ consists of: power supply
  oscillator
  resonator

The cycle of opening & closing—vocal cords acting like vibrating lips—feeds a train of air pulses (Beating of the veins) into the vocal tract. The train of pulses produces a rapidly oscillating air pressure (throbbing, dilations) in the vocal tract—a sound.

The sound chopped by the vibrating vocal folds & generated by the airstream is the voice source. It is the raw material for speech or song. It is a complex tone composed of a fundamental frequency & a large number of overtones.

Messiaen identifies mode no. 2 with violet.

Complexes of resonances replace the concept of chords.

1.10.83
& I await the resurrection of the dead?

dehisce   (to yawn)
                to open spontaneously when ripe
                opening of (fruit) capsule by valves, slits, or pores
                splitting into definite parts

einode   das Westgerm
                poverty, want, give oneself away
                jewel heimat as home (not heaven), homeland

Ezekiel: the voice of the Almighty, the voice of speech
                a voice that was over their heads
                don't fall on your face/no voice

129

These never unravel their own intricacies & have no proper endings; but in imperfect, unanticipated, & disappointing sequels (as mutilated stumps) hurry to abrupt intermergings—

That profound silence, that only voice of our God...from that divine thing without a name, those impostor philosophers pretend somehow to have got an answer; which is absurd, as though they should say they had got water out of stone; for how can a man get a Voice out of Silence?

The room (finite, resonant chamber) opens out onto the desert.One side or wall *is* the desert.

pt 1 of poem   =a)   train through the summer night, alone in a room, violet tongue (get rid of?), a waves, & Ezekiel (voice & sapphire throne)

            b)   desert blood dried to dull brown (perhaps have terms of brilliance, but all put in negation, cancelled use   hymn tune

            c)   train

In a system of multi-rhythms—to keep your step—you have to hear the beat that is never sounded (hidden).

rule of repeats repetition reveals depth of structure
                (should be more, as *immediate*, in b)

fiction of audience supplying a beat to which I respond, use as basis for elaboration

the gaps: where & how big?
                (never at same place on successive lines)

1.12.83

Looking at the last paintings ('68-70) Rothko did, I'm tempted to stop. Shouldn't the poem—which may be the last one in the collection—be grey, not red or violet?

The gaps in the first section of pt 1 don't seem right. They're at different places on the line, but feel arbitrary. Why should they all be five spaces?

Good rhythm fills a gap in the other rhythms and creates an emptiness that may be similarly filled.

1.13.83

Adapting Chernoff, the open quality of the rhythm becomes a deception; if the call isn't actual, then the response must be strangled. A deceptive call to strangle the response. The organization should *look* open.

So: first pt appears open, to invite response

       second is oblivious, completely closed

       3rd returns to acknowledge, in terms of 1, that the possibilities are gone (same words, different tone) or that the very same calls are made in this final pt, but they're given without hope. Problem is intonation (on the page).

Re Caputo's comparison (Heidegger & Meister E): an experience with language can lead out, does lead out into "the world."

Term in his letter: *wiederholung*   retrieval of what somehow gets said in the work, not necessarily what its author intended

The difficulty isn't in the cancellation, but in providing something after the x-out. I think this will have to show up in the second pt. This won't alter what comes in the third, i.e., disillusioned repeat or near repeat of pt 1.

perhaps mention the poem is a late thought, something unexpected, added on to the collection

1.14.83
Time to consider what should go in the middle section of ten lines. One thing: it must be continually dense, very tight rhythm.

Think about feeding the Rothko quote (when red does appear, it is like a flame of self-immolation) throughout.

The idea of dried blood as the dominant color, color of the desert.

This is *after* the train doesn't come.

You were waiting alone in a room for the train, in a resonant chamber. One side or wall of the room opens out to the desert. The room, in fact, is more a number of perspective lines than an actual construction of walls.

This section should be so dense that the reader or listener is immobilized, unable to move.

1.15.83
could begin with "were you"

That the section of 10 lines be "about" the closing up of the gaps, that gaps themselves—with perhaps some quotation from Chernoff—be a reference.

unresting

Or: leave first part as "fiction"; then the following overlays operate as commentary (gaps, chernoff, the revisitation of the messiaen poem)

> explanation re lips, tongue
> that the bk. was supposed to be done

Went back to Spanos' essay last night. He argues that Ishmael, contra Father Mapple, uses language interrogatively. Presumably this connects with Heidegger's thinking as asking. He borrows Derrida's process of supplementarity for this as a process of repetition which always delays a final measuring—defers presence & thus allows the thing to go on living. Thus mystery is kept or enacted in an active way as opposed to the French always mouthing off about *mystère*, etc.

A naming that's an interrogation of Naming? Does he mean a questioning of the Word, provenance of His saying? One form would be to doubt, but not *the doubter* per se, member of a sect in itself. It seems possible that this is what occurs with the active use—more than "use"—of metaphor. What separates it from the New Yorker decorators is that it begins at the beginning of the poem and continues, as a process, throughout. Not merely incidental modification of cast-iron noun structures (always false, whatever the comfort). This may be connected with Ashbery. When I say I want the poem to fail, it's in terms of offering that assuring structure in new & winning ways. Now the interesting thing is to appear to offer just such ways and still make the structure, hope for & claim of structure, fail.

Always erring *words*, not the original/abiding Word

Ishmael has a disaffiliative enterprise

a careful errancy. When Spanos says that seeming for Ishmael is always seeming, the statement affirms that function of active metaphor. This way it's understood that poetry as the formal profession (?) of metaphor will continue—forget the question of audience—because of the nature of metaphor itself (unresting), the end of any single poem or the volume of anyone's collected works no more than a pause, parenthesis that will have to be open-ended on the right-hand side.

per etymology of *Dia-bolos*, poet as scatterer, disseminator, dissimulator—the finite, eccentric, dialogic voice that repeats & retrieves the *dia-spora*

to give undecidability a positive value (negative capability) to bear witness, to be a witness (this doesn't, contra Olson's emphasis on the topological—as if everything happens in terms of space & surface—refer only to object and event.

There *is* the mind, theatre of the mind.

un-name the beasts

tears at his clothes
keep throwing away, speed
up the decay process

1.16.83
Gk ereuthein = to redden

at the least refracted end of the spectrum
color of blood, fire, poppy, rose & ripe fruits

sky at dawn or sunset
of the cheeks, lips

dyed with red   red flag

forget violet

You were

1.17.83
By chance saw the Tarahumara dancers on TV!

1.18.83
Idea for overlay—section 3, over the middle 10 lines—attack the embrace
of the father, embrace of the soul by the father, at the end of B's
Jerusalem. That this—after the picture is given—somehow won't happen,
that the Word, contra E, won't be born.

Pulses make sound, and the sound becomes the Word. Perhaps use some
of Ong's statements on the word as sound.

(For bottom overlay: note that the words—were you ready, etc—are the
same, but the tone's changed.)

1.22.83
lines like puffed sleeves

mention the fiction of the broken glass?

This is a dense pattern of sound & not a system of gaps

Melville: imperfect unanticipated disappointing sequels mutilated
               stumps hurry

Xenakis: a book of screens equals the life of a complex sound
               each screen is made up of cells or clouds of grains

135

no room inside for movement

Augustine on repetition: a mode of assuring the seeker that he is on his way, and is not merely wandering blindly through the chaos from which all form arises

the train carries & is the voice, is the Word

God speaks his word in the birth of the son

true language=a response to the Word which the Father addresses to us (response=letting the Father speak his Word *in* us)

all human language must be silenced before the Father speaks

verbum cordis, silent inner word

through song the singer & the listener become identical

Father's son/word is personal & *breath-given*

word is in speaker as seed in source

>   the only source of flames
>   whose tongue pierces and
>   gathers the taste for the
>   Word

(last section can deal with the question of whether there's anything left after the negation)

We don't have the promise of the next breath—Jerry Lee

Gloomy Sunday!

Decided to leave bottom of the first page as it is, a repeat of the opening. Yesterday I thought it would have to be changed in the interest of variety. But, as I come to see, this is an eye demand. When I speak the parts, they're different, i.e., the opening fairly brisk and aggressive, the close slower and tentative. The real question is whether there should be, as in music, reading notation or instructions of some sort included, put in the margin.

new poem: How To Read Me

section 3 = 13 lines 1 overlap from 2 & 2 lines in the space between

Ives was trying to protect a fading transcendentalism behind all the noise, no? *That's* the unanswered question.

1.24.83

What is the connection between the train—train time & being fed the train—and dancing in the gaps? Turned around, what's the connection between there being no gaps to dance in and the train's nonarrival?

In the top & bottom sections, there is the promise of the train to be fed inside by the tongue of the father. Granted, this is past tense. (Pages after the first should be in the present?) If the gaps are closed, there can't be a dance or only a confused attempt. If you can't dance, you can't join the assembly.

First 3 lines deal with the gaps; beginning with the 4th they modulate back to the train or allow some sort of show-through from the middle section.

137

Perhaps even those lines, the first 3, shouldn't refer to the gaps because the thrust of the second page is clear enough. But: have to keep the last one for the overlap. Their disposition would be completely different if the first of the 3 begins with something other than "if."

Joining the dance=getting on, being part of the train?
Just say no gaps no train
1st line: carried over from 2 with some addition
2nd & 3rd: transition (gaps — train)
4-13: train (use Eck., possibly Ong)

1.26.83
Looks like the whole deal of there being no gaps—or that the gaps have been closed by the song in the air—will have to go in the last section as a series of questions.

2.6.83
"Were You" finished? Happy enough to type it up and clear off the desk of notes and the big cardboard sheets. Final section of 5 lines could go this way:

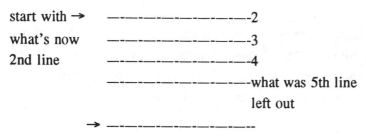

start with →   —-———————————-2
what's now   —-——————————-3
2nd line   —-——————————-4
      —-————————————-what was 5th line
            left out

      → —-————————-—-—--

      new line takes note of disappointed, unhappy sequels

But: may be wrong to want more of a da da dum end. Enough to pause a bit in reading the last line as it is. Let the past tense do the work. Important that the tone isn't too harsh; it shouldn't sound superior.

Were You

Were you ready   ready ready   ready for train time
       were you   were you
time to be fed   tongue   to feed train inside you
       were you   were you
train in   in waves of a as in father   amen train
     were you   were you

you were ready you were you were as you were as ready as you were
ready as you could be ready for ready for train time the violet
train you were as ready as ready for the love train "let's start a
love train" you were ready to pull the train ready as could be
to pull the train through the summer night "let's start" ready for
the end of the song "come on come on" ready for violet tongue to
tongue to feed violet train inside train in the train of pulses in
pulses inside you "come on come on" inside you in waves of a
waves of a as in father ready for the end for the father's tongue
you were ready for the father father's tongue to touch your teeth

were you ready   ready ready   ready for train time
       were you   were you
time to be fed   tongue   to feed train inside you
       were you   were you
train in   in waves of a as in father   amen train
     were you   were you.

Were you ready to place your foot in the gaps
were you ready to place confidence in the gaps
were you ready to enter a trance in the gaps.

Were you ready to enter a trance in the gaps were
you ready to do the locomotion in the silent gaps were you
ready to be entranced in the silence in the gaps ready
       read-ee-ee-ee you were you were "could be ready for"
       you were as ready as rain you were ready to pull
       the train through the sum of the song "come on come
       to feed violet train inside inside you "come on come o
       fa as in father read-ee-ee-ee-ee-ee ready for father
       to give the word train of pulses is a word ready to
       be fed to be given the inside secret word *verbum cordis*
       not say a word hushed to let father let father feed
       feed give speak the word hushed in response soul's
       language is hushed language of response you were ready.

Were you ready to listen and to understand in the gaps
were you ready to understand with a dance in the gaps
were you ready to do the dip with father in the gaps
were you ready to be embraced like Jerusalem in the gaps
were you ready to give birth to the word in the gaps.

Rachel Blau DuPlessis

On Drafts:
A Memorandum of Understanding

I cannot romanticize poetry. It is hard to make up words about it. For me poetry is the creation of a necessary object made in and of language. As a poet, I work with language and its critique—words, their histories, the play of social materials and discourses, the twangs of nuance, neologisms, aphasias, syntax, and the notion of continuities by sequencing, the groundswell of letters and the falling apart of language; I work with poetic conventions and their critique—line break, metrics, rhyme and other marked sound, sonorities and overloads, genres and their uses, motivated allusions to the cadence and turbulence of past materials, all the rhetorical resources I can muster, wild or tame; I work with textual conventions and their critique—punctuation, capitalization, the look on the page, the page space itself, the notion of "poem." Making poetry is real work with an intractable substance and intricate social institution (language) which is at the same time a medium with which we are all too familiar, being saturated in its blandishments and banalities every day. One works IN art with a manifold of conflictual traditions and IN the language with the manifold of exacting resources and IN genre with its vectors and suspicions. But also—works out of all these categories because they may prettify, hobble, or confine. Works with the visceral surges and material densities of language. Works with excess, to excess.

What makes any writing into poetry? Poetry as a specific kind of writing is distinguished essentially by segmentivity, that is, by the choice and division of its material into lines. One makes meaningful lines by the negotiation of kinds of temporalities (speech, meter) and kinds of markers (such as rhyme, hinge, blaze, bridge or gap) in interplay with syntax and statement. Line segments, as George Oppen proposed, construct the "sequence of disclosure" by "separating the connections of the progression of thought."[1]

In an objectivist mode, technique is the test (and text) of a person's sincerity. This makes an ethics of writing emerge simultaneously with the making of language. The basic "rule" of technique is that every single mark, especially the merest jot and tittle, the blankest gap and space, all have meaning. "Craft" and kinds of craftiness follow the intensities of the writer's need, for the poem or the writing. At this moment, making poetry, I like best the tactile quality of moving language around, sculpting it into shapes, making bodies of syntactic manifolds that suggest...meaning flickering in and out of focus, within and against the enormousness, and the enormity, of silence. When a poem is finished, and good, there is that comic, dastardly sense of satisfaction and pleasure that can be summed up as "The devil sold me his soul."[2]

The problem of memory is the largest motivation for my poetry. However, the sheer memorializing function attributed to poetry, especially as that singles out female figures to be surrounded by "the male gaze," has been an ethical and intellectual issue for me since the early 70s. This stance, which also involves the desire to criticize and undermine the lyric, to wring its ideology out, and to envelop it in the largeness of another practice, has been consistent as a motivation for twenty-five years.[3] It does not necessarily lead to feminist declarations in my poetry, but to questions, the research of cultural materials, in short, a feminism of critique. This commitment to analysis within the poetic act and text creates a powerful force field for me. This impulse to critique had long been joined with a tonal and structural interest in what I was calling (from about 1981 on) a "Talmud" poem, by which I meant something like midrash—doubled and redoubled commentary, poetry with its own gloss built in. My idea was sidebars, visuals, anything to create "otherness inside otherness." This formal issue, evoking Hebrew textuality, was also, as I was to find, of central thematic meaning.

It was also clear that my practice of essay writing, since the late 1970's with "For the Etruscans," created an opening my poetry. For example, I wrote this diaristic letter to myself in 1985 that illustrates the melange of feminist critique and issues in textuality as spurred by the essays (such as "Otherhow"): "My problem with 'being a poet' is stated in 'Otherhow'—I cannot believe in the perfection of lyric, the separation of lyric, the selectivity of lyric, the purity of lyric, the solitary language of lyric & cannot imagine what to 'do' next. NO! I *can* understand what to do next....a deliberate intermingled generative midden of a voice...a voice which accumulates all the pressures of its situation. And it means that what will therein appear could be, generically: a poem, an essay, a meditation, a narrative, an epigram, an autobiography, an anthology of citations, a handbill found on the street, a photograph, marginalia, glossolalia, and here we go here we go here we go again...." This note marks the beginning of the project that has been the focus of my attention since.

"I fumbled a size 8 paradun onto my 3X tippet and waded in. A businesslike boil 30 feet upstream drew my first cast." In 1986, I began, with fair abruptness, to write two intermingled canto-length works, and I recognized that a project in the long poem had begun. Like any cast, this project had a long pre-history. The question of length, extent, duration, ambition, desire, commitment combined with the calm one needs to face such a project had simply come into being. The claim of the long poem on myself, I recognized by virtue of establishing the title *Drafts*, a suggestive word for the title of the whole, and each. "Drafts" are never final. "Drafts" are freshly drawn and freely declared, as if a preliminary outline or sketch. In "Drafts," completion is always provisional. "Drafts" involve the pull or traction on something, a drain upon something, conscription into something. Therefore "Drafts" are an examination from the ground here, not elsewhere. No matter what.

Drafts, then, are a series of interdependent, related canto-length poems on which I have been working since 1986. The first two "Drafts," along with "Crowbar" and "Writing" appear in *Tabula Rosa* (Potes & Poets, 1987). *Drafts 3-14* was published by Potes & Poets Press in 1991; *Drafts 15-25, The Fold* is expected in 1996. These poems began over and over for many years before 1986, and a tracking of their origins is a tracking of vectors and sources.

o"Drafts" began in 1964, when I first read *Paterson*, or a little later when I furtively and pleasurably read the whole of *Spring & All*, a work at that time available, in its entirety, only in a Rare Books Room. I was reading that when all the lights went off in New York City—the great blackout.

o"Drafts" began in response to the unfinished issues in my intractable dissertation, *The Endless Poem* (1970), on *Paterson* and *The Pisan Cantos*. This was an awkward and academically marginal attempt to name the objectivist poetics to which I was connected, to explain how "imagist" poetics could have generated the modern long poem. Others, less in the dark than I was in the later 1960's, have written very effective books on these poems, but I was then unable to write satisfactorily on a topic I nonetheless felt as vital, joyous, and festering. This ambition to register the impact of Pound and Williams has subsequently migrated forward in time, affecting me in various ways during those 20-25 years. I am not sure in what spirit I offer these exorbitant numbers of years. It is not quite pride. Gratitude would be more like it.

o"Drafts" began in about 1981, when, after (repeatedly) teaching *The Waste Land* and seeing certain modern art, I had the vision of a text on plastic laminate sheets, layered one over the other, which could be read through, could slide relative to each other, and thus make changeable configurations of materials. This was also like the notion of a "Talmudic" text.

o "Drafts" came from a pivotal pre-"Draft" poem, a serial work called "Writing," dated 1984-85, whose concern with the first months of a child's life was deeply influenced by the originality of Mary Kelley's *Post-Partum Document*. In this poem, which cites from Williams' "January Morning," everything was "happening on the side."

o"Drafts" began in the fall of 1985, in Nijmegen, when I first read Beverly Dahlen's work *A Reading*, whose scope, passion, and design struck me with pleasure. Later I wrote about Dahlen's text, and noted her "heuristic establishment of form by the reading of those words she

146

has 'happened' to write." (*The Pink Guitar*, 118) Tracking the intricate meanings of one's own accidents—a practice related to H.D.'s writing practice in *Tribute to Freud*—gives rise to a midrashic layering and linkages of interpretation, where the production and productivity of meanings is continuous.

o "Drafts" began in the nourishing brown marbled-paper Italian notebook given to me by Kathleen Fraser, in which I (January 1986, just back from four months in Holland) "drew" or "drafted" words into the page, making a sketch-pad of language. I was teaching Creeley's *Pieces*. He claimed (it was said) never to revise. But it wasn't so much that permission, as the alert, nuanced present-ing he achieved, a series of shifting weights and balances on the page, engaged in the momentary registering of flicker. Suddenly, even on the luscious paper, in that extraordinary notebook, I felt free simply to notate words and sounds. To set meaning down. To write stops and starts.

o "Drafts" began on Solana Beach, the other end of the States from my home, on 17 May 1986, in the Sonia Delaunay notebook bought in Buffalo in 1980, but hardly used until that moment. I sat on the beach, a whole day writing, continuously, but in spurts, with an intense self-consciousness that was neither paralyzing nor aggrandizing, but business-like, and almost flat. I had been at La Jolla, at the Archive for New Poetry, reading George Oppen's papers for my edition of his *Selected Letters*. His words: "You have your own pencil and your own piece of paper and you're on your own word by word from scratch." It was true.

I cast myself off into "one." The first one was mixed with the second one; but once I named and separated, it was clear that I needed to write them and number them simply in the order in which they came, trusting to the fact of ongoingness. One began where "one" was. "One" was where one was writing.

At first, it seemed as if my plan was going to be the investigation of some "little words"—pronouns and pronominals ("it," "she")—the shifters. But such a conception eviscerated itself. Anyway, one had to be true to the "moving along," or on-goingness. What was learned from the

first ones was that there was a lot of "it" out there; that it was all "it."
And, one way or another, "she" was going to have to deal with "it."
Those first titles were, in fact, an amusing version of the project. Then
prepositions presented themselves ("of," "in"), which identified sites in
which there was participation and vectors of direction. Still, I had no
intention of writing a poem per pronoun, or for each preposition. So it
began to seem as if every scheme for settling the poem, for controlling
its processes of continuance, was self-devoured. Schemes became
inadequate to themselves virtually at the moment of their conscious
declaration. At about this time, I stopped worrying about what parts of
speech my titles came from, about what pattern they made, and about
what I was doing in any ultimate sense.

I could always point to or invent patterns of address among
groups of works, and it was interesting to do so. For instance, a group
of titles from 1988-1990 seem to intimate the materials of writing:
"The," "Page," "Letters," "Schwa."—"Letters" with the qwerty
keyboard foregrounded as alphabet. But these observations were no
sooner made and sustained than they too were eroded by and in time.
After this, there was a time when title words indicate genres and
grammatical little words ("Haibun"—a Japanese diary form of prose
mixed with haiku, and "Conjunctions"). The examination of textuality
is ongoing ("Title," "Traduction," "Incipit," "Segno") but this focus is
not exclusive, for I am also interested in work, and mapping, and their
results ("Working Conditions," Cardinals," "Philadelphia Wireman,"
"Findings"). In the poems subsequent to "Draft X: Letters," there is an
undercurrent of the sociological/poetic practice called (in the 1930s, in
England) "Mass Observation." In all the works, the distinction between
the discursive and the imaginative, between the analytic and the creative
is certainly frayed. Being willing to cast yourself off into it—this no
longer seemed odd or awkward. I assumed it. It had advantages. The
thought remains buoyant.

Let me return to memory, since I have a bad memory—maybe
I haven't talked about memory yet. Bad memory, like "bad dog!" I have

lived, for many years, with the losses of shadowy memory. Mourning for it. But in the poem I found that I was building the space of memory or a replica of its processes.

There is a repressed and barely articulated grief—the extensive killing that has formed the places in which we reside. Begin with the Middle Passage or the ridding and near-extermination of many First Nations and indigenous peoples during the colonial expansion of Europe. Begin with the Armenian genocide, or begin with the Holocaust. The accelerating firestorms of aerial bombardment. Begin with the first World War or the Second. Begin with the deaths of diversity—bio-diversity or linguistic diversity. Begin wherever you want, back in another century, or in ours. Begin with modernity, in any event. There is a ghost in our socio-cultural house whose specific outlines depend on a particular set of identifications and histories, but whose presence is palpable. The ghost is there—a "transgenerational phantom" (as Abraham and Torok say).[4] It seems as if poetry is the institution (a conduit, a bridge) through which this phantom can speak. Can make sounds. It can recognize and it can grieve.

How? Because of the thick layering of implication that words in poetry generate, because feelings are trapped in the rich matting of language, and as well because poetry acknowledges silence.

How? Does so thru words. Words which remind of other words (metonymies across a reaching plain). Words suggesting. Words that recall words used before. Words which contain the mysteries of the unspoken.

If Walter Benjamin argues that hope and memory are the epic experiences of time, what happens if you have only little hope and sporadic memory? My answer is this work. I consider myself a writer of a post-Holocaust era. The relation of this to my poetics is straight-forward: I try to write so that if a single shard were rescued in the aftermath of some historical disaster, that one shard would be so touching and lucid as to give the future an idea of who we were. It is like our reading Sappho after her almost total erasure. This kind of thinking sets a standard for the work. It is, of course, an impossible standard, but not the less compelling for that reason.

"Plenty of debris. Plenty of smudges."[5] These are poems challenged by—moved by—the plethora, the extent, the intricacy of the sites that seem to be at stake in their composition. Here is a typical situation: small to large, tiny to largest. It is about the plethora of stars, that vastness, and the dot or yod, the most miniscule mark. That it is. That we can read it. That it defines us and we barely know what or how. An absolute and a-human sense of scale into which these works get swallowed up—a dot, a point, a little flicker. These situations—of awe and amazement—are part what generates the poems.

In form *Drafts* are closest to collage, with its ethos of accumulation, clarity of the excerpt, preservation of edges, and juxtaposition. (In my vision, Schwitters, perpetually. And I think of the essay called "Marianne Moore" by Williams, in which the poetics of collage is analyzed.) But at other times, the works seem symphonic, declaring a vast performance space in which interesting sounds occur, develop, and reverberate. Structurally, the works are linked by subtle forms of repetition, presenting the reader with sets and bits of recollections, or the evanescent sensation of déjà vu, its rhythm of gap and recall, or the sensation of forgetting and being half-reminded, as if the poem, as I said, constituted the space of memory.

Drafts could be described as heterogeneric, making allusive loops around and through concepts of genre which the poems both appropriate and disturb, genres such as midrash, elegy, ode, autobiography, and meditation. In texture, they are heteroglossic—open to a range of voices, tones, verbal textures, social codes, and rhetorics. Definite motifs and thematic materials are at stake. A representative, although incomplete, list would include home and exile; writing and the scenes of writing; the minutiae of dailiness; death, and the dead linked with the living; silence and speaking. And as well the question what positions and discourses are adequate to speaking as a gendered "I" while at the same time, there is a distinct downplaying of any "I" (a word, incidentally, that rarely appears), and no more overt discussion of gender than of anything else.

Gender issues, however, do suffuse the formal and discursive choices that underlie my resistance both to continuous narrative and to lyric. Whether or not there are, in the poems, particular comments about being a person gendered female, it is clear that gender matters for the ground of these poems, and is their *sine qua non* in my commitment to a critical rupture of the standpoints and ideologies of the lyric: intact "I," bounded by yearnings for female figures, climax, epiphany, desire for beauty, consumable narratives, neat length. This type of poem, to generalize briskly, offers repetitious positioning of the self in predictable poetic/political situations but via brilliant language. I have argued (both in critical prose and in poetry) that the problematic of the lyric is acute for the female figure on whom poetry has had, historically, a number of designs. These poems are my response—an attempt to appropriate the sound, music, and nuance of the lyric but to criticize the issues of beauty, unity, finish, and female positions within these ideas, and to instead articulate the claims and questions of Otherness—not as a binary to something else, but rather as a seam opening inside existence. I use the nonce-word "otherhow" to indicate a space, a practice, a further distance implicit within method.

Thus these long poems are neither narrative nor lyric, although they propose both narrative and lyric elements. I want to use what these modes give me, but otherhow, in another sense. So my resistance to lyric or narrative, my critique of their normalizing and naturalizing of gender, of causality, of trajectory, of telos, of memory is a porous resistence. It is riddled by holes through which leak these discourses and their rich histories of use. *Drafts* are the sites of these struggles, the site of my wariness.

The individual "Drafts" are deeply related to each other. Structurally, the works are linked by subtle forms of repetition, presenting the reader with line sets and phrases, images, bits of recollections from one "Draft" to another. This creates resonances when things come up again and again, in a new context. The structural relation of the poems is also accomplished by the building of a long-term pattern of reference netting the works together, but especially from one "Draft" to the "Draft" exactly nineteen poems later. The issues, or ideas, of images, or some materials of the "donor draft" are reread in the next work of the fold. So "Draft 1: It" moves to "Draft 20: Incipit," and "Draft 6: Midrush" to "Draft 25: Segno." The strategy of the fold means that each newer work will correspond in some sensuous, formal, intellectual, or allusive way to a specific former "Draft." The strategy of "the fold," this layering and reconsidering materials, creates a regular, though widely spaced, recurrence among the poems, and the possibilities of linkage whose periodicity is both predictable and suggestive. "The fold" is my way of facing the insoluable problem of the long poem—essentially the question what holds it all together.

"The long poem, then, is a rereading of writings, a rewriting of readings...."[6] The writings I reread are sometimes the prior writings inside the poem, and by rereading them in the poem, as the subject of the poem, I can rewrite them. And, although no genre is the master mode in a poem in which genre is continually at issue, the description of layering and reconsidering, of allowing the work to create a texture of multiple and matted glosses does connect the work to the genre called "midrash."

Another genre analogy is certainly the ode. Curiously the same word characterizes the political and the rhapsodic (Horatian and Pindaric). It is a genre without many guidelines (three parts about sums it up) but one which assumes some stance of commentary and exposition, but also keening, bursting and other kinds of high feeling. I also think of my odic impulse as "ex-odic," on the analogy of Exodus—a bringing of a disparate, complaining, sloppy, backsliding, and suspicious set of materials into a "poem." But it's also an ex-ode in the sense of going out, a going away, a turning away from the normal bladishments of (let's say) civilization, or genteel writing. An ode that exits from the ode.

There have appeared, as the work goes along, a number of

allusions to elements of Jewish tradition. It's a creolized mix: certain holidays and customs; certain compelling Hebrew scriptural stories such as Jacob and the angel; some words in Yiddish; a pervasive and incurable nomadism and sense of the exilic; a number of humble shadows of the Holocaust. Can this be summarized? The poem is inflected with a peculiar (and of course resistant) "Jewishness" because it is about text and textuality? about debris? about "anguage"—a cross between language and anguish, and maybe anger?

As I have already made clear, *Drafts* are a large-scale project with several of the monumental works of modernism haunting their author—poems that might (with some yearning, if not total justice) be described in Pound's words, as "endless poem[s] of no known category." This raises the unsolved—perhaps insoluable—problem of representation and extent: "the whole knowable world" (in Williams' phrase). Knowing and unknowing clash interestingly in these two citations as do termination and the interminable. Both speak of a decisive yearning to produce an encyclopedic work of grounding that explores socio-political and spiritual forces with collage, heteroglossia, citation, accumulation. No one could now claim anything resembling this ambition innocently, yet the question is still fresh after eighty years or more. What to do about the long poem?

Since teleology had already been taken, I am not thinking about ending at all, or endlessness either, but about whatever materials come, or are figured, in the site which each poem declares. When there is some rhythmic or emotional realization, the individual "Draft" stops. There is ending for each of the poems taken individually, but no end in sight for them taken collectively. The poems do not stand too far above or over anything. The vistas here are always lateral, local, immersed. I look around at the plethoras and crossings. The random strewing of debris always moves me.

But the heroic force of the artist? The sense of a poem as a bildung? The "growth of a poet's mind"? The exemplary nature of "me" in my encounter with anything? All of these were undermined both by my belatedness as a writer and (though it is amusingly self-contradictory

153

to say it) by my humility in the face of many precursors in words. Especially when one is in the midst of a work—who can say the "I" is exemplary, historical? One just writes as best one can. The vow is simple, although it may have taken years to recognize: "to work in one's time." Time and history are the situation and ground, work is the medium and the response. The ins and outs of the self are just part of the design.

At the same time, the project has its own duplicity. The "form" is ambition—not otherwise thought of structurally or as a genre. But it may well be an incitement to both. Is the very nature of ambition, no matter how constituted—biographical, literary-historical, socio-political, elegiac, intertextual—the nature of a claim AS claim? Does the thing most extrinsic to the work finally make one understand that "where one is going" is to make adequate marks? This "mark of ambition" (otherwise known as work) marks the dissolution of the poet into the poem.

Notes

1 This work is a revision—both an expansion and a cutting—of a statement under the same title published in *TO: A Journal of Poetry, Prose + the Visual Arts* 1, 1 (1992): 72-77. With thanks to the editors Seth Frechie and Andrew Mossin. George Oppen, "Statement on Poetics," *Sagetrieb* 3, 3 (Winter 1984), 26.

2 In the words of the twelve-tone composer invented by Randall Jarrell in *Pictures from an Institution: A Comedy* (1952). New York: Meridian Books, 1960.

3 I have investigated my resistance to and my play with the use of the female figure in culture for a number of years, both in poems such as "Crowbar" (in *Tabula Rosa*) and in such essays as "Otherhow," "*Pater-Daughter*," and "Sub Rrosa" in *The Pink Guitar: Writing as Feminist Practice*. New York: Routledge, 1990.

4 Nicolas Abraham and Maria Torok, *The Shell and the Kernel: Renewals of Psychoanalysis*, Vol. 1, edited and translated by Nicholas T. Rand. Chicago: University of Chicago Press, 1994. See especially "Mourning *or* Melancholia: Introjection *versus* Incorporation" and "Notes on the Phantom: A Complement to Freud's Metapsychology."

5 Williams to Zukofsky, *The Selected Letters*, edited by John C. Thirlwall. New York: McDowell, Obolonsky, 1957, 94.

6 Smaro Kamboureli, *On the Edge of Genre: The Contemporary Canadian Long Poem*. Toronto: University of Toronto Press, 1991, 99.

Notes to the poem: Most of the "Drafts" are between 5 and 7 pages in print; a few are longer. To give a sense of the work to date in a few pages, or to track its repetitions and internal relationships from poem to poem is not possible in a selection. The author has chosen one fairly recent work that clearly presents several of the themes and textual issues in her statement of poetics. When she reads "Schwa" aloud, the italicized portions are whispered. "Gunish helfin" is a Yiddish version of "gar nichts helfen." "The unsaid," M. M. Bakhtin, "Methodology for the Human Sciences." "Metamorphosis" and "petrified human desire" from Marianne Shapiro, *Hieroglyph of Time*. The line "Wer, wenn ich schrie," translated severally from Rilke, *Duino Elegies*, I.

Draft 11: Schwa

The "unsaid" is a shifting boundary
resisting even itself.
Something, the half-sayable,
goes speechless. Or it can't

and Inbetween

> what is, and
> that it is,

is ə Inside

. . . . . . an offhand
sound, a howe or swallowed
shallow. Sayable Sign
of the un-.

. . . .

Not the exotic
that is strange but this *strange* puzzle
coil cup "here" where time goes forward

> floats by
> *boundaries*

a memory *of half*
sayable vague,
and textured *what*
. . . . . . *and that it is*
rose or knit or mother-of-pearl

156

goes speechless
 marks the child *makes* letters,
a signature graffiti, film stills,
saffron light on a west soffit, *Inside.*
And Inbetween

. . . .

lost objects, a tiny doll
and her SWEE-TOUCH-NEE
tin tea trunk of frills.

. . . .

There was a set of girl hankies, saying Monday, Tuesday,

it

the glimmers over 7 new days.

Wednesday, veiled,
those patches of old ice
swampy around tree roots,
low, soupy grey now
so that a great mist covers what was
dirty embankments,
clouds glowering in the nooks of soft valleys
as I rode or ride
so away I do not recognize the vacuum
. . . .
walls of dreams
. . . .

A Thursday, some small good girl
speechless

twirls her plaid umbrella, Friday,
the details.
Struggle tableau:
squeezer-siphons suction out the mucusy sinuses.
Framed from the outside, the flailing
careens thru schwa time
a darter from the murk of silence.

Are lost. Most.
Things of which.

Old familiars, hook toes in amber.
"as still aware as"
Bits matching or unmatched
"gunish helfin." Can't helf or heft
can't scarcely help
the looming empty weight of emptied time.
Carry an eviscerated bird.
The rubber chicken of a melted past.
Whose kosher yellow feet cut off
stuff up the vacant cavity.

. . . .

Lunchbox Thermos
shatters slivering into

All little tiny "it's" and "its"; there was
a shifting boundary *that is strange*
Open the drawer *speechless* Of all the lost things
never reseen
hardly bearable never
recoverable, here is something!

An orange blotter! on which brighten
cough syrup bottle- and bird- profiles
edged with a tiny ruler.
WAMPOLE'S CREO-TERPIN compound,
Conjunctures detailed and lavish, Mott Avenue,
Far Rockaway, some of the ten birds
(nested, pecking, chirping, or in flight)
became, in the four decades interim,
endangered.
Other conjunctures blank. Years
this incredible life in time
"simply" erased.
yet day by day the bits and crumbs
wiped up *by what invisible vectors*
lost *not lost; half lost,* and lost.
A random swirling pulse of bronzed leaves
breath of a wind intense and subsiding, so
some *falling* here, some over there. . . . . .
like Betelgeuse and Rigel, 200 million,
where the light lands
whose faded thread chance calls
the pulse more powerful more bright
its factors more unfathomable
than any thing we know.
And we know nothing.

Yet the blue twisted inner
tinkle of milk poured out the broken Thermos
in which mirror-like glass bits splintered. . . . . .

      YET WHAT?
      Is this

159

rubble accountable? Half-memories, memories half
empty, schwas of memory,
Things, half Things, Things'

effacement. Shadow somber lesions
slopped and filled by creamy prime, so that
almost, they are drawn back
to the stretched silence of canvas.

. . . .

Made in China,
marked down sweater
now marked down half again
to really cheap:
 that I,
whatever that is,
can,
without particular investment in it,
stand in the mall,
drawn and quartered like a heifer
trying this
thing in which filiations
(geopolitical, material, and narrative)
thread, and are stored.
Signs readable, but also embarrassing.
"It's so now." Just
a Knitting whose rich patterns
shuttled thru dark labyrinths
"punch up your Look."

How many miles
have its bumpy acrylics travelled

to have come thus far,
to Springfield Mall,
adrift from its pence-paid maker. . . . . .
The weave of its wefters, its shunters, its buyers,
its filmy yarns' dictation and direction

       Who can
       must Credit.

And the bright tags and the price codes are tacked in plastic string,
and anchor it

a sound halfway between articulation and disappearance
a sound falling out
or beginning to fall out,
voiced, but seemingly voiceless.

. . . .

Unheard vocalics taken for granted
are making, are mocking up
words, that
no one can put their finger on, yes
abrim with scrambled schwas
and unfathomable glissades.

Just as a febrile distracted
ichneumon bug, the leggy one,
wavers shadowy from corner to corner,
flies panicked, and climbs treadmills of wall,

this loss seems irrevocable.

I quiver in my pinhole time
where bits of voice are buried
in broken, unrecoverable objects,
the flowered butter dish, a-smash
Trip films torn from a stolen camera, and dumped,
bits and turns, the buried sounds of stifled voicing.
And were I to cry that out, who'd want to hear me do it?

            Gap and glut
            "most people"

remains between the two
"unwritten."

And cried out
who would bother to listen
among those frantically fluttering angles?
. . . .

            Bunched up.
            If only.

Thus, travelling hungry, I lost my sense of direction,
with "metamorphosis"
and "petrified human desire"
my dearest companions.

                              June-November 1990

162

C. D. Wright

Provisional Remarks On Being / A Poet / Of Arkansas

I consider my background, my upbringing, relevant to every line I lay down. None of the adjectives that can be applied before the noun *poet* can do more than crib, crab and contain the noun. Usually these adjectives go further—they dwarf and deform, they idealize, mythologize, and push the noun out of its rightful solitary position. I consider myself a poet of Arkansas. If the ear is tuned just so, the ear can identify the source. Once, I wrote just so, naturally. Later, unnaturally. Now I choose when to, when not to. It is just another strategum though I came by it naturally.

+   The division between urban and rural is the only serious border left to us. One serves to undermine the other. One could just as easily serve to mine the other. I am a serious border-crosser. I like the sticks; I am, if you will, of the sticks. I like the ruins of New York City second only to the sticks of Arkansas. I am mostly a spectator at the Friday night fights of poetics; I return to the preserve of the white page hungover. I wake up slowly. I wake up almost ready. I make myself ready.

+   I am fortunate to be from the Ozarks. My family is there. My original family. I am glad for that. The trees are there. The trees true me. I hear from journalists in the state of Arkansas that the present policy of the national forestry service is to chainsaw the redbuds and dogwoods in the forest, then to poison the open stumps to create a more uniform woodland. Naturally the posion runs off. Uniformity, in its motives, its goals, its far-ranging consequences is the natural enemy of poetry, not to mention the enemy of trees, the soil, the exemplary life therein.

+ Conscious Southern identity is a bromidal fallacy. The conservative force of that line is an abomination. The most radical individuals I have ever known come from below that blood-soaked line. The most rearguard poetics and the most radical poets. Some of it is great stuff, the stuff from the back of the bus. The raw, strange beauty of the tale and the tongue, what Agee called "the cruel radiance of what is." Some of it is godawful, but is nevertheless offered up as literature of the New South, a maneuver to promote tourism.

+ I seek to be pulled up by my hair roots. Don't all who bother with this rootbound art.

+ I poetry. I write it, study it, read it, edit it, publish it, teach it.... Sometimes I weary of it. I could not live without it. Not in this world. Not in my lifetime. I also arkansas. Sometimes these verbs coalesce. Sometimes they trot off in opposite directions.

+ Narrative is. You have to know when to enter in, when to egress, when to provoke, when to let be, be. However, narrative is overly identified with Southern poetry; it is a global condition not a literary convention. Poets should be willing to exploit the rind of narrativity, and be more than willing to be lost at the heart. Exceptional intellection is being exercised to decry narrative. I am not learning much from that line of refutation.

+ I don't know how a Southern lyric might express itself, at least in terms of definition, but I am attempting to initiate my own practice of the same. "One does what one knows before one knows what one is doing." I think Charles Olson said that. "A poet would show little thought to say poetry is opposed to—since it is added to like science." Zukofsky said that. Here, here.

+   Almost none of the poetries I admire stick to their labels, native or adopted ones. Rather, they are vagrant in their identifications. Tramp poets, there you go, a new label for those with unstable allegiances.

+   If there is any particular affinity I have for poetry associated with the South it is with idiom. I credit hill people and African Americans for keeping the language distinct. Poetry should repulse assimiliation; each poet's task is to fight their own language's assimilation. Miles Davis said, "The symphony, man, they got seventy guys all playing one note." He also said, "Those dark Arkansas roads, that is the sound I am after." He had his own sound. He recommend we get ours.

+   I am not convinced poetic camps serve the purpose of non-assimilation as well as they purport. I think they just put more heavy-handed poetry cops on the beat. They jump down your throat for commingling and they jump down your throat for having a good time and learning a new step and they jump down your throat for moving a few rocks. I have always acceded to poetry as a free space.

+   I do not mean I do not recognize the value of formal constraints. Form is a high poetic value. Whose form is another question. I have never been keen on inheritances, excepting that I think they should be heavily taxed. (Our schools need the scratch). In as much as Southern poetry is yoked to rigidity, Tradition, received forms—I think it cuts itself off from growth, change, astonishment. Some say form is the primary poetic value; some say, the creation of new forms is the sole business of the art. "Indeed, can there be a new thought in an old form," Fanny Howe queried. I think the potentiality of the art resides in form. I think the business the result can achieve is various.

+   The urge toward monumentation in poetry has always been sepulchral at best—how the maker is to be remembered, not how the making is to be achieved, not how the poem is to be discerned, not who will sense its percussion. A participatory corps is required.

+   There is as much enmity in this starry field as any other. Sometimes the susurrus of grass steers one's thinking—upwards.

+   I do not know if I am trying to do something new, but I know that I am trying to learn something new. The doors fling themselves open. Follow the light of your own skull.

+   For a long time the critical quesion has been, can poetry survive. Is it mutable, profound, sentient, resplendent, intense, stalwart, brave, alluring, exploratory, piercing, skillful, percipient, risky, exacting, purposeful, nubile, mirth-provoking, affective, restive, trenchant, sybaritic, mad... enough? Can it still enkindle or enlarge us? And even if yes, yes to all of the above, is it enough? Among poets this inquiry is persistent. And if the answer is nay, all this and more is not enough, the question becomes, with what then, will we hail the children.

Yours
Provisionally,
CD Wright
Providence, 3/29/94

I believe in a hardheaded art, an unremitting, unrepentant practice in one's own obstinate terms. I believe the word was made good from the start; that it remains so to this second. Even the humble word *brush* gives off a scratch of light. There is not much poetry from which I feel barred, whether it is arcane or evident in the extreme. I am ineluctably pulled by the extremes. Yet I believe the word used wrongly distorts the world. I hold to hard distinctions of right and wrong. I also submit that antithetical poetries can and should co-exist without crippling one another. They not only serve to define the other to a much more distinctive degree than would be possible in the absence of one or the other; they insure the persistence of heterogenous (albeit discourgingly small) constituencies. While I am not always equal to it, I appreciate the fray. I am neither too old for it yet nor too finished. Important, I believe, to resist closure in one's own work while assiduously working toward its completeness. Detrimental, I think, the dread of being passed on the left as is the deluded and furthermore trivializing notion of one's own work being an advance over any thing or any one. Truthfulness is crucial. A continuous self-criticism is demanded of the effort without which only non-art gets made, that is manufactured. I would contest those writers whose end (reviling-all-the-way) is to prevail.

The box this comes in
(a deviation on poetry)

is not beautiful, at least it is not aggressively beautiful, meaning the workmanship, as it was formerly called—regardless of whom took up the tools, but also generally reflecting to whom the tools were entrusted— falls on the faulty side, connoting the work shows: nail heads, cuts which exceeded their mark in insuring the fit of the lid, steel screws securing brass hinges, and especially the irregular tooling of the conventionalized flowers. Though the flowers are suggestive of tulips and dogwoods they are apt to be fleurs-de-lis and marvels-of-Peru. Because the work shows I favor it more. It likewise follows, lacking mechanical perfection the box was made by hand. Possibly for someone in particular rather than for sale. If the object was wages not affection, it was nevertheless made with the same two hands; practice rather than mastery guided its making. If true to tradition the pay would have been unduly low; for motives ruled by affection the making would have been its own reward. The box was given to me by an old flame, now a virtually unbeaten trial lawyer. Flame is a hotter word than truthfully applies since we were bound by argument more than passion. In the end I was the wounded, but throughout I inflicted my rude, overbearing manner on him. Memories too keen to dwell upon. The first woman it was made or bought for has long occupied her own box. So does the maker—occupy a box of his own, that is if we follow the gender assumptions of the period in which it was made. On the other hand, the flowers are on the austere side, not overly feminine, perhaps it was meant to hold a man's effects. There is no loitering odor of cigars or of perfume. The wood is dark. The lining vanished but for the residual glue tracks and morsels of fabric attesting it was once faced with gold velvet. It measures 6 7/8" x 11". The interior space offers an inch less in length and width, again to insure the lid's fit. The box stands 3" tall.

Allow me to date it this way: the woman, who I won't try to picture in detail, must have had a bundle of hair, as when it was bought for me 15 years ago, the dealer told my friend it was approximately 60 years old. Circa 1914. This would have been prior to the bob, a coiff forbidden to this day according to an Arkansas statute. Little Rock is where it was bought but not where it necessarily originated. The antique dealers in that internal capital get around to wherever dealers in old things convene, and they venture out on their own: estate sales, flea markets, bank auctions. A dreamy novel could be written about the alleged maker and the alleged recipient, but merely to dream them up in period clothing, in love and trouble, does not stir me. I am more drawn to cold, factual things such as diet, income, fertility, abilities with animals, plants, interstellar links.

If I knew my woods once felled and fashioned, I would tell you what wood this is, what polish to apply. Generically, my guess is fruitwood, if this does not infer too gorgeous a grain. With trees in leaf or bloom, I am on a first name basis with an impressive number, even the paulownia, resembling the catalpa, which alongside the mimosa is treated as a nuisance tree in the little towns in the mountains as their frilly flowers damage car finish. Where cars are inviolable, totemic. The bodark remains my personal favorite—it being truly hard, burning blue in the fireplace and standing out by itself in a field with its extra half dozen monikers: hedge apple, horse apple, mock orange, osage orange, bow wood, bois d'arc, not to mention its bizarre globular fruit and lascivious smell. Diagonally across the lid stretches an ugly scar, unprofessionally repaired. The result of some lapse. Even from the underside the injury appears in reverse. The flowers which lace the lid and sides have been tipped with gold paint. Hopefully the painter did not wet the brushes with the inside of the mouth to bring them to a fine point in order to articulate the scrolling stems, because odds are that the pigment is tainted with a pretty poison.

The box holds a modest inventory of things kept in spite of their inverse relation to value: two bowties, one solid avocado green but patterned, one with lavender and pink diamonds on a purplish field (from my father's springy days). Three battery-operated watches, a strand of phony pearls, six or seven nondescript drugstore barrettes, one Italian butterfly clasp (for my sheared head). Clay beads from the Chrysler Museum shop in Norfolk (because they were a dollar and I was burning to buy something). Three flowered handkerchiefs from Mamo carefully folded inside her last birthday card to me—of the type she has carried in her handbag since she was a young woman to blot the lips, tamp the brow, blow the nose (although I can't for the life of me see myself blotting, tamping, much less blowing on them). One has been folded so as to bloom from a breast pocket. A black ribbon for an armband when the occasion calls (last donned Election Day). A strip of day-glo survey-or's tape pierced by an ordinary nail which belonged to Frank Stanford, poet, land surveyor. According to the late Stanford, the tape derives from a vegetable base, cows love it, causing the line just surveyed and flagged to vanish behind you. Also one notably odd handkerchief brought back for a souvenir of Seoul: short, parallel pink and aqua bars on a white cotton field surrounding a square frame which features a pig in a zoot suit. The pig stands in front of a tractor parked before a limelighted city. A poems inscribes the picture: "Listen, Can't you hear the Manhattan Blues? / Howdi? / Smoky Night. Moody shadow is behind my back. Slow ballad / is in my glass. Black trick is a sweet thing. City light is only my God." My notion of Seoul nights is undoubtedly as accurate as the Korean poet's of Manhattan. One fabric gardenia, misshapen and discolored. Three woven friendship bracelets, an enamel and pewter cross once on Frank Stanford's key chain. A silver dollar from Mamo, tin dragonfly from Jean Kondo, two frosted hair combs bought in a jewelry store in a small-town mall on the eve of my wedding. One star-shaped turquoise pin, one beaded leather ring I cannot remember borrowing or buying, neither of which I like even a little.

The box maintains an honored place on my sewing machine bought at the sewing center on Broad Street because it is there, which is near, and because I imagined myself sewing, curved over yards of wash-able silk, giving the balance wheel a spin and treadling until the dress was done. Then I would put it on and go where, to the policeman's ball?

"Howdi, Smoky Night." On my rickety Mamo's one and only visit to Rhode Island she showed me how to thread my Singer. I did not progress beyond threading, nor did Mamo's recollection extend to stitching. The only one in the immediate family who can barely claim current use of a sewing machine is my father, retired jurist, who bought a White at a yard sale. Actually Judge persuaded my mother to make the purchase for him while he sat in the car feigning manly disinterest. The cemeteries are rife with people who knew how to make them hum. The Singer itself has been retired to the attic. Over the well, I placed a jagged slab of green marble fallen off the front of a building downtown. On top of the slab a covered glaze bowl from the kilns of Gubbio—where we waited out a sudden, fabulous storm before a lengthy, fabulous supper— filled with cotton balls. Also on the marble, an array of shapely jars and bottles containing clarifying lotion, moisturizer, emollient, eaus de toilette. Propped against the the wall behind them, a tin mirror from Mexico. I perform my ablutions there. Of a morning and an evening, I face myself, a poet of forty. Within the limits of this diminutive wooden world, I have made do with the cracks of light and tokens of loss and recovery that came my way. I can offer no more explicit demonstration as to what my poetry is. The box this comes in is mine; I remain faithfully, CD.

171

Poems from *TREMBLE*

Floating Trees

a bed is left open to a mirror
a mirror gazes long and hard at a bed

light fingers the house with its own acoustics

one of them writes this down
one has paper

bed of swollen creeks and theories and coils
bed of eyes and leaky pens

much of the night the air touches arms
arms extend themselves to air

their torsos turning toward a roll
of sound: thunder

night of coon scat and vandalized headstones
night of deep kisses and catamenia

his face by this light: saurian
hers: ash like the tissue of a hornet's nest

one scans the aisle of firs,
the faint blue line of them
one looks out: sans serif

172

"Didn't I hear you tell them you were born
on a train"

what begins with a sough and ends with a groan
groan in which the tongue's true color is revealed

the comb's sough and the denim's undeniable rub
the chair's stripped back and muddied rung

color of stone soup and garden gloves
color of meal and treacle and sphagnum

hangers clinging to their coat
a soft white bulb to its string

the footprints inside us
iterate the footprints outside

the scratched words return to their sleeves

the dresses of monday through friday
swallow the long hips of weekends

a face is studied like a key
for the mystery of what it once opened

"I didn't mean to wake you
angel brains"

ink of eyes and veins and phonemes
the ink completes the feeling

a mirror silently facing a door
door with no lock no lock

the room he brings into you
the room befalls you

like the fir trees he trues her
she nears him like the firs

if one vanishes one stays
if one stays the other will or will not vanish

otherwise my beautiful green fly
otherwise not a leaf stirs

Like Peaches

change   speak   sway
keep lingering smell
protected by a succulent seal   a burr
yield one's earthly wand   one's earthly sac   into this vessel
trace   blaze   clear
the foliage at the wrought gate
the serrated tongue   rescinded   along with the dream
of urinating in three streams
sunscalded

Forever Lynne   riddles the water tower   of a dying town
ripen   cling   drop
what would it be like to fell   this mess of twigs   to graft
the shaking body   to lyric   the seasoned body   to stem
to shake   the lyric body   to season
the stemmed   to trail   the fallen...
slather   shudder   lower
drupe

things that are not written in this book
don't go boring your nose in the fork of a tree not even present
arise   refreshed   wormed
pulpy   opaque   ecstatic
lingering innocence
of perfect nexus   shave the epicarp   collect the juices
we orchard

one steps forward   under a sifter of light
   holding a globe   in ungloved hands   we share
the experience   of dying   in snow   pages turn
   on illuminated fragments   we become   aware
of the extremes: joy   and   revenge   the fierce
   confusion therein   one form senses another
when there is pressure   from all sides   and wasn't the light
   seminal   tilting toward us   nay,   labial
we knew from the start   the center was within us   this blizzard
   this conversation   could go on   for years: should you
go   should you stay   no shoulds about it   no matter why

   the hole was made   the task is not yours   to fill it
why standest thou   so near   to the brink   how old were you
when you first lay down   before the god of love   what was
the objective: a staff   against the wolf   of reality
nay,   to get warm   only to get warm   would you be
   let down again   if I said   it were not the one true god
but only a candle   of the same   where were we in the middle of a phrase: we froze we fell we went to a gilded hell
   I only have escaped to tell you   though I have come to be lost
   I do not ask you to lose your own self   in my triangle   only
to keep watch   yea,   to keep watch   over the shaping
   of the sky   snow orbiting   all   abide abide

a car   that could not pass inspection   an expired license
like someone suddenly overtaken   with a need to see them
again   moving fast and in formation   she could feel
the white lines
streaming by   the radio tuned to the road   like someone
crying in the bathroom   she attacked her own idiom
welcomed
the distraction of corporeal detail   a toenail on the tile
some hair   the drain could not swallow   according to
the legend   not a long way to go   books thrashing
in the trunk   unpowered steering   the arduous turning
around
and skies   amassing at the border

words appeared
by which she wanted to live   not singularly but
companionate
in a wandering and guilty life   everyone makes
orthographic errors
while her face slept in her hand   her mind saw him
sitting at his oak plane   with his new pen
he wrote steadily into the night   thinking the next paragraph
would surely snuff out   the destroying angel
thinking the sequel to the rain would be a gaining movement
focused between two cones of light
like someone driving to Texas

they surfaced   gradually   until the center cooled
male and female colored differently   like dinosaurs
colored by impurities   autochthonous
sprung from inner earth   or ancient seas
without names   sunscreen   honorary degrees
given the climate
and the silence   except for continuous wave action
intermittent screeches
a strange yelping   impervious to   oarlock
axstroke   gunstock   out of pressure   heat from above
and under

continuous wave action   impressed with ferns
quarry me   uplift   butterfly me   micturate
across the flat of my back
it had to be a dawn horse
crag   fracture   cleave
fingered   sniffed   specified
by luster   hardness   coarseness
the caught and faceted light
rubbed smooth   by continuous wave action
in the very beginning   was only fucking
hunger   poetry   breath   shhhhhh

Like Horses

in their long black coat   they love the back roads
show their teeth   in a heartbeat   breathe in breathe out
don't fool around with them   their involuntary nervousness
beasts   of draft and burden   they are naturally
nervous   saps for the sweet sop   left buttock rubbed
against bark   and barbed wire
she ungulates   whence their fire   sweat like ballerinas
and stink   during the intervals
cannot help but be anxious   for the morrow   don't trust
anybody
they are helpless lying down

the young husband stands
on one foot   in front of the blackboard   the wet banged
equestrian students   breathe in breathe out   the sugar apple
on his desk   cannot help but be anxious
for the morrow
he ungulates   don't trust anybody   never have
they never will

Flame

the breath	the trees	the bridge
the road	the rain	the sheen
the breath	the line	the skin
the vineyard	the fences	the leg
the water	the breath	the shift
the hair	the wheels	the shoulder
the breath	the lane	the streak
the lining	the hour	the reasons
the name	the distance	the breath
the scent	the dogs	the blear
the lungs	the breath	the glove
the signal	the turn	the need
the steps	the lights	the door
the mouth	the tongue	the eyes
the burn	the burned	the burning

Albert Cook

Poetic Purposes

What are my purposes as a poet? Do these poems cohere into a unity other than retrospective—or crucially prospective as I keep trying to forge ahead? The very expatiations of my bulky critical commentary on poetry, which I have always thought of as an endless prolegomenon to my own poems (whatever else they have been), tend to displace the integrative center of my purpose. My masters are themselves a large and various chorus whose voices I am hoping blend with my own.

Working towards a poem is working through a poem, is working the poem together. I ruminate, and I broadcast. When a new music pulls at my ears it tends to be a sign that a poem will be a long one, first *Midway*, and then a decade later, for more than a decade itself, finally *Modes*, which I thought of as the last of this series employing the "syllabic module" and at one time came to think would last me my whole life, on the model of Pound or Olson (or for that matter, Whitman). My way turned out to be different, thankfully, and lo, along, slowly, came "Prophecies," then "Dooms and Inclinations," and then the still unpublished "Transfers." And then there is another large poem on the boards which may be two hundred lines and may be thousands, I don't yet know. I also don't know of a nascent poem at first even when it will turn out to be only epigram-length, or only a haiku; most of my many haiku start out headed for more expansive expression. As I perpetually do too. In the inch as in the mile.

What You Don't Want is to Be Reminded

"The streams of Forethought lie afar."
                              Pindar

What you don't want is to be reminded
of a mastery slipping away before you have properly
centered yourself in it, for all your ardor.
The pear tree goes on producing
pears, tough on their stem and green, yellowing
gloriously to a fullness so soft the morsels
melt in your mouth, and there is another brown-grained full
group of yellow pears on the table, perhaps gracing an imitation
Majolica bowl of ornament curled
on a darker yellow ground. The window is open. The door
is open, and the fine sand on the floor tiles
bespeaks an ease of bare feet coming and going, tanned. Such days
pass softly into the memory,
distraction married to fulfillment, simplicity
seducing and forbidding. Where you are
is where you were not and will be again.

Thwarting the Wise Bracket

Thwarting the wise bracket of his balm
For what is less than humdrum, trusting
The last recrudescences,
Bleak in the resurrections
Of his bargaining
He is thrust
Into gladdening rooms
Out of forlorn spaces.
The old reminders
Do their work
Blinding his orts
In a weaker darkness
Beggaring
Dissection.
His apologia
For a fool's errand
Is equal to the porings of the wise.
The hail-mothered
Underplayed
Come to their consolations,
It and he
Gathered on.

What You Don't Have to Know

What you don't have to know carries you far There were openings
in all directions past the fruit-shiny leaves of the apple trees
the bends in the road and the bends in the river the clouds
in the sky and the slant of the buildings These are the various
shining exempla a rounding in becoming a rounding out

So many untoward motions untutored satchels of convenience

Tautness was just a memory by endless preparation forestalled

Taking care taking time taking hold between takes taking it back

These are the maw you have been parallel to
the women who expand equanimity as a lung
expands but without the natural redress of exhalation

Being of all things the most in controversy The giant lid
is on me the light does its harrowing one day at a time its harvesting
over a longer stretch If you knew what you meant to be saying

A manifest witholding reverses, condign comminglings
come before nothing gnawing and nattering if they found
themselves to be listening tower tear tire incipits of gloom

Parts of my life of processing assimilations the good feeling
of one who has carried off enshrining his caprice modified
the offerings and clarified the leavings Where were
the reassurances if not in the palm of such a person's hand

The morass of equivalents would leave them further on without
    advancement

Without embarrassment foursquare in the thick of new diatribes

They're going to do what they're going to do pressured, pressurized

Heady as the dark of a love flowing over from its pitch of coming

Scathed and Diminished

Scathed and diminished
in the elusive loveliness of living,
the self-resurrecting hands
are ravelling out
the vein of self-deprecation.

The sing-song of sweetened
conversation invigorates them.

Overtone and assumption
of a round.

A blaze of tranquillity overtakes them.
They brace themselves for the tall buildings
And over-reliable circuits,
given a hearing and an airing
in rum benevolence.

The signs of a skewing order
leave them on the defensive.

These are the wild
objectifications.

Harnessing the invisibility
under the form of inevitability.

He is Not Unworthy

He is not unworthy of the lost art

Who performs with a flourish
The last act, drowning

And horns in on Necessity
As might a timorous,
Authoritative elder.

And, name-cabled
To its recognition, has his art
Rehumbled and alive
To transcendences, open blue
Originality sheepish for its share.

In the leaves of a thousand trees
His tension is fading.

Shame bears its repletion
Of another age
And buries
More than it shows,

Thwarting the cold
Relief of the hunter
And the kind flanks
Of the dazzled guest.

The Time Has Come

The time has come and brought what you
                    bargained for.
The dirt road is in eclipse.
One man's garden is another's square.
Old brass buttons bear tiny coats-of-arms.

Go forth to meet charitably
Each single arrival and all the arrivals,

Hurrying to bring together
All and enough of it.

Insecticide laces the egg
In the nest of the bird of prey,
Infanticide tightens the bonds
Of the hunting tribe.

Live out the truth
Of the story.

Daily the self-cripple holds himself back
From the wide swathe he longs for,
Orpheus at the Orpheum a memory,
The wing-ding sell of Jean Cocteau.

Laugh and be free.

Lies paper it over.

The wrong tone
Swallows you up,

Pommelled into sincerity,

The base brunt of cities,
The many fields,

Slambang
Destinies
Heady and venturesome.

Give up the weakest and dearest
Part of yourself,
Riding high
A willed amazement.

Then what good is succor if the grief
It engenders, live?

Coming Through

Squeeze through a mountain or a mirror and be brought to believe
in the lapse of time it is all one whether you go that way the sages
have drawn up the tables of blame in a pinch you are guest and victim
A driving impulse will get you to sleep through pilasters
and torrents, patching plaster as the home you inhabit
crumbles, the time is ripe, rife with red arrows, they
will not inhibit your shambling all over again weathered
into headier semblances, rest like the loosened stone
away from anybody's stare in a nest of hybrids
If the dreams made a difference you would be heeding them
for life no matter you are headed athwart a blaze drumming
you alone call it a dream for you the heavy doors open
heavily you can get through them weighting the trice
scotching the truce between here and there now and then, numbed friends
forgive and forget, plasticene cards slapped down until marred
expectancy has checked a docketted future You are wanting
to be like nobody else light through the cleft of the wheel jarred
to a rifted circle a man let through into revivified life until
the green nap of a tablecloth brown shell of an egg bright spoons
        modillions
in sunlight pass into shadow the crowns of elms shade vivid passersby
in the heart of it an isolated member you won't be amiss or amazed
heron and boar reed and mountain courtyard and field
sailboat and scythe sharp confrontation aching memory
gathering and grinding the starry night its freight of labile
fright mangling the miracles wondering what it is coming to
where re-experiencing benevolences of fading
preparing to understand and honor the supersonic voices
you are tending by the sea your short-term garden in a life
winding down while the boom boxes wander on the beach below
yellow light appearing and disappearing in its reassurances

taming through hives of wildness good times till it spoils or blossoms
plumping rarefied forms of life for what they are worth whirl-worms
porcupine fish conger eels horseshoe crabs dolphins anemones
"Guarded time taxing a stout heart swamps a weak one"
taking for good and all the strident tangle in such stride as would happen
to further concepts of amelioration, true-blue evergreens
putting you inland, every lake purified of its faint film
of oil from the milling spurt of random motor boats smooths
its bosom in the bosom of the year teeth brushed your clean mouth
moves into day and your clear head takes the dark of the wood
to its limits hinting of darker wider woods in some other
dispensation dumbfounding those who would bother to ask
and be kept awake nights getting for an answer only such echoes
of places they might wade through or not depending
on the worn stones of your looking, losses cut, the lacking
supplies easily dispensed with, the landlocked cities
festival-radiant at their times riding over rowdying and ready
founding up such energies for the breach of a mirror or a mountain

The Syllabic Module

In metered verse, the design of the lines as a recursive pattern dominates the instances of the statements, which flow along by the process of natural language. In free verse, this balance is inverted: the process of instance dominates, and the recursive pattern of design, present in most cases from the mere fact that verse orders its words into lines, takes on a random character, even when the relation between design and instance grows very complex.

Now the randomness of verse instance can be subordinated to recursive patterns without being made to comform to a simple linear meter. In the principle of the syllabic module, as exemplified by the poems in *Modulars* and *Modes*, every syllable is enlisted both horizontally and vertically. The line unit is bound both horizontally by syllable-count in the line and vertically by recursive series from line to line. At the same time, the line, within its limited number of syllabic alternatives, remains free, as free verse is free, to choose, at every point, the particular alternative for the particular line.

In the syllabic module, the lines are all syllabic lines. But in addition they are subjected vertically to a series of recursive rules which totally determine their function in a larger pattern, one which retains the processive freedom of free verse because the alternatives are never closed.

For the poems in *Modulars*, an elaborate example is "One-Way Mystery," where the vertical pattern is a total one; every stanza must contain no fewer than 24 syllables, and no more than 48; every stanza must also be divisible by eight, the base module. But individual lines do not use it. They must be of 3, 5, 7, or 9 syllables, and there are further rules outlines in *Modulars*. So every line moves further towards closing out possible alternatives. But the stanza-progression remains open to alternatives, and hence it does not lose the aleatory character of free verse, for all its elaboration. The lines are open too: a line of 3 syllables must be followed by one of 5 syllables, but a 5-syllable line may be followed by one of 3, 5, 7, as a 9-syllable line may. Pairs are determined, but at every point in a stanza there are alternatives of the succeeding pair.

The ninety-three sections of the very long poem *Modes* have a module based on 3 (3 or 2 x 3, or 3 x 3), with steps permitted within a strophe only by one three-syllable jump (the progressions 3-9 and 9-3 are not permitted).

from One-Way Mystery

The clairvoyant survivors
Are burning to find an open field.
The grey mayor means
To restore his summer place
Before making rounds.
His interests are self-shelved.
His soft wife
Crochets and crochets.

He resigns himself
In tea-sweetened confusion
To becalmed knowledge
Of the long wait come,
Having learned
That is all there is.

Mellowing and mellowing,
Every full man is a king.
Hate's reverse is
Activated fate.
The body and the spirit
Remand the to-do on other grounds.

One dream to be scored,
One throw to be known,
One turn of mortal squaring
To return a mortal share.

So many pained-out well-wishers,
So many hilarious
Lovers pie-eyed in a pied meadow,
High on the blare of music,
Easing for a drumhead festival.

If the sure end is a long detour
who is going where the dead of night
at high speed? Something about a plain
queers a confidence in azimuths
to live by, given half a chance. Brakes
soon wear out their linings. There is a
split lodging a membrane between what
we see and what we are, renderings.

Flash-slabs thrown up by 'an
earthquke in an ice-house'
if not framed
even when
dreamed again
slide on by

Equilibration, trust,
greensickness, stringsaving, the long rooms
of the Oneida Community
where intimacy was decreed, self-
chosen lovers forced to run away
if they were to keep space
from wreaking harm while stretching the soul.

A man comes back to his starting point
finds the questions loaded he had posed,
and posing already takes its toll
in leaden attitudes, consequence
of pushing for clean ground, raillery,
solemnity, and the ingrained calm
of steadying interiors. Call

for ashtrays, the window-cleaning spray
and a settled demeanor to touch
the white salt on the edge of a plant
in an earthen pot by the window.

A rug is on the floor where it happens
of steadying so the open void
of falling away would do no more
than fall away in continuing.
Outside dark leaves on the darker ground
stay in place around the motions danced
in progressions of forthcoming blue
notwithstanding the bobbing boats and
grand slaloms of inconclusive years.

The mind 'a fading coal'
conscious of all, resists.

A mountain
of years at his back
and at his beck nothing
so sweet as such an air.

The gateways lead to tombs
set rounded on their own even space.

The world stays in place through hydrangeas,

Rounded cuts of green water pouring
over Niagara and the spray-
doused caverns underneath.

LXXXVI

If I have been fulfilling the roles
Another dark role overriding
My actions with its plot
From before history
Holds its net
Over high points lightly
And inescapably

It comes through in a dark
I have been angling for

To see how Odysseus doubles Christ
in the supernatural *virtù*
Of bringing the underworld to bear
On reconstitution
Of a real home and strong horizon
Setting all in its place

I am barricaded
Who want to open up
From a stronghold within

Memory and affect
Trick me into retaining burdens
Of failure to forgive
When the shining faces
Of the old wrongdoers
Are pleading for release
The vigorous sorrow
Of half coming to terms with the past
Evades the issue by meeting it

Ovid was never more Ovid than
At the fishing station so remote
His glib tongue was useless

Except for bringing up
To supreme expression
The huge poems he had brought along
In the long ship outward

What was new
On that exacting coast—
His expressed dossier of sadness

The apostles of softness take hold
Shamefaced visionaries

Dooms of love
Leave children
Doomed to love
Other ways
Brighter rooms
Cramp the praise
They dream of
Bog and den
Haunt the ways

The displaced dancer swelled
Away from him, more drink
Swelled in him

No other
Was to come

"Goodbye my friend goodbye
Nothing new's in dying
But in life's nothing new"

By the mother's plain house
The old cow in the field
Keeps on munching away
Nothing in her large eyes

It was the underworld
Odysseus visited
To learn from his mother

And the Theotokos
At the end
Stood aghast

LXXXVIII

Whose life would you have been dreaming if
being planted amid
a family's demands
had not opened space for conifers
and bewildering roads,
many-storied buildings
and sulphur-tinged regrets,
subways, doors, bookcases,
knives of large and small blades,
cars, prop and jet airplanes,
well-stocked stores, gas stations,
doctors' offices, labs,
cabs, lounges, beach houses,
flower beds, queen size beds.

The history of objects will not
yield to mere redeployment in space.
Enough has been said, we have looked long
enough to have excerpted their force
and not be content with even time,
scrollwork on the silver box, steep threads
on the shining screw, struts and guys on
the pylon, irrecapturable
glaze on the Sung vase, microscopic
measurements on the computer chip.

Baths, second cars, long drives,
second houses, dogs, long
silences, friendships, stalled committees.

White cup full of water
clear tea glass
foamed beer mug
dark shot glass

Exhibition table
varnished tree root table
table of plexiglass
table of ships' menus
table of stainless steel

Families pass on furniture

Whom I have to outwit is myself
crowding under the wire
of man's allotted time
suppressing all thinking
to hear hidden music

A lifetime brush with fatigue
must be known

Robert Creeley

Was That a Real Poem or
Did You Just Make It up Yourself?

As I get older, I recognize that my thinking about poetry may or may not have anything actively to do with my actual work as a poet. This strikes me as no thing cynically awry, but rather seems again instance of that hapless or possibly happy fact, we do not as humans seem necessarily aware of what we are physically or psychically doing at all. One thing, therefore, that does stay put in my head, as something said in youth, is "we live as we can, each day another—there is no use in counting. Nor more, say, to live than what there is, to live...." I did not feel that a pessimistically argued reality back then, nor do I now. It is very hard for me to live in any projection of reality, in a plan or arrangement of the present moment that uses it primarily as a 'future' term. I have long experience of my own restlessness and impatience, and have managed quiet and a feeling of centeredness only when the *here and now* literally discovered it for me. Elsewise I have battered myself and the surroundings with seemingly useless energy, pleased only that something at least was 'happening.'

My writing seems to me no different. Of course I learned as much as I could about the *how* of its occasion. Like many of my contemporaries I felt myself obliged to have defense against the authoritative poetry of my youth—whose persons I'd like now not to recall just that it's taken me so long to forget them. So, from that initial, crotchety purview, I've continued, finding and choosing as heroes men and women who must at this point be familiar to anyone who has read me at all: Williams, Pound, H. D., Stein, Zukofsky, Olson, Duncan, Levertov, Ginsberg, Dorn, Bunting, Wieners, McClure, Whalen, Snyder, Berrigan —and so on, being those I can almost see out the window if I look. Put more simply, there's been a way of doing things which found company with others, and in that company one has found a particular life of insistent and sustaining kind.

That has been part of the situation of 'what poetry means to me,' but dear as it is, it has not been either the largest part nor the most significant. A few months ago I was sitting with friends in a lovely house on a lovely afternoon, and we began a collaborative poem, on impulse, using an electric typewriter that was on a nearby table. It took me real time to get to it because it intimidated me—I've never used one particularly—and also intrigued me, and so my feelings and thoughts began to singularize me, isolate me in relation to the others. But I've always been able to do that, so to speak. But is it some necessity of my own working? In any case, my contribution to the poem stood painfully clear in its twisted, compressed statement—even the spacing of lines shrank to a small fist of words, defensive and altogether by itself.

No wonder that I've never forgotten Williams' contention that "the poet thinks with his poem, in that lies his thought, and that itself is the profundity...." Poems have always had this nature of revelation for me, becoming apparently objective manifestations of feelings and thoughts otherwise inaccessible. Did I love Mary—a poem or story would quite usually make the answer clear, no matter it might take years to know it. A pleasant woman met this spring pointed out, for example, that "For love—I would / split open your head and put / a candle in / behind the eyes..." was a literally violent proposal that was not demonstrably involved with the usual senses of "loving" the recipient. Yet I had always felt that poem a true measure of an ability to love, and possibly it is.

As a young man, then, moved by poetry, feeling its possibilities as inclusive, bringing all the world to one instant of otherwise meaningless 'time,' I wanted, not unexpectedly, to participate in that wonder. We struggle with them a good deal, mutter, mistake, but *words* seem even so significantly common and in that respect accessible. My own commitment to them was not easily understood. Was it that nothing else was open to me? Did I turn to them simply that no other act or substance permitted me such occasion? I know that I felt in those years now past very often useless in other attempts to find place in the world. As so many of that time, I married primarily to reify what might be called my existence. The fact of wanting to be a social person, as well as a private one, seemingly demanded it. Again, there was nothing I otherwise 'did' that argued my relevance to a general world.

In short, I was markedly self-preoccupied, lonely, inarticulate at crucial points in my relationships, and again, and again, restless. If they did nothing else, words gave instant reality to this insistent flux, which otherwise blurred, faded, was gone before another might in any sense witness it. That poems, stories, fed on this experience of reality was of great use initially. Just as I had used reading as a place to be, a world of volatile and active nature yet also 'unreal,' not 'flesh and blood'—and yet that surely, how else could it be—so now the possibilities that words might engender became a deep preoccupation.

At various times I've put emphasis on the fact that I was raised in New England, in Massachusetts for the most part. So placing myself, I've argued that that fact clarifies my apparently laconic way of saying things, especially so in my early poems. But might that use of words not come also of feeling tentative with them, unsure of their appropriate significations—as though there were a *right* way that was being distorted, lost, by fact of one's ignorance? I sense an aspect of this dilemma in Williams' plaint, "many years of reading have not made you wise...." I know that he did share with me a tacit fear of the well-trained, academically secure *good English* he felt the comfortable equipment of various of his contemporaries. We both depended, it would seem, on enthusiasms, rushes of insight or impulse, read only to a purpose if the appetite underlying would settle for nothing else. I was delighted, for example, to realize that Williams did not spend long hours researching *Paterson* in the library but rather, as Michael Weaver first told me, got his information from a lovely, old time *local* historian. To this day I am so intimidated by the *nature* of libraries, the feel of them, the authority of their ordering of books on shelves, etc., that I rarely if ever go into them. I feel toward them much as I feel toward telephones, that their function is disastrously limited by their form, no matter what efficiencies are also clearly the case.

But why worry about that? If one has spent close to thirty years writing books, in effect, why be so fearful of this one place they may come to rest? Why be afraid of *poems*, for that matter? Thinking of that world 'out there,' and recalling my own tentativeness in trying to find my own use in it, always the *general* measure of reality can hurt me, can say, in short, 'of course *you* like it, you wrote it—but what about other people, don't you care what they think or feel or want?' More specifically, why not write poems the way they are supposed to be written—as a simple acquaintance with poetry as a *subject* would easily define. Thus, if you seriously want to be a poet, you study the prevailing models of its activity and you set yourself to their imitation as diligently as you can. And slowly you acquire, or do not, the requisite ability.

I don't believe it. I *know* that attention to what has been written, what is being written, is a dearly rewarding experience. Nonetheless, it is *not* the primary fact. Far closer would be having a horse, say, however nebulous or lumpy, and, seeing other people with horses, using their occasion of said horses as some instance of the possibility involved. In short, I would never buy a horse or write a poem simply that others had done so—although I would go swimming on those terms or eat snails. Stuck with the horse, or blessed with it, I have to work out that relation as best I can.

Posit that music exists despite the possibility that no one might be consciously able to make it, that what we call *poems* are an intrinsic fact in the human world whether or no there be poets at this moment capable of their creation. That would characterize my belief—which gives me no rest, which, too often, causes a despairing sense of uselessness and ineptitude. Why can't *I* write them, fall in love, reveal the actual world, and be the hero in it? Isn't it *mine*? No. Yours? No. Theirs? No. Ours? No.

Days, weeks, months and sometimes years can pass in that sad place. Nothing gets done, nothing really gets even started. A vague, persistent echo of possibility seems all that is there to depend upon.

Perhaps tomorrow, or later today—or even right now. To work. Useless paper, useless pen. Scribbles of habit and egocentric dependence. But you did it once, didn't you—they said so, you thought so too. Try again.

Sometime in the mid-sixties I grew inexorably bored with the tidy containment of clusters of words on single pieces of paper called 'poems'—"this will really get them, wrap it up...." I could see nothing in my life nor those of others adjacent that supported this single hits theory. Dishonest to say I hadn't myself liked it, haiku, for example, or such of my own poems that unwittingly opened like seeds. But my own life, I felt increasingly, was a *continuance* from wherever it had started to wherever it might end—of course I felt it as linear in time—and here were these quite small *things* I was tossing out from time to time, in the hope that they might survive my own being hauled on toward terminus. Time to start over, afresh, began to be felt at first as increasingly limited, finally as nonexistent. The intensive, singularly made poems of my youth faded as, hopefully, the anguish that was used in the writing of so many of them also did. I was happier? Truly pointless to answer insofar as I lived now in another body and with an altered mind.

More, what specific use to continue the writing of such poems if the need therefore be only the maintenance of some ego state, the so-called *me*-ness of that imaginary person. Lost in some confusion of integrity, I had to tell the truth, however unreal, and persisted toward its realization, even though unthinkable. So writing, in this sense, began to lose its specific edges, its singleness of occurrence, and I worked to be open to the casual, the commonplace, that which collected itself. The world transformed to bits of paper, torn words, 'it/it.' Its continuity became again physical. I had no idea of its purpose, nor mine, more than a need to include all that might so come to mind and survive to be written.

My tidinesses, however, are insistent. Thus forms of things said moved through accumulated habits of order, and I felt neither ease nor possibility in the jumbled or blurred contexts of language. No doubt I will repeat the manners of small kid with mother town nurse and older sister most articulate in West Acton, Mass., 1930 to 1935 forever. Only the town is changed, to protect the innocent.

If one were a musician, the delight might be sounding again and again all that composite of articulation had preceded one, the old songs truly. In poetry, the dilemma of the circumstance is simply that some*one* is supposed to write some*thing*, and it becomes a possessive and distracting point of view. It is interesting to remember that Archilochus and Sappho are known to us because literacy comes to 'write them down,' no necessary concern of theirs nor of lyric poetry more generally. Yet I am very much a person of my time in wanting to leave a record, a composite fact of the experience of living in time and space. It was Charles Olson's hope to make an *image of man* in writing *The Maximus Poems*—not at all to write some autobiographical memoir. I use all poetry to write anything, and only wish I might know more of its vast body, which is seemingly as vast as the earth itself.

What *is* poetry? In a dictionary I've hauled around for almost as long as I've been writing (*The Pocket Oxford Dictionary of Current English*, Fowler and Fowler, in a "New and Enlarged Edition revised by George Van Santvoord," 1935), it says to my horror: "elevated expression of elevated thought or feeling, esp. in metrical form...." If I turn to a more recent dictionary, *The American Heritage Dictionary of the English Language*, 1969, I'm told that poetry is "the art or work of a poet," which has got to be a cop-out. So all these years people have been screaming that one was not writing *real* poetry—and it turns out nobody, certainly no one in that crowd, knew what it was to begin with. No wonder they insisted on those *forms*! They wouldn't know it *was* a woman unless she was wearing a dress.

So now I will make up poetry, as I always have, one word after another, becoming something, as sounds, call them, as beats, *tum tum*. All very familiar. But each time I take the bus I do see something new, somehow. Eyes possibly? Certainly a turning world. Verse turns, and takes turns in turning—which are called *verses*, in my book, like changes —and not those *stanzas* or stops, standstills. *Onward then, multiple men, women too, will go with you*—boohoo. Which is a poem because I say so, it *rhymes*. That was a primary requisite for years and years. But so lovely when such rhyming, that congruence of sounds which occur in time with sufficient closeness, to resound, echo, and so recall, when *that* moves to delight and intensity, feeling the physical quality of the words' movement with a grace that distorts nothing. To *say* things—and to say them with such articulation can bring them physical character in the words which have become them—is *wonder*.

It is equal wonder when the rhythms which words can embody move to like echo and congruence. It is a *place*, in short, one has come to, where words dance truly in an information of one another, drawing in the attention, provoking feelings to participate.

Poems have involved an extraordinary range of human and non-human event, so to discuss that fact seems pointless. We will talk of everything sooner or later. Americans have had the especial virtue in the last hundred years of opening both content and form in an extraordinary manner, and the energy inherent continues without apparent end.

But again, one lives a life, and so, personally, one speaks of it, and of the people and places it was given to find. I cannot say that my children particularly respect or find other interest in my being a poet, and, at first, that bothered me because I wanted them moved by what moved me. False hope, I now think—although it might otherwise come to be the case. At times I hear the niggard comment that poets seem only to have other poets as an audience. It is certainly true that the dearest company I've had in reading has been so. But many people otherwise have heard too, through no intent of mine. I couldn't predicate they would, in writing. As a young man I questioned that anyone would ever hear at all, although it did not occur to me that I might therefore stop writing.

The tacit lament in this way of speaking strikes me as pathetic. Getting a purchase on writing, so to speak, was for me a one way ticket to bliss. I've never really come back. In those long, lonely nights I've wailed the sweetest songs, possibly, certainly those most designed for my own pleasure. Years back, again, Williams said, why don't we make clear we write for our pleasure, that we *like* doing it? It's a fair question. Nobody wants their pleasures criticized, and that fact no doubt explains why nobody really wants to be explained, nor wants to explain either. And I suppose that's why one uses either a tendentiously 'critical' vocabulary in speaking of 'his work' or else pushes clear with a, gee whiz, fellers, it's really nothing.

At first I was intent upon getting *anything* to hold, so that the experience in reading had the same qualities as the impulse in writing. But then I don't really know, nor have I ever, what's being said until it comes to some close, and it's now there to be read through, as one thing. Elsewise I trust the location implicit in feeling it's going well, opening, moving without a sense of hesitance or forced intention. I don't want to write what is only an idea, particularly my own. If the world can't come true in that place, flooding all terms of my thought and experience, then it's not enough, either for me, or equally, for anyone else. It must be somehow *revelation*, no matter how modest that transformation can sometimes be. Or vast, truly—"the world in a grain of sand."

The title for these divers thoughts comes from a lovely story told me about 1960 by John Frederick Nims in Chicago as he afforded us a charming lunch in his role as editor of *Poetry*. It concerned a friend of his, another poet, who had been on a tour of readings in the Middle West. And, as was his wont, he invited questions from the audience at one particular college, on completion of his reading. And a guy puts up his hand and says, tell me, that next to last poem you read—was that a real poem or did you just make it up yourself? Terrific. That's stuck in my head so lucently so long! Much as the phenomenon of another friend and student at Black Mountain in the middle fifties, who in truth could perceive no demonstrable difference between a cluster of words called *poem* and a cluster of words called *prose*. She felt the typographical form of the poem was all that apparently defined it—and that of course was a very arbitrary gimmick, to her mind. I tried everything, "Mary had a little lamb," tum te tum, clapped my hands with the beat, pulled out the vowels à la Yeats, probably even sang. Still it stayed flat and arbitrary. She felt the beat and texture of the sound was imposed by will of the reader and was not initial in the words themselves. All the usual critical terms were of course useless, far too abstract. Finally I truly despaired of gaining more than her sympathy and patience. Then one day, we were reading Edward Marshall's "Leave the Word Alone," and for some immaculate and utterly unanticipated "reason" she *got* it, she heard all the play of rhythms and sounds bringing that extraordinary statement of primary humanness into such a density of feeling and song.

Would that all had such a happy ending—and 'American poetry,' like they say, soared on to the stars. Senses of progress, also familiar, really want that in the worst way. Meantimes one's brothers and sisters are out there somewhere wailing on, to make the night a little lighter, the day a little brighter, like. Bringing that sun up and bringing it down again, every time. I don't know where it's supposed to 'get to' in that sense, more than to persist in the clarity of human recognitions and wonder. Poetry, as Duncan says, comes "from a well deeper than time." It's 'contemporary' in the way that fire, air, water or earth might be said to be particularly involved in any apprehension of present existence. Sadly it can, as these, go away, be lost to other appetites and acts. Talking to Michael McClure a few days ago, thinking of the primary *stances* in the arts, to the three most familiar (Classicism, Romanticism, and Surrealism) he felt a fourth might be added: the Beat, which, distinct from the other three, does not propose 'the world' as a stable, physical *given* but, in ecological terms, realizes its fragility and thus the need for human attention and care.

As a poet, at this moment—half listening as I am to the House Judiciary Committee's deliberations—I am angered, contemptuous, impatient, and possibly even cynical concerning the situation of our lives in this 'national' place. Language has, publicly, become such an instrument of coercion, persuasion, and deceit. The power thus collected is ugly beyond description—it is truly *evil*. And it will not go away.

211

Trust to good verses then... Trust to the clarity instant in being human, that knows and wants no other place.

Bolinas, California
July 31, 1974

Nothing New

Whatever's the case, such fact as I presumed the world to be at twenty-five or six is no longer even remotely actual. I keep thinking of that shot in one of Fellini's movies, the one of the helicopter flying over the roofs of the city, with people variously down there, sun bathing, carrying on, waving, and all becoming smaller and smaller as the helicopter lifts up and away. That's where it was, so to speak, down there, in some other quickly fading world that even the endless horrors of the Second World War and all the trashed decades since haven't managed to put clearly in anyone's mind as what, after all, did happen.

I like, rather, am caught by, that sense of history deliquescing, becoming commentary on its own agencies of recording, a schizophrenically dividing pattern of of multiple *realities*, all contesting, all "right" from their own demanding perspectives. A friend spoke of the hermeneutical phase of history, that stage where it becomes the study of its own meaning. And then the baroque, and then the post—. Pound quoted Santayana as saying, "It doesn't matter what books they read as long as they read the same books." The banal commonnesses we would all quickly recognize and tacitly accept, physically depleted *place*, diminished determinations of *work*, increasing despairs of any imaginable "solution," whether political or personal. Who can think of "progress" in a terrarium, which, at best, seems what our lives "on earth" may prove to be.

Poetry, like anything else, speaks to whoever will listen and respond in the desired manner. Hey, man, I'm talking to you. It's a familiar pitch. Poetry presently is probably no more "experimental" than it ever was, Wyatt shifting the beat, Chaucer getting it on in the local, or Villon using a kind of patois that was way under any imagination of street talk. It wasn't just words, it was *mind*. Like first century Rome, Plautus, or Catullus, really disliking certain people.

"Mine eyes have seen the glory?" Enough to stay open, certainly, but it had little to do with qualified "great moments."

Somehow our elegantly secure cat Aphrodite having her kittens just as the first human stepped out on the first moon ever to be walked on is something I'll remember most specifically of that event, like they say. Is it that the so-called "personal" keeps drifting back into "self," wants the home of its own habits, recognizes even in vastness its own familiar hat and coat? I don't really know, and *I* is fading, intermittent signal, batteries running down. "Oh build your ship of death, for you will need it…" D. H. Lawrence got to me, he made sense, he made clear that feeling, touching, holding, seeing, being with other people in every sense, was the fact of life, what it was, literally. You could think anything you wanted to or could. Still you wouldn't, and couldn't, go far.

Anyhow I don't really want any more separation from anything, even the disasters, cheap as it seems to say that, or to be so glib about what I know so meagerly. I don't want to be a poet who writes "about" "things" or will have a "poetics" to be "affected"—which returns to the questions of that time, "What did Hiroshima mean to you poetically?" "Did the Holocaust alter your imagination of audience?" Everything, God in particular, gets trivial if you try to make that proposed content singular in the apparent world, the diverse plurality we flounder in without ever having a clue as to what it means, other than the "meanings" we give it: "Names we have even to clap on the wind…" (in Hart Crane's words). Or dear Wittgenstein: "If you give it a meaning, it has a meaning." No teacher will ever grade all those papers.

Nor will the roles be played as if they were choices, as if people wanted to be doctors and lawyers and simply became them, fulfilled those roles and played them to the hilt. If all this is a play in Shakespeare's sense, and we thus "actors," our parts will be simply assigned. *You get this, you get that,* or probably more aptly put, *this is what you get, that's what you get,* and *that's* that. No refunds. Do it or don't do it. Nobody's watching anyhow.

So what's the point, baby? If you were alive all those years, what would you say happened? Did you like it, or didn't you? Did you want ever to trade it in? The answer is, it doesn't come in a package, you are there all through, stoned or not. You are not an exception. If there was a puppy playing with a ball, you'd not be confused. Yet your own delight, just the same, seems to need reasons. "Can you afford not to make the magical study which happiness is?" So Olson translates Rimbaud, his last poem I believe. Did he fade out into heaven? I don't think so.

How best to say it. I.e., "I am a post-communist, vegetarian, unemployed, overworked, illiterate and de-signed, spiritualized, abortioned, computed, technified, e-mailed, voice-mailed, MTV'd, virtual almost surrealed person," etc. I thought we passed 2000 way back there. I must have set my watch wrong.

"Are you ready for the rapture?" Remember that? Always a pitch but at least someone's talking to you. Smile...

Poetry will make you happy, put hair on your chest, shoes on your feet, get you out there and swinging. "Recorders ages hence...," bro, those "happy few" of 1835 Stendhal was then talking to, all that crowd like everybody's waiting for you, to get it on, get up and go.

...Thank you for your time; I'll look forward to hearing from you. Please call or write with any questions or confirmations of submission. And all you poets of that vast future out there, don't you ever forget to enclose a self-addressed stamped envelope. You hear?

> *Nothing new*
> *I wasn't going to*
> *do to you*
> *nothing new*

[1995]

Four Days in Vermont

Window's tree trunk's predominant face
a single eye-leveled hole where limb's torn off
another larger contorts to swell growing in around
imploding wound beside a clutch of thin twigs
hold to one two three four five six dry twisted
yellowish brown leaves flat against the other
gray trees in back stick upright then the glimpse
of lighter still grayish sky behind the close
welted solid large trunk with clumps of gray-green
lichen seen in boxed glass squared window back
of two shaded lamps on brown chiffonier between
two beds echo in mirror on far wall of small room.

.

(for Maggie)

Most, death left a hole
a place where she'd been
An emptiness stays
no matter what or who
No law of account not
There but for the
grace of God go I
Pain simply of want
last empty goodbye
Put hand on her head
good dog, good dog
feel her gone.

．

Tree adamant looks in
its own skin mottled with growths
its stubborn limbs
stick upright parallel
wanting to begin again
looking for sun in the sky
for a warmer wind
to walk off pull up
roots and move
to Boston be a table
a chair a house
a use a final fire.

．

What is truth *firm (as a tree)*
Your faith your trust your loyalty
Agrees with the facts makes
world consistent plights a troth
is friendly sits in the common term
All down the years all seasons all sounds
all persons saying things conforms confirms
Contrasts with "war" equals "confusion" (*worse*)
But *Dichtung und Wahrheit*? "Wahr-" is
very ("Verily I say unto you...") A compact now
Tree lights with the morning though *truth* be an oak
This is a maple, is a *tree*, as a very truth firm.

．

Do I rootless shift
call on the phone
daughter's warm voice
her mother's clear place
Is there wonder here
has it all gone inside
myself become subject
weather surrounds
Do I dare go out
be myself specific
be as the tree
seems to look in.

        ·

Breeze at the window
lifts the light curtains
Through the dark a light
across the faint space
Warmth out of season
fresh wash of ground
out there beyond
sits here waiting
For whatever time comes
herein welcome
Wants still
truth of the matter.

        ·

Neighbor's light's still on
outside above stoop
Sky's patchy breaks
of cloud and light
Around is a valley
over the hill
to the wide flat river
the low mountains secure
Who comes here with you
sits down in the room
What have you left
what's now to do.

.

Soon going day wanders on
and still tree's out there waiting
patient in time like a river and
truth a simple apple reddened
by frost and sun is found
where one had left it in time's company
No one's absent in mind   None gone
Tell me the *truth* I want to say
Tell me all you know   Will we live
or die   As if the world were apart
and whatever tree seen were only here apparent
Answers, live and die. Believe.

Stephen Rodefer

Closure

Squint stock dot mate
    laud nil writ drink
nab plain timbre
    tongues make just

world's great hive
    takes smarting
cropping husbands
    maladroit

what does not feel
    like it does not
feel like it felt
    to so many real

natural birth misses
    arms part from side
keeps touch from hem
    fled from roost's sleep

paper panned in speech
    readable one day
counted as slid
    from nimble's memory

loss next and still
    summer giggling comes
pills bearing sheets
    plastic paying

lackaday states
    what does not
still changes...
    the will to change

Preface [from *Four Lectures*]

> *Writing and painting are deeply identical.*
> —*Paul Klee*

My program is simple: to surrender to the city and survive its inundation. To read it and in reading, order it to read itself. Not a doctrine, but a public notice.

The city, which even before Baudelaire had been a ready-made collage or cut-up of history, constantly remaking itself—a work of art, founded on an anthill. And every art grows out of the same collective desire which informs and compels the idea and reality of a city (Latin *colligere*, to tie together). A district, or a ghetto, is a segmentation, an alternative version which both resists and embodies in a different fashion, that is with an opposing ideology, the original model. Hence, dialect and civil strife are alternating codes of the same phenomenon: the city does not hold together. Language, which also binds together and extends, including as it isolates, is a city also.

In such a metropolitan of history, in which the city is literally the mother, the greatest art is painting, if only by the sheer weight of the temporal. Without a city and its structures there would be no painting. The only thing precedent to painting is caves—the Gilgamesh is not as old as Lascaux.

The Greeks had painted sculputre and from the start all cultures have painted their deities. Today we have painted cities, painted conveyances, painted apartments, painted roads, painted people, even painted food. Is is not time for painted poetry as well?

A poetry painted with every jarring color and juxtaposition, every simultaneous order and disorder, every deliberate working, every movement toward one thing deformed into another. Painted with every erosion and scraping away, every blurring, every showing through, every wiping out and every replacement, with every dismemberment of the figure and assault on creation, every menace and response, every transformation of the color and reforming of the parts, necessary to express the world.

Even the words and way of language itself will suffer the consequent deformity and reformation. The color beneath, which has been covered over, will begin to show through later, when what overcame it is questioned and scraped on, if not *away*.

Political revolution answers the same process. Shapes and lines converging and diverging will formulate new ideas, the true statement of which is not fully disclosed, but fully embodied. There is a continuing direction felt within, but ordered from without. When the oppressed whole is dismantled, the parts will find a new place, more proper to them, or else all fails. In the future it will be said of such a mode, regarding its material and its language, to adapt a phrase Augustus used of Rome, that it found it brick but it left it aggregate. Deliberate decomposition is required in a state of advanced decay.

Marble is no longer the style of course. Our era promises to make the late Roman look small time, if not benign. In a world in which there are more photographs than there are bricks, can there be more pictures than there are places? I'm told that soon there will be more people living than have ever died. In innumerable ways we exist in an incomprehensible age. It is entirely unnecessary for this argument (though ultimate) to mention nuclear weapons. The signs are otherwise quite enough.

In art, just as in life, significance tends to emerge tentatively, as figures in an abstraction, or a seascape in Kandinsky, even as the figurative element reveals new structural relations which then re-define the abstraction. For example, say, Rosso Fiorentino, *Nosferatu*, or the latest improvised quartet.

Such a poetry as is suggested here is not a new concept, any more than poetry as music is. In *our* world it's been around at least since Blake, and was revived by Klee, Huidobro, and Picabia. My decision to take up the art again is simply carrying on, which is of course the meaning of tradition. Painted poetry is probably as ancient as the absence of machines, and with good fortune will survive the ends brought on by them.

The old form / content play has always been self-contained, like Hamlet or any good Polish sausage, somewhere between metaphor and metonymy, as the linguists would remind us, or Gertrude and Laertes. The modern world began with the first contiguity disorder, i.e. at birth, when things become wrenched from their similarity. But bent out of shape is also bent *into* shape. New replacements are expected, and they always come. We start to be fed things forcibly. We can throw up, not eat, or fold the spoon in half. Several wars are going on at once, but there is also one big war. The peace that is won with difficulty at times out of this condition will necessarily always be partial; the map will ever be fragmented and changing. The same territory with a different name makes no more sense than a different state with the same name, though we are asked in the so-called post-modern world to swallow this kind of malfeasant pitch all the time. The word itself sounds the end.

The events and systems that embody this swarming *state* of affairs have become so mixed, complex, and unconscious at once, that what is required to read it is the ultimate painting. It can be made in any number of ways, but there is no way now that it can be anything but apocalyptic. A vision is intended, rather than an explosion.

For writing is a graphic art, and a word projects either stroke or color. As it is born, a poem is drawn. It can begin with a figure or a line. It can begin to clothe a cartoon or *about* the idea of anything. It begins to paint itself. It can be made with a pencil or with a knife, with a pen or a recorder, or with a keyboard contraption that strikes the paper. It requires patience, approach, observation, technique, impulse, intent, alternation, energy, and obsession. It can be attacked by history, as well as attack history. It can be unknown and done only for itself and nothing other. Its meaning can change in time, and *always* does.

Completed, the art object is nothing but the fantasy of a given artist at a particular time. If fully worked and read totally, it will reveal all there is to know about the life of the artist, the conditions in which it was made, as well as implicate the development of art up to its example. It is shape of mind, as such. The formation of the work will literally imply the history of the species (*imply*: to fold in, envelop, embrace). Hence it will take its place at the latest point of a tradition that it will then be *carrying on*, no matter what.

Tradition as *borne*: not only what speaks to us across time, but that which we *drag along*, what we lift into the picture as well as what by a differential operation we "unload." Footstep, tread, trace, track, path, thoroughfare, method, practice, market, peripatetic *trade*, TRADITION.

I consider the enterprise of poetry therefore to be musical and graphic at once, more than literary. For how much more illuminating and amusing it is (MUSIC / MOSAIC, belonging to the muses) to compose language, or to paint poetry, than simply to write it.

As should a book be as deep as a museum and as wide as the world.

Prologue to Language Doubling

Boris Pasternak (older than Mayakovsky and alive *after* the Allen anthology) speaks somewhere of the necessity for writers to disregard the approval of their admirers, lest their writing be tempted to repeat itself. He speaks of the urge for perfection as the mark of the imitator. Writers of course can imitate their own original maneuvers—what is practically an epidemic malady of the trade. Pasternak offers that the real exploration of new territory is constantly marked by abrupt change and barbaric intuitions, calling for still another *contrary* genius to appear, intuitively and without notice. The thrust of the argument is that too much rationale can turn an original idea into so much ration, a new form into simply format, ignoring the richness yet to be mined.

Now, of course *all* art partakes of some usefulness of the artist as recorder and transmitter of an external world or an internal one, according to his or her idea of how best to do it. Limits are what any of us are inside of, find a form to accommodate the mess, etc. There is of course usually some motivating force in operation (what is called an ideology or a moral belief, depending on which side of the sphere you're on) which is ordinarily more than numerology or circumspection. On the other hand, an account of *almost everything*, inside or out, in any given historical era, is hardly too small a goal for any art to embrace.

Perhaps embrace is just the point. Passion, not compulsion, is what is meant. It seems to be the function precisely, say, of the *Iliad* or *Canterbury Tales*, of Shakespeare, Tolstoy, or of Melville—at *least*. As generally the 'special' interests in such great writers behave as *pluses*, rather than as focus, in the greater design.

Who could care the archaeology in Homer or the eating habits in Chaucer, for instance, the invective in Shakespeare, the manners in Tolstoy, or the detail of the whaling industry in *Moby Dick*, or for that matter the Fibonacci numerology of Ron Silliman's *Tjanting* or the marginated presentation of Steve Benson's *The Buses* (making marvellous internal white spaces that look like Illinois), were it not for the greater force of the overall work—a condition required of any writing if it is to be more than an accumulation of its parts. What is crucial is not the ingenuity of a verbal work, nor the relentlessness of it, nor the versimilitude of it—not the formal innovation, nor the meticulous care for detail, nor the working out of schema and intent, however much these may contribute—but something absolutely vital no matter what else is present; I mean that power to lift us out of our seats *and* keep us in them. Perhaps that old church purpose of literature to be *uplifting* is not so far off in a varied sense. To disclose in short a design and a vision which impel us to a greater apprehension of where we are situated as inhabitors of room on this globe, larger than us and smaller than the universe.

The world is full of writers whose main idea of what to do with the act of writing is to sell it or get noticed—verbal art as commercial venture or job application. But what good is it to get caught up in some fix (as to *idée*), if there is not some more urgent purpose inherent in the consciousness. The question is pertinent to Aeschylus or Shakespeare, to Ovid or Dante, to Dickens or Dostoevsky, to Swift or Dickinson, to Kokoshka, Stein, or Kafka, as it currently is not least of all to current examples.

Then how that detestable phrase *post-modern* sounds the end by almost bomb-like assuming it. And so we must fight against any writing which prescribes or predicts any goal at all...except what lies beyond. In that sense it will remain the writer's job to exist *outside* any mode of any centr*alizing* discourse, especially that one projected by the writing already written.

Enclosure of Elk

I wrote words on the brow of home and around the corners of its mouth—waiting for those days which wait for life to engulf them. The silhouettes of Pompeii were made and excavated for me. I take them personally. If embarrassed by my work, I turned to satire. What will never be position will nevertheless struggle, like a wild animal by night, a dog by day. The epigones are slashed, the elective affinities are not dice. The work is nothing now but a pencil motif, vulgar yet important. It dedicates its orifice to pioneering the handling of modalities. It will be a hero with one wing. But it will never be content with any view of the world except as it may proceed to its essentials. Even when they are hidden from view, it will hasten to make them materialize.

The fault of all endeavor every day will be to attempt too much, never too often. Our art is unimportant, but that does not matter. We were born to this means and we must make more of our situation than at first it will seem ever to allow. Decide what will be the use of forcing oneself to do things beyond one's power. Acknowledgment advocates laughter; reason, its forgetting—on a carpet of memory.

Though it is not to be despised that marriage should be a great relief. The bride and groom find that place full of nothing in which they still fall down with emotion. The source of all happiness afterward will be to live without pretension. Who will not? My father, who lives here, gave me my sailboat, my train, my puppet theater. I dressed like an alchemist lover at the sea, though you took me merely for an instructor. If I am not a Bohemian, you still can think that I am somewhat odd. And so is art history the falsification of facts which as they occur are neither factual nor historic. As the movement, of which I am a part, is nothing but a part of my own development.

One liberates oneself through work, even on the eve of catastrophe. How long can you continue to delay the true nature of sensations? We must refuse to be beggared by orderliness. True nature creates combinations to defeat naturalism. There will always be on the table, if you look, a vase of intentions.

Wherever you go, there will be nothing but lines and surface rhythms. Then let never will speak word. For we all live as happily with the dead as with the unborn. Nearer to the heart of creation than is usual, but not near enough. Reality will be invisible always. The visible world will be nothing but a special case, the very one we have come here to overthrow. After the die of fate is cast—and who is to say it has not been —it is pointless to tolerate anything inferior.

Perspective then will make you yawn, opening a hole in nature. While the dark shades of the landscape visible through the film are nevertheless full of promise, the cast is still weak at the top. The contracted pages are to be rigorous and substantive. But the words devolve to be persistent and unique. No element is dominant that wants to allow the cultivation of change. The idea among others of love and its concomitant time took too great a hold on everyone, its program of everlasting appeal, that the chance for greater inclusion would have to be squandered by the more willful deliberation to fantasy and drive. Independence would be the interim fake name for all these new states.

What a lot of things, after all, would be required of us to make art. What a lot of things besides being a maker of art an artist would have to be, in order to make art. To make that which made visible, they believed, that which was not. Some kind of enclosure, some initial fence or extra latch, seemed to be the necessary first step.

But now imagine that you have been dead for many years and that at long last you are permitted once more to glimpse the earth. And all you can see is an old dog, cocking a leg against a lamp post or wall. Still you can't help sobbing with emotion. Because of this my light burns sometimes so hot that to most people it seems even to lack warmth. Like the festive evil it could be said—it could be *drawn*—of a zeppelin flying over a cathedral. But I am absent.

I do not belong to the species. Though my sun and chair are necessary, I remain here dumb and bristling, in a suburb of children. Let the sentries comment later on the hospitality of the region. Though the species is in me, I am neutral.

The Library of Label

for JG, MD, JP and LCS

> The Library is a sphere whose exact center is any one of its
> hexagons and whose circumference is inaccessible.
>
> Borges, "The Library of Babel"

Duchamp gave up painting and became a librarian in 1913, at the Bibliothèque Sainte-Geneviève in Paris. Picabia got him the job. This was the
beginning of Duchamp's "getting theoretical." It was a line. In *Memoirs
of a Fool* and *The Roofing Ceremony*, Strindberg wrote with that one-
eyed Nordic pathology of his stint at the Royal Library in Stockholm.
Aren't we all. And of course—Borges, king of the blind librarians and
genius of the idea itself. There are many others.

A writer in a library might be a thrilling proposition, if it
weren't. You'd have to follow her into the stacks to see what she was
after.

Libraries like bookstores have a way of making you a little
nervous, probably more so if you are a writer, though almost everyone
in a library is a writer. Like the world. A sphere full of millions of
things and you, you want one of them; maybe two, perhaps eventually
several. What is life but a number of hours in which you find out which
are your few things. Then the body exits the texture, it leaves the estate
of the library. The day of its death is like any other day, only shorter,
as another bookmonger put it.

And the library is the world. When I am at home, I'm in the
library. When I'm in the library, I am at home. Forget the Library.
Librarians, with one or two stunning exceptions in a hundred, live up to
the anemic stereotype with a relentlessness that is flabbergasting. Para-
mount couldn't do it any better. And librarians are about as likely to get
over the disappointment, as they are to administer, or give meaning to
the life of letters. Their function really is just to manage the staff, as
though *it* were some kind of necessary, low-grade nuisance infection.

230

Books in fact disappear, the better they get at housing them. What was meant to be a museum or a seat of learning converts perfectly into a "storage facility," or a target for an incendiary first century Alexandria or twentieth century Los Angeles, similar cities in the likeliest of centuries. The corridors, stairways, and hexagons, like the functionaries themselves, come to their predictable ends. And others certainly replace them.

The best thing about being a writer is when somebody happens to read you and finds that instance to be happening. The best thing about a Library is when, for instance, you don't have to go there to find out what's happening.

The universe, which others call the Library, is composed of an indefinite and perhaps infinite number of hexes, where one may sleep standing-up and satisfy necessity. Paranoia is the logical exaggeration of what is called "being careful." You can slip a disc, and the record is erased completely. Strindberg thought he had enemies trying to subdue him with electromagnetic fields, yet he was the Shakespeare of Sweden. I was once the Shakespeare of the local collapsible hexagon labelled the Library, the synergetic ranch. It is a name loved from birth but married now to the inaccessible circumference.

Having lost the ability truly to revel in the proposal, they're tearing down all the trees soon and planning a huge underground annex. The Library bunker. A place to bury books and, like an abbey, even writers.

A dinosaur now, pushing up flowers from time to time. But hard to tell the plaster from the bones.

Statement for Reading the Prioresse's Room

I thought I might be able to read it perusal—overconfident or wary, what difference—the English lyrics, most of what saw daylight in the last couple of years, here and in other states. You're always attached to what's left you most recently—in the stillness especially—inevitably. As you leave your mother at birth.

But then I thought that would be too literary or passed on. Hence —and thus—when I am writing and not writing, which is a lot lately, I burn through a fair correspondence, to manage the low-level elevation and maintain the groundswell—to avoid the burial of print. Or mount it.

And always I have loved that sense of lit'rature which transcribes, simply enough, "letters." Perhaps not so belle as such, but still we are prepossessed—and letters are the post proctors of the possession one imagines. Make no apology. I've always hankered after that position. But one can do worse than look into the reasonant page and write. So long as the placard doesn't start to look too bloody lumpish.

There is the dyslexia of a hole, in some organ or other. We plug it with our best fish & chips, while others argue mutton, and hope for the best—agog at the sublime sea-foam outside us. Much good may our harm, may our sight reading, do us.

There are letters, if not post-its or readings necessarily. They don't arrive here merely as some *correspondence* to writing. All this is much and more. Posted cards can lead to the apotheosis of the prosaic, and to something other, more, or less.

For what is writing, but a marker of what one loves or is confined to. The first, the only call from gaol *allowed*, once you've been subject to arrest. Why the bars are so satisfying, inspite of the tendencies. They narrow your direction.

And writing and letters are, in the course of that, more often identical than poetry and writing—or poetry and letters for that matter. They contain distraction and direction—cheers, saws, or apotheoses. Everyday a pain is out their window, however barred. For we live—and how could we not—in a country where flesh is a chair, bread is pain, to rent is to love, and Villon is a fancy shoe store.

It's all a ligature of bed, food, desk, walk, company, flight, arrest and dream erasure. And the interlacing cells, the arenas of flood, house, temblor and street lights—the images scrimmaging—make precisely, if feebly in the end, a detail of the larger confinement of existence. Which is certainly ours, but of all conscience. All that is known together. One can make a company of solitude, but not a community— except a pathological one. I mean, some hemorrhaging of history that is beyond, not about, history.

Of course what you receive is not always what you get, or got. Goodness knows what any of us does not get. Recently they have taken me to emending photocopies. And like a proper diarist, dearest readers, de-arrested for a second, become freed or recaptived, what difference. Not to mention the writers—well, their names most of them get erased along the route.

Thus the poetics of reading is always "self-selective." Though with some, if the address were only Pepysicola, tenth muse, Dykersville, the letters would eventually get there, against all confinement and delay. One can think of countless exceptions to this ideal postal service, of course, but just wait. Or get to work, find a revised delivery system.

For it is nothing but an allegory of textual remains in the end. At least it warms the imprisoned colonel to think so. Letters are the last things managed to be scribbled or ascribed. Of course, one wishes they were always at the snood before the fire. And the blood in bed. The ordinary ecstasy of raw cloth in its place.

SR / Jesus College / 4 21 94

Brief to Butterick

The tooth of time is black to the root...
I have done all I could
to appear mirthful

About suffering we are always wrong.
It doesn't dawn on us what day it is
who shave our children's heads like frigate birds
subversively, as scholarships to dreadnaught street,
as waxwings, as envelopes...

                       and Allusion

is use

       but that which is not

               stills something.

Why should a dog a rat?
who cannot write. Why should a poet laureate
nationalized and public

               have TV breath

old boy piss

          retiring to his Connecticut
pasture, some alumnus to be
the rector of poetry

             to play some tennis
while he can and putter around
his garden waiting for a poem
to hit him on the head.
Looking for them we are a zoo.
Our faces halve our heads, the song
sticks and it collapses. No poem
will hit no one no head no more.

Which is the letter of the letters' letter
now reduced and deferred. Why should Bankier, Bartlett,
Benson, Bergé, Berkson, Bernstein, Bertholf,
Boone, Brainard, Bromige, Bukowski, Burke
have use of letters, which will be outculled
and the grass breathe on something instantly amiss
like a molecule for a season
or a monarch butterfly in love with vessels.

Still, in the midst of the mess
there are intervals of life
and the heavenly bodies that dissolve at night
they are not casual in their demand for Strega
for they have come to cook up something more
than a cauldron of feathers—
loathesome particulars of afterwards.

The writer says he hopes that Ingram reads this
rather than that high-hatted rabbit at a tea party.
For pep flickers in the step down to Susan's
at the pond's edge, where Martz lives (*Louis?*
George wonders, among the freezing molecules).

Then who could gather all those sources,
who could read all that Carl Sauer and turn
the max into an ark, no bigger—
an exemplary and its repartee.
The line packed and shipped now to us all.

While the grasshopper invasion reaches
biblical proportions and our headless
body may be that of the lost witness
subject to deterioration

from the weather
and mutilation from animals and other
editors of the body, as the obit arrives
with the new Norton, replacing Oppen
and Riding, as it does, with pinafores.
Insult were it not negligible to the trade.

When friends and poets carry on
their tedious wars at the backs
of magazines and institutions
and language associations go wall eyed
with a view to canons
                    the rest
of the world continues its fight with death and sloppiness,
which is the rest of the world.

As though the whole world hangs on the color of a vowel
you made the car that goes from there to here.
You sharpened with pencil and an eye
the animal devouring teeth that speak.
And we who still can say know what increase,
what cease, prowling among the accidents.

For there is tempest, screendoor, passport, sea—
planest model, earth's dusty guest who gossiped not.
Young winner, shaper, catholic strider
who built the deck, righthanded history
and its letter of projected bric-a-brac.

A ship that scholars float on now with us
out to sea in the city street...

7/29/88

Pretext

Then I stand up on my hassock and say sing that.
It is not the business of POETRY to be anything.
When one day at last they come to storm your deluxe cubicle,
Only your pumice stone will remain. The left trapezius for now
Is a little out of joint. Little did they know you came with it.
When nature has entirely disappeared, we will find ourselves in Stuttgart.
Till then we're on the way. The only way not to leave is to go.
The gods and scientists heap their shit on Buffalo and we're out there,
Scavenging plastic trees. When nature has entirely disappeared,
We'll find ourselves in the steam garden. Evening's metonym for another
Beady-eyed engineer with sexual ideas, who grew up eating animals.
Do you like the twelve tones of the western scale? I prefer ninety.
I may work in a factory but I slide to the music of the spheres.
My job is quality control in the language lab, explaining what went
Wrong in Northampton after the Great Awakening. So much was history.

My father is a sphinx and my mother's a nut. I reject the glass.
But I've been shown the sheets of sentences and what he was
Really like remains more of a riddle than in the case of most humans.
So again I say rejoice, the man we're looking for
Is gone. The past will continue, the surest way to advance,
But you still have to run to keep fear in the other side.
There is a little door at the back of the mouth fond of long names
Called the juvjula. And pidgeon means business. It carries
Messages. The faces on the character parts are excellent.
In fact I'm having lunch with her next week. Felix nupsit.
Why should it be so difficult to see the end if when it comes
It should be irrefutable. Cabin life is incomplete.
But the waterbugs' mittens SHADOW the bright rocks below.
He has a resemblance in the upper face to the man who robbed you.
I am pleased to be here. To my left is Philippa, who will be signing for me.

Codex

That is the glebe and this is the glissando. The future is nothing.

But a flying wing. You must make your case either with names or with an
unfolding.

A position or a disclosure, a microbus. The corridor, the cascade, what stuck.

Glacier notes over the tops of hills. To be close again, as it was in the leanto.

Lengthen the line and increase the leading. These are the helloes of progress.

At the kitchen table the books are pored over, much as a neighbor will bum a
cigaret.

The bungalow, radioed and occupied, has no other path to follow but the
venture,

The undeniable yielding turmoil mapped out for us for life.

Somebody might ought cook someone a square meal. Life in our adulthood

Is mistaken for wanting completion. What it longs to do is continue being.

The BEES are sleeping beneath the pergola. At the end of each lesson is the
vocabulary.

If one opening clouds, another will clear, so long as you both will breathe.

Where's a shovel or something, I say, what can dig, or a trowel? Language
pointed

To its content. A crowd of people at the beach screaming "Tuna! tuna!" The
evening

Breeze, trembling trees, the night, the stars. And there you are, in a manner of
speaking.

So at sunset the clouds went nuts. They thought they were a text.

This language of the general o'erflows the measure, but my brother and I liked
it alot.

I think I'll just pause long enough to call God a bitter name.

Ripeness is all right but the lip is a couplet and nobody knows fuck-all about it.

The THREAD has always been bias. There are alternatives to purchasing goods

To recruit admirers. Right, but is it what Verdi would have wanted?

Nor is it enough to be seen by your youngers as having carried the tradition

To a good place. Given disasters everywhere, don't drink from the tap.

And for what reason make anything that is not for flight?

These are treatments to keep your retina from becoming detached but for what—
To see this? Why, there are things about Israel not dreamed of in the Bible.
How could I miss you when my aim is dead. The goal is sea sounds not yet
    writ.
All right. Enjoy the heads of your beaches. I'm not going in order
To get tied up on spec, but I wanted you to meet your fellow brains. Thank you,
People of destiny, for your brilliant corners. I like your voice. Look where it's
    come from.

Child of Faust

Whether veins amok play school-like
The swarthy dreads of lost anarchies
And balk upon submission with a stamp
Whether next door to ecstatica
A freckle surfing in a drift of hair
Owns twice the reed bop at the arch
And scrawls a bunting on the bed
Whether an apocalypse of earth's great confiscation
Of clock time, cup tea, rakes all to withers
Whether scotch dandies roof the rubble
With the Quebecois of Lenin all pristine
In lyric nature's film revival day

The generosity of the second sense
Of sense beglozes in a swoon of big return
None other than the great cool beating wood
Where berries pile up unswerving to be et

Our

We've the doesn't.
This suspension. This this.

Then but.
Back at a.
If the: here which, now why.

Because they.
Out.   Mode they.
They they.

That I we've.
We've risking.
We've and.

[from] A Letter to Paul Metcalf (jan 7 1972)

Wellsir, maybe I put you off a bit talking *SPACE* as "spychedelic" (oops) or whatever—actually I recall the word Olejonathon used was "electric," but neither (term) is actually here nor there as opening to the book. Natch I hope one can read into it without any preface, get a feeling of my feeling of words anyway, which is near the crux, "options open" ain't bad either—it seems indeed a catch to find *any* new options for words these days. & I really didn't want to dive into a vast aesthetic discus here in letterform, easir (easier) in person, talky mebbe, if you're interested. I like Barney Newman's "aesthetics is for artists as ornithology is for the birds" still in such regard. As you might figger, I've had many years pleasure & turnon "at the hands of" the NY 50's painters, & Gertrude Stein, whose proposals (from back in the teens) still seem untaken-up by almost all writers in English: just what are words & what do they do?

Here's a few notes I jotted down reading your letter & thinking (artists ain't too good at that mode?) it over again for you. Take 'em or heave 'em over thebackfence—it's all still a matter of what you can & cant use I guess Ezz??!!!?

    —the Necessary Negatives: 'cause the subconscious gets so
        loose.

    —Creeley's "you want/the fact/of things/in words,/of words."

    —DeKooning's "it's very tiny, content"

    —to work at the zone of interface tween unconscious &
        frontbrain   (thought / word)

    —the Language as Present Fact

    —I'd rather the Fudge than the Shine.

    —Reversing the Syntactic Polarities arcs new energy across the
        blocks.

    —Composition by Unit: read it that way.

    —I'd rather risk destroying the whole language than bore
        myself.

—Give myself something to read.

—"expressive," "rhetorical," "descriptive," "explicative"
whatever statement is too abstract to me (by that I mean:
removed, vague).

—I can't add to all those books.

—Differences, edges, oppositions, polarities, twins, offshades,
silences, blanks, erasures, shrubbery, echoes, strata,
repetitions, phasing, plain it.

—If you got something to say you should be a *speaker*
("something to say," "whether he tells the truth", etc
= all part of the Oral Tradition anyway).

—I want a movement of language that stands for me as sum of
all the axial drives in universe.

A Possible Range

manipulation of language particles	resultant new aggregates of "meaning" elements	forces of all aspects of language structure as "metaphor" for (as-yet-unseen?) physical states-of-matter
	→	→

(1972)

[from *Mine*] XIII

I wonder about things and the people between us. The currents, the feedback, and the whelms. The sharp cracks between trees, and the tolling between the knees. The world is sharp, narrows, and perhaps lost. But I was born on an avenue, though perhaps too short for the name. Now I skip the yard plots and end up in these wood lots. Do you wish me to tell plots, to pronounce names. A walk in the woods would last a while longer than some of its beings. They die loose since they never came up with time. Step over by and around and sometimes on the small things being a history of this world. Shout, as you're shutting the book on the roles.

Nobody has said to me Stop when it mattered. And I go on doing what I had been doing in a manner that keeps its lights trimmed. Push the finger into the woman at the point of lash control. As in sleep we lose lives in ourselves. Time to matter. Time to cancel the fly-over. Time to fur the wand. Is there time for control of the slowest, as we know there might be in the fast. From which we speak we are hidden, as the lines of the walls have the parallel power of candles. I lie down abed and imagine your body in all its positions at once. This is a speech from which, as in gnarl of chemicals, an act will proceed. Time seems insistent on the singular. If not mere alone one is next.

The woman rises, her breasts never the same. A man's wife's body is the greatest mystery. Each time it is revealed. Do you know me? Each glimpse a start, each stare another. And the removal of tight silks is a peeling away of skin to expose the more sensitive flesh beneath. What was your name before you were born? I wish that only I will know it. Standing unclothed across the room you are sensitive only to my eye. And when I cross to you and enter you I will infuse you with my sources. A kiss of my extremity speaks with you inside. Then is the world shut down for awhile.

The world is coming up to us all the time. It has its chicken and lands. I see a greatness in dull whacks, light boards and snooze. The buckle on one's carapace, who can assemble it? Pirates have stormed the land from the north down to the cove. The new lights on your itching wrists are the sealed product of rice. A nova occured at the black rim and brought them. There will be a ruby soon, it will be the robber of dense.

I have no call to say this but I think you should store my place. Needles are required and a shut solution of darkness. The chickens will chime then and the warts on a pickle rise adroit. You have no sun here but often a moon, it curdles the wicks that singe dreams. And the constant drawing toward and away limns a hotness. The man stands on his own hands in the backwards, a land of longness and told gaps. Buzzings in the nose the toes and the penis. Lights that at night are holes in pitch, turning you each center whichway. Each one writes a novel which is a stream at the bottom of the yards behind the houses. In the way that no one can hold in the mind what is constantly on the move. And the hero will be kneeling in the turns on his mind. He will be the Borealis of the Wheatrows in brown corduroys.

A Sex of Lists

"structural horror and flouting"

Breast seeped into from the side
A bit flattened and in purple intransigence
The skin holding it
The fine things
the Catalog of Dwells
That it is almost loose
Dawdles and dims and divines
Pendulums that never quite come to rest
Anywhere at all in the lounge of it
Not quite anywhere
The breaking back of sight from a clasp
And hit from the underside
And the bit through straps
to apply firm but flexible lines to the body
The juice not poured but squeezed upon
The coming "out"
The dwell in lapse but sheening flame
Underclothes as positions
The hands beneath, the hands to the sides, the hands lost
A curling sort of flame through silk slices from one side
The bringing of the body to one state
Though always to be "seen" from all angles
Tipping within
Crushed berry
Internal sap, risen
and the side-to-side *drive*
Breasts flattened while withheld
The suturing
From the armpit to the first flesh of breastside

The candleflame waits at the tip
The crease as handle
Everything is suddenly too small, too far

Three things in the hand
    at all times, from all places
        these dwell
Mixing the cunt with a brash speech
Colander under
Bright metal and the squeaking it makes
Certain spots
Held lights
The loaf of dampness
Rate of task
The mumbling bell

The tongue wound

From Notebooks (1976-1982)

"movement"

        has that arrow edge nerve to it

"motion"

        sounds like a washing machine

      .

Perhaps art is merely the translation
of the external into an obduration
of mind that erodes neither to the
side of memory nor conception.

      .

The worst danger for an artist's work:
assimilation. And this is a country of
highly refined assimilating mechanisms.
To make *like* (how I hate that trait),
to leaven, make digestable, democratize,
ultimately strip of individuation.
Art *is* isolate. Its obduration is
unacceptable. At its deepest levels, art is
an attribute of nothing else. It may not be
defused in attribution to. I would prefer
hatred, obscurity, misunderstanding. In fact
it is my right to be ignored, maltreated,
discomfited.

      .

The history of 20th century art is so much one of
assimilation, that art itself is finally becoming
inseparable from the main mechanisms of society:
business, education, government, the church.
Therefore the artist must reject art to keep clear.

      .

248

At the same time there is the plethora,
proliferation of all forms, making a muck
unforeseen previously. Beckett's statement (1961):
"To find a form that accommodates the mess, that
is the task of the artist now." seems pointed
exactly at our condition.

.

Criticism is divergence, immediately.
I know, when I have written, that there
is no other possible state of this matter.
They have only to begin "This is..." to
be off the mark. And in the wrong voice.
In fact in *no* voice. They write in a mode
that does not speak. But I must remember
that when they write *about*, that "about"
means only "around," not on. And I know
that I am capable of wounding myself
far more deeply than they. The beginning
and end of my work remains here.

.

To create is to make a pact with nothingness.
The void exacts its tribute. What price do
I daily pay for maintaining sufficient
ignorance to accept forms when they emerge?
Writing, I sometimes feel I am working with
nothing. Where are the words? Certainly not
here on this page. Their only firmness seems in
sorts of motion. I am constantly emptied
by their infernal obduration! Cursed forever
to listen to the voices inside there is no
stepping back from. Where silence is a
blessed hell.

.

I am jealous of my own doubt.
To say *no* to everything, what a wonder!
To set in motion, contains its own stopping
point. I glare in at myself to start it all
turning again. I have often opened my doors
to find the small flame of my doubt my only
light. Sometimes I shelter it with the mass
of all my works. I cup it with my acceptance,
blow upon it with satisfaction. I am vitalized
by all it has killed.

.

Obduration.　　Hard Time.

.

A sentence is a collapse.
Time on itself. Lands. To resurface,
and stun in.

.

We now have to peel the skin from
the cup, in order to lap what's wrought.

.

The miles will topple me, and I
will be reached.
Put in my placed in my will.

.

There are walls in the mind's time, and
I would live in the breach.
I would crack myself open to what?

.

What I want from the world is the freedom to
need what can't be given but must be taken.
I want to *stay* in motion. I want the first thing

to be the last, every time.

        .

Alternate: L. alternare, to do a thing
               by turns; change; hesitate
So, alternatives are *hesitations*
along the way.
Thus, he who finally accepts alternatives
is lost.

        .

But, in art, he who takes but one step,
in any direction, is already lost.
Sometimes I feel I could speak but one
word, and thus disappear from the one
I am with.
Again, art is a disguise?

        .

I want everything to come together.
And then I want it all to go away,
leaving behind one thing that was never
in the pile to begin with.

        .

The world is not enough. I want something
else to appear. Only I can cause this,
only I can hate what I have done
enough to destroy it.
                   Only I can stand at
the point of my own collisions.

        .

Are the mistakes, the chips that fall from
these catastrophes, pieces of the void?
Blurred puffs of time, like cigarettes?

I smoke *and* burn. I am moving in
opposite directions at once.
Like a sentence, when written, seems to
move backwards to complete its hold
on itself. The dialectic of forward
and reverse. Weighted on which end
will the work be completed today?

.

The void gives no opening when one is
inside. It is all of the world again.
The feeling of everything giving onto
oneself once again.

.

On the inside of the mask there is nothing.
My eyes slip from the holes,
and I go to work.

.

When I give them my works, how pleased
they seem with degrees of failure.
The only applause I could accept
would be the sound of them all
going to work from disgust.

.

[From] Regarding Morton Feldman's Music and Wherever It All Now Goes

To reach that point at which no other points.

"I feel that in my life I'm trying out another option. It's not philosophy. It's the option of writing very long pieces that are very difficult to play, very difficult to hear, and have to do with the life of the piece, whatever that means and not the life of the performer, or what happens to an audience when they go hear it. I'm trying to see what happens when the work does not depend on those other very important, very rigid factors."

What is this art that has nothing of something else in it? Surely there is too much easy connecting of art with other procedures. Standing in the friars' cells of Fra Angelico in Florence it seemed correct (even novel) to return to the image (the note, the word) as object of solitary contemplation, cut off from all those extraneous vitiating pursuits that are supposed to make us feel so good about our involvement with art. "I think we lost that religiosity about music, about *sound itself*. We don't want to live in a convent."

Think of thing, not of them. "If you need an audience, we don't need you."

I wonder even more about the continuing viability of *writing* as an art form, it being so bound to the engines of explanation. This writing here is a huge frustration, since it can never embody what it is pointing at and swirling around (discussion) I should just shut up. It could just shut itself off? Feldman stopped writing his essays...and one could usefully wonder at just what point in his music?

All quotations taken from the essays, lectures and interviews of Morton Feldman.

"But you're not supposed to *understand* art. You're supposed to understand *culture*. Culture is mutual understanding. That is not communication. Communication is what I have in my music, with myself. Communication is when people don't understand each other. Because then there is a consciousness level that is being brought out of you, where an effort is made."

What is the story? No, what is the subtext? No, what is the substance? And what is all this going on between the masterpieces?

Doesn't it seem that the musical structures have become lodged, like grammar, in the same connectiveness, leading us always back along the same definitions to the same conclusions? Couldn't we afford to lose a lot of this purely connective tissue? But who wants to fact up to *a* tone, rise or fall?

Are you in a misery, or agony of doubt, or just a mild malaise? Said complaint, whatever region or even form of relaxation, tagged to be relieved by a certain shelf-life music? It drips down the sides of the cabinets. But your job is not to fence or lap it up. Leave that to the border cats. The job is, perhaps, to ice it.

"I like the long pieces because you don't drink it, you sip it. You get saturated more and more. The only way you get deep color in rugs is to dip it over and over. You can't put Z against A in ten minutes. It takes saturating. And time is the liberator."

Feldman's music seems never to manipulate, as if never overdetermining its destination, so not rushing to insure the most ease (audience) in getting there. An absolutely non-rhetorical music ("I'm the Master of Nonfunctional Harmony"). A music without god or stain. A music as dependent on you as milk on the sky.

His makes all other music sound anxious for more space, for higher speed.

And he reminds me of what writing has never quite been able to get away with: Lost in that field purely of nouns that verb and stretch and edge, a radiance which comes when things are not used, not used with other things.

"The Abstract is not involved with ideas. It is an inner process like another consciousness. There is a real fear of the Abstract because one does not know its function. The Abstract Experience is only one thing—a unity that leaves one perpetually speculating. Whereas the literary kind of art, the kind we are close to, is involved in the polemic we associate with religion, the Abstract Experience is really far closer to the religious. Collision with the instant is the first step to Abstract Experience. It cannot be represented. Once you make the leap into the Abstract there are no longer any definitions."

And silence for certain matters. The core function of art will not be defined. It operates according to what appear to be other than consistent laws.

This cannot be said.
This cannot be said.
There are no words.
There may be notes
but they are in another realm.

"You just have to forget about yourself."

25I88

[From] Letter to Peter Baker

28 june 94

Dear Peter,

I'll try to say something about Bernadette then, though it's getting to be hard to remember precisely that far back, 20 years or so now. I do recall that from the very first work of hers that I saw I knew her to be a compatriot in this writing. No doubt at all, just FLASH, right! I had taken some poems of hers for the last issue of JOGLARS, 1966 I guess, and had actually met her briefly in Ted Berrigan's presence in NYC in 1966, though we didn't actually "meet" till she came to SF in 1969, right. Immediately then started long talks that lasted through a decade at least. Letters too, when we all had that writing and *letter*-writing energy. In fact, if you were to do any extended work on her you should read through her end of the correspondence with me which is now at SUNY Buffalo, I don't know what she's done with my end. We certainly encouraged each other a lot, I recall that. Always to go further, no matter what reaction, or lack of, by anyone, known or unknown. I remember us agreeing that we were probably "crazy" and had very little to do with "poetry" as it was then understood even among the NY School forefront. We'd say, Why not just call it "writing" then, trying to avoid the whole problem. We wanted endless works, that would zoom on & on and include everything ultimately, we'd talk about hoping for the "Everything Work," which would use every possible bit flashing through our minds. We'd try to give much longer readings than were acceptable at the time (early 70's). Probably 2 hours at most, which doesn't sound like much now or maybe it still does? I recall taking some flack for length: who wants to sit that long, etc. There was finally a reading series at the Paula Cooper Gallery downtown, I forget who arranged that, maybe Larry Fagin had something to do with it?, where there were no chairs but pillows scattered over the floor so people could lie there and even fall asleep and wake up and in and out like that, where

I read my Polaroid in its entirety for the first time and Bernadette was there writing her Studying Hunger Journals as I read, and then a few weeks later she read a couple hours from that manuscript. People thought she was being "rude" (!) to write while I was reading, but I thought it was totally great, I couldn't imagine a better response. I think those readings were in 1974, there are tapes of them somewhere. I suppose we both suffered from people's shortening attentions spans, a lack of desire for that total immersement in the writing process which we had both learned from people like Kerouac and Stein and thought was perfectly natural and exciting and ongoing in the art. I suppose that situation is even worse, if anything, now. I remember people being more intimidated by Bernadette's work than by mine and puzzling over that, in fact I still wonder, I figured at the time it had something to do with the fact that she was female in a male dominant poetry climate and she was feisty and wouldn't take shit from any of these guys, wanted the same opening for her work. [...] How did I first react to MEMORY? The original gallery installation, grid of photos on the wall with the spoken text constantly playing on tape, was amazing: you felt like no matter what photo you were momentarily focusing on the voice was commenting on exactly that image, until finally you were enveloped in a dream continuum of total contingency. I recall it's being reviewed by the photography critic of the Village Voice, very positively, but not talked about that much by the poets. I wonder how many actually saw it? Bernadette has always highly valued one of the best aspects of the NY School: collaboration. So we always wanted to do more of that. We once did 3 videotape works with Ed Bowes (Filmmaker she was then living with) which were shown at St Marks Church and people criticized us, saying "What!?! You're not going to actually READ?!?" I hope those tapes still exist, they shine still in my memory. Our cave collaboration is beautiful too, it ends up with a dialogue Bernadette wrote between me as Melville and her as Hawthorne (!), but nobody has ever wanted to publish it. It strikes me odd how collaboration is never taken as seriously as solo work. [...] Collab has always been a sort of poor sister I guess. One of the best

257

aspects of the Language group was how/when they met together a lot and gave talks and fought and criticized and did collaborations. Maybe that kind of ferment can only last a few years at best? Guston used to say, any scene is five years, tops. We were always more interested in the process of it all, the working with others and taking from other media (music & movies especially), and not so much in focusing on promoting our writing as "career." Maybe amateurs, in the best sense? The writing should always be going on no matter what ever else was happening in our lives. And that's been pretty much the case. Probably not too many people have seen as much of her work as I have, so they can't really know the extent of it, the forms she's made, the inclusiveness. Certainly, nobody has ever taken dream-writing as far as she has. And it's all always so lucid, no matter the chances taken, the speed of the transcription. I've been disappointed that New Directions has chosen to print a scatter of excerpts, make silly distinctions between "poetry" and "prose" in her work, when they should be printing her longer works entire finally. Thank goodness Desires of Mothers is finally coming out. Now if somebody will only take on the mammoth Studying Hunger Journals! Mind of Hour! and further! [...]

Well, I hope this is of some, rambling, help. I do tend to shy at critical works, believing as I do that poet should protect himself against interpretive reception. But I try not to be too doctrinaire about it and do like to see things. I recall Michael Palmer showing me a copy of your book in SF once briefly but I never got to read it. I would appreciate a copy if you've got one extra. So far there isn't any more During done but there will be, I've made plans for at least seven sections. If I can only finish (!) up all the things that have come between and get back to that impulse. I better not wait too long. I like the Baudelaire quote by the way. Let me know if you do anything on it. There have been no reviews that I know of. But some very strong reactions from poet friends. Which, of course, is fine with me.

[from *The Book of During*] XI Letters

Dear Long Battle Creature, attacks are possible, perhaps
insurmountable, but dangerous is as dangerous does. I will meet
you in the door.

Dear Bad, my lights are well known. And I climb. I am hired
then gone, bruised all over by a weather as radiant as your eyes
when you speak of a change. When I think of you supple I am
adored, nearly overreached. I go to bed with a lot of shameful
things, shameful with a rope or other instant access. Hot pills,
flushed stockings, the proportions of a cold cigarette. It is
understood.

Dear Mop Bone, I am too tired. I try to leaf through the
stockings but my room is too long. Your dreams as nothing to
think on, a white fluid.

Dear Integument, sharp as an illness crowded as my life. I love
your crudeness, the green value of no leaves.

Dear Over, drop your drawers if you want silence, your mouth
to the glass.

Dear Blood, it's in the wood. Do we measure each other there?
Your hands are in my rhymes, your play to end at the sea in
baseness. I have to nod off here and cover the sperm. Where
there are eyes in your legs, head at all costs.

Dear Acquaintance, there is variety, a book by Freud. Is your
bite a tunnel, do you misconstrue my whole face? The limp of
your crush, I'd eat the sex open to some hilt, some trouble with
the light at arch breasts. Your hem is a cover. And with that in
mind, a container, I kiss you all over. Will you come back safely,
and to this house that would speed but for the gel it contains?

Dear Carpenter, put the far away lights out of your image. I see
your body's photos and I clap. I wrote poems of such backlit
glances that in the blank room the head is ill.

Dear Cinema, your elastic souses me and I lie up in the grain of your genius. I hope to love to leave you and will phone you slim. Use my head as it helps.

Dear Death, I'm going to see the doctor next week. I'm coming to some dream rooms, lightly rounded and furnitureless.

Thanks for the pretty stick in a pile of hot American junk. I got your license and a bed with a very good mattress. I saw you from my window but you were equipped with windows.

Dear Form of Love, I'll have to go you one bit further out to not be so alone. I adore the fracture of your functions. I'll put them on the wire. Are these endurable days? Of slips in damage and every need a gramophone tune to understand. I'll take care that the eyes of this sex be forever new. Cover your hand with the larger part of my letter.

Dear Address, I wrote some poems too, frankly of this damned apartment of the domed painting of the bumper cars. Good weather as quickly as you like but where is the other hand? Can you bend at the join and always be severe? Is your hair as naked as wings in the snow?

Dear Figure, about what street corner is the telegram that brought me nothing? I have arrived at the wire of a bitter dream. Make sure your toe is bolted, a sweater for tomorrow. But this work, is it executed near your sex?

Dear White Place, she is gaining strength.

Dear Animal Delight, I was a child myself. A whole bottle of dolls ever more sweetly disturbing. But now there is a tear and my ghost is so full of you. You should take a red cloak and spend the night. The black ones are old and in utter disrepair, though still as disturbing. At your breasts I resign myself to the difficulties. If I could only speak to the population that is escaping. The runs toward shadow in the wood where I live.

Dear Heart's Face, our sights have scattered in mistaken distance. Your cherry as good as anybody else's. Spending your

days for the movies to cease, an alarm of blossoms. I see you at
the bed to good effect, but was mistaken.
Dear Pay, you are the title of my little green house.
Dear Cloud of Poison, put me out on your rocks. I have a
picture of your sex. A bird will laugh, nothing will fall. Are you
anxious for the money above all?
Dear Foretold, please be so kind as to follow the cloud of
kittens to Spain. I leave tomorrow, but the horizon has wings.
Dear Thoughts of Sex, abandon those colors. Everywhere I look
I see it empty.
Dear Fire's Been Lit, dear still in pajamas, dear let it get you
down. I have papered the walls of your room all filthy to the
good.
Dear Fuck To Be Stopped By.
Dear Helmet Without Its Head, bullet strikes the severe
overhead poppers, numbered exactly to the pile. I don't imagine
anything anymore and this is not for you. In pencil added to
your garment, a clutter of which then disturbs the letters. An
oiled nomenclature left behind, trying to write on muslin in a
ward-taken temperature wind. Leave it up to Gerard which
mountain stops beyond the film.
Dear Leave Which, the lair is off the avenue, all told subsided
from the snare.
Dear Such As This, move.
Dear Threatened With Loss of Garments, I am your creature.
But I've quit smoking and it's still very cold. Then yours will be
a poem, I'll love it and abolish you. Or vice versa and I'll take
both, till we've worn down either end of the wick in this wind.
Dear Endless Banister, a cube driven into the sail we depend on.
Dear Out, even more.

XLII Last

It goes there. How does it come to you?
Braided mirrors to their holes in effect. Sight gaps.
Where newsprint surrounds the fuck, the place of full webs.
Could play her brush like a flute, what is backward in the dark.
Haven't seen you there and then have. Disappears into her
drapes. Head lock, draw limb, gone away and back into. Held it
all down with the head back. Auroras in wait. Do you think I
painted for it? Nothing but blackness drawn in the act.
Trounce, then parade the parts. Popeye the painter, Barnacle
Bill in utero. And holes become jewels

Could you be doing it while? Lift those things that hold us
back. Where towels are wishes, lights crawl under the bodies.
And what she has there, so elaborate. Even left alone it grows.
Pick it between, the fingers don't grow. And then his gaze
lights. I elaborate she says pinching.

They make all these blocks come up in oneself, slots.
Down there where she is going she is already. It exists of her
taking. I had nine numbered things, now you have another.
Parties of bristling fanciers overflown in direction. Parts of it all
so flowing so distinctly he recorded them. It's a made up thing
that reaches you now. I would have to fuck it out for you to
greet in paint. Rollicking samplers that nothing but. Got all
caught up into her treated her, traced then like a jarred comet.

She could be presented with something, an article herself in the
act. Did I come on too? We shuttered these things in our own
smooth landing. Down from that a cap on the light, a nose on
the fan.

There he has made it avid. Hands upon it broken thing. Open one.

I think that later you want to see *them* do it. But there is no expression. And the entrance grows more elaborately crested, captioned. Make yourself them seeing it. Open them all.

Michael Palmer

Active Boundaries: Poetry at the Periphery

For my own sense of poetry, I would like to examine a series, a "discrete series," as George Oppen would say, of sites or *topoi,* places and pages, boundaries, junctures and margins. By "poetry," I mean that poetry often marked by resistance and necessary difficulty, by a certain rupture and refusal, and by the use of exploratory forms. Such poetry has come to be identified, very loosely, with an enduring counter-tradition that encompasses both critique and celebration. There are other poetries, of course, and other poetries of value; that is not the argument.

I think of that *"communauté désoeuvrée,"* "idled community" (hard to find an adequate translation) of Jean-Luc Nancy, and of the "imaginary" or "negative community" as defined by Maurice Blanchot, in fact not so much defined as imagined, in all its resistance to definition. *"Communauté impossible"* then, existing at the margins of thought, as the poem so often does, and as the poet all too often exists at the margins of material society. Such an imagined site would be, as much as anything, a place of contention, fractious, even dystopic. As "a community of those who have no community" (Georges Bataille), a community of differences, it is the space of encounter of the poetic imaginary with the social, the space where the poem may be said to disclose its desire for the world, for nothing less than the recovery of identity from loss, and language from the discursive mechanisms of power. It is finally, I think, as one projects it, a site of passages, full of noise and its silence, what Clark Coolidge refers to as "sound as thought."

The title of this talk, meant I suppose in part to disperse or decenter the idea of a subject as such, is "Active Boundaries: Poetry at the Periphery."[1] It derives essentially from a conversation with Charles Bernstein some months ago, where it turned out that the Heideggerean notion of *peras*, of the active boundary, was on both of our minds in relation to a sense of form, but also to a more social sense of poetic activity as it exists in the margins, along the borders and, so to speak, "underground." It is a term I put to use often in the years when I first worked with dance, and for me at least, it then connected with notions of composition by field so important to the Black Mountain poets, and in particular, Robert Duncan. It suggested to me (how distant this must certainly be from Heidegger's intent is another question) an anti-hierarchical structure of language and perhaps hinted at a politics of poetic form as well. Its origin in this respect, in Heidegger, is not finally determining and may well be deceptive, given his sense both of relentless hierarchies and of poetry as truth or *aletheia*, poetry as disclosure of unconcealment, disclosure of the world. That is, I would strongly disavow his idealization of the poetic function, though I'm not always completely sure, as this talk may disclose, whether my poetic unconscious feels quite the same way. Certainly the issues raised or implicitly alluded to by such a title go back to topics addressed by both the German and the English Romantics, though many have been passed on almost osmotically (and here particularly skepticism is called for). They are concepts which underlie much of the content as well as the rather nomadic form of this talk, as much as they inform, positively or negatively, much of the work of our century's modernists and vanguard-ists. I think, for example, of the problematizing of the subject and the privileging of the fragment among the Athenaeum poets and critics, as discussed by Philippe Lacoue-Labarthes and Jean-Luc Nancy in *The Literary Absolute*. Equally we may think of the changed relations between poet and society, which the Romantics immediately recognized, in the formative stages of modern middle-class culture. The title suggests an "elsew(here)" which includes the word "here," as well as a "nowhere" which can be read "now here." Such is the power of juncture, or silence. Here and elsewhere, here as elsewhere, elsewhere too as here: a space or region of paradox, contradiction and polysemy, a space, one is tempted to say, of poetry, where the words we hear are both the same and different, recognizable and foreign, constructed in fact like language itself on the play of identity and difference.

266

I would like arbitarily to begin, or continue beginning, or continue deferring a beginning, with a sequence of images, images in a sense of the invisible and in another sense of the unrepresentable. First, an overall view of the Serra Pelada gold mine, Brazil 1986: an almost unimaginably vast and deep open pit, with tens of thousands of mud-covered workers clambering with sacks of dirt along its floor and up the network of almost vertical ladders along its walls. At the time, the mine was said to employ 50,000 workers. Next, in a close-up, a number of men from the mines surround a member of the military police. One holds him by the hair, two others clasp his arms, another displays the pistol which has been taken from him. His face is swollen from a severe beating, and blood runs from his nose and mouth. Then an image of an American slaughterhouse: pigs have been crowded into a room. From nozzles in the ceiling a shower of water descends, in preparation for their electrocution. In the refugee camp of Wad Sherifay in the Sudan, starving children lie on rows of cots or palette beds. The desert light burns through the doorway and through openings in the walls. Mali, 1985: a cemetery for refugees on the outskirts of Gao. Since there is no wood for grave markers, scrap iron is used. One grave is marked by a half-buried steering wheel, another by what appears to be a rusted brake drum, others by pipes and unidentifiable metal fragments. In the interior of Brazil's Northeast, a child is prepared for Christian burial with eyes open, so that she will be better able to find her way through the underworld.

Such images of elsewhere in the work, the life project, of the Brazilian photo-journalist Sebastião Salgado, evoke a complex series of often contradictory responses. The scene in the Serra Pelada gold mine verges on the incomprehensible, both in its visual scale and its human implications. At the same time it is, one gradually realizes, entirely familiar, a vision of hell prefigured in Dante and the painters of the Trecento, as well as the earliest of the Russian icon painters:

from Inferno XVIII:

"Luogo è in inferno detto Malebolge..."

There is a site in hell called Malebolge
made of stone the color of iron
like the wall encircling it.

At the exact middle of that evil field
opens a pit both wide and deep
whose plan I will speak of in its place.

(my translation)

What we had thought of as oneiric, product of the visionary imagination, was in fact an image of the world, an entirely possible world. World as it is, somewhere. Other echoes are obvious: the beaten military police-man, with his swollen and distorted face, brings to mind Lee Miller's photographs of Auschwitz guards, similarly beaten. The children in the refugee camp, near death from illness and starvation, are twin to earlier images from earlier camps. Nowhere/now here. Yet here, now, means the walls of a museum of contemporary art in San Francisco. Here, now, there occurs an almost inevitable aestheticization of Salgado's (as of Dante's) "moments." One notices the surreal beauty of the desert cemetery, the exact rhyme (deliberate or not) with Tchelichev's *Cache-Cache*, or Hide and Seek, in the picture of children in Thailand playing in a tree. One takes a certain uneasy pleasure...

There is a tension between context of viewing and source, between here and there, which Salgado exploits to focus attention and to ironize the act of viewing itself. The subject of Salgado's photojournalism, we must continually remind ourselves, is *not thère*, is in fact not the visible but the invisible: what has been repressed and will not be spoken. It appears always at the edge of the frame or in the uneasy negotiation among the space of origin, the framed space of the work, and the social space to which it has been removed, which is also a cultural space, of the aesthetic.

268

Here the paradox of Paul Celan's struggle "against representation" comes to mind. It is that in the search for an active mimesis, *Darstellung* or presentation, the work may be drawn further and further from conventions of affect and accepted norms of narrative, those very devices which function as a kind of agreement or tacit contract (or complicity?) with the mainstream of culture. Let me quote a few passages from Celan's complexly layered and ironic talk upon receiving the Büchner prize. Its title is "The Meridian," and the translation is by Rosmarie Waldrop:

> Ladies and gentlemen, it is very common today to complain of the 'obscurity' of poetry. Allow me to quote...a phrase of Pascal's...: "Ne nous reprochez pas le manque de clarté puisque nous en faisons profession." This obscurity, if it is not congenital, has been conveyed on poetry by strangeness and distance (perhaps of its own making) and for the sake of an encounter.

For the sake of an encounter. The poem speaks "on behalf of the other, who knows, perhaps of an altogether other." A little further on in the same talk:

> It is true, the poem, the poem today, shows—and this has only indirectly to do with difficulties of vocabulary, the faster flow of syntax or a more awakened sense of ellipsis, none of which we should underrate—the poem clearly shows a tendency towards silence. The poem holds its ground, if you will permit me another extreme formulation, the poem holds its ground on its own margin. In order to endure, it constantly calls and pulls itself back from an 'already-no-more' into a 'still-here."[...]
> In other words: language actualized, set free under the sign of a radical individuation which, however, remains as aware of limits drawn by language as of the possibilities it opens.

In vastly different circumstances and with different means, Salgado and Celan are both drawn to ask, what are the exigencies of witness, where must you go, where is the margin, where the (invisible) meridian? To Celan, the margins may mean margins of language, a necessary distancing from the center for one who in life is already, forever, *distanced*. (Yet such distancing, or estrangement, seems to me radically different from the strategic subversions of a self-conscious and self-designating avant-garde, whose other is often none other than the center itself, to which it incessantly calls like a wayward child. As Lyn Hejinian put it very eloquently to me recently, "It is not only a matter of where you are standing, but also of the direction you are facing.") We can measure degrees of distance by placing a poem by Celan from *Mohn und Gedächtnis, Poppy and Memory* (1952, the early collection which contains his "Todesfugue") beside another poem, and a similar form of address, published in the 1976 posthumous collection, *Zeitgehöft, Farmstead of Time*. From 1952:

> Aspen tree your leaves glance white into dark.
> My mother's hair was never white.
>
> Dandelion, so green is the Ukraine.
> My yellow-haired mother did not come home.
>
> Rain cloud, above the well do you hover?
> My quiet mother weeps for everyone.
>
> Round star, you wind the golden loop.
> My mother's heart was ripped by lead.
>
> Oaken door, who lifted you off your hinges?
> My gentle mother cannot return.

From *Zeitgehöft:*

> Walking plant, you catch
> yourself one of the speeches,
>
> the abjured aster
> here joins in,
>
> if one who
> smashed the canticles
> were now to speak to the staff
> his and everyone's

blinding
would be revoked.
(Translations by Michael Hamburger)

In the former, however elliptical, orientation is still possible without too much difficulty. It is work fully realized in an elegiac mode quite characteristic of the poetic literature of the Holocaust, for example that of his friend Nelly Sachs. The latter poem more completely acknowledges, or perhaps inscribes, unrepresentability. It presents the unutterable and leaves the text, in any conventional sense, incomplete or broken. "Tell all the Truth but tell it slant— / Success in Circuit lies," writes Dickinson (#1129), a poet whom Celan translated extensively. But what of the untellable, what is the nature of such witness whose center is, necessarily, silence?

It is sometimes forgotten (I'm thinking here of various polemics, notably in Germany and Italy through the 'seventies and 'eighties) that there is a profoundly historical and social dimension to such hermetic[2] speech, that it is its own form of intervention, and that its resistance to meaning, to paraphrase Stevens, is shared by many types of poetry including some of the most avowedly public and/or "transparent." Before the contradictions and paradoxes of the real, including the quotidian, those very paradoxes and contradictions may become agents of articulation and the reassertion of meaning. I am thinking of a poetry that "asks to be questioned," a poetry whose means remain in question. I am afraid that this is all too obvious, yet much remains invested in its denial. One is drawn toward ease of assertion and consumption, toward a formal nostalgia and the comfort of the given, the given self and its terms of reception and address, the beloved other always the same, a certain neo-romantic aura, a moving and mysteriously articulate aporia; in short, the standard-issue sublime, the Wordsworth of late age still among us, slouching from workshop to workshop, waiting to be reborn. A poem called "Ne'er so well expressed" or "I looked at myself and there I was."

I have mentioned that the title for this talk arrived during a conversation with Charles Bernstein a few months back, but its actual origin dates to a visit two years earlier, with the photographer Ben Watkins, to the Eliot Square cemetery in the Roxbury section of Boston. (Ben was then in the process of documenting its restoration, along with that of several other local historical sites.) The graveyard was in an extreme state of neglect, with broken gravestones scattered about and others which had been removed from the ground and were awaiting repair. Ben indicated a particular eighteenth-century marker lying among the weeds. On the decorated part of the stone, that which would have been above ground, were the spare "hic iacets" for a husband and wife ("Here lyes ye body of..."), followed by dates of death and ages at death.

The cemetery had served an affluent, initially exurban community from some time in the late seventeenth until the early nineteenth century. (The eponymous Eliots were in fact forebears of the poet's family.) Now the graveyard, surrounded by a cast-iron fence, was itself enclosed by a struggling and impoverished African-American and Latino ghetto.

On that part of the stone which would have been beneath ground, had the marker been in place, Ben pointed to two meticulous lines of letters, amid a scatter of other letters. The two lines, he said, were practice alphabets, the product of an apprentice stonecutter learning how to work the granite. They had been buried when the stone was put in place and only rediscovered during the current repairs.

Practice alphabet, alphabet of praxis, alphabet underground, the letters invisible beneath the conventional memorializing sentiments. Layerings and contradictions, both diachronic and synchronic, of the site itself. The stark social reality of the present, things coming to light or not.

The "above" and "below" of Williams' *Kora in Hell*, echoed in "Homage to Creeley," the opening section of Jack Spicer's *Heads of the Town up to the Aether*. Which the signifier, which the signified? What of the line between? Is it as bar?

Where does one practice the art, and how does such an art respond, in its relative invisibility, to things? And to "things as they are"? Is there a counter-logic in the poem, a possible other voice, which can talk back, cast some light? Or, as certain contemporary theorists have proposed, gathering their accusations under the reductive and deficient rubric of "post-modernism," are the strategies and subversions of contemporary practice merely symptoms of the contradictions themselves, a kind of schizo-mimicry of a desiring machine which has lost its wheels?

I think of Zukofsky's long poem "A," finally published in its entirety only after his death. From "A-12," a passage about his father after his arrival from Russia, where syntax, the "orderly arrangement," is drawn into music, so that both survival and mourning can be sung:

> The miracle of his first job
> On the lower East Side:
> Six years night watchman
> In a men's shop
> Where by day he pressed pants
> Each crease a blade
> The irons weighed
> At least twenty pounds
> But moved both of them
> Six days a week
> From six in the morning
> To nine, sometimes eleven at night,
> Or midnight:
> Except Fridays
> When he left, enough time before sunset
> Margolis begrudged.
> His own business
> My father told Margolis
> Is to keep Sabbath.
>
> "Sleep," he prayed
> For his dead.
> Sabbath.

The path is that crossed and recrossed in "*A*": from the domain of labor and the social, to the world of spirit and family. The one is overseen by a very personal and idiosyncratic Marx (to whom reference will eventually disappear), the other by Zukofsky's omnipresent Spinoza. The syntax is flexible, at times perplexing, and the prosody post-Poundian, a highly disciplined free verse (though of course elsewhere Zukofsky will also work with fixed measures, both simple and complex). It is worth considering the economy of such presentation and the effect of its music in the evocation of the marginalized subject. The narrative itself exists in tension with the ellipticality and lyric condensation of the work. A further tension is that between his often stated objective of "rested totality" and the restless multi-directionality and complex layering of language, the "invisible" Zukofsky rendering the invisible subject, "lower limit speech/upper limit music." Here I would guess that it is the music of the Psalms he hopes to suggest. In the following part of the passage, there is also the barest, delicately ironic hint of the poet/son's lifelong experience of a minimal audience for his work:

> A shop bench his bed,
> He rose rested at four.
> Half the free night
> Befriended the mice:
> Singing Psalms
> As they listened.
> A day's meal
> A slice of bread
> And an apple,
> The evenings
> What matter?
> His boots shone.
> Gone and out of fashion
> His beard you stroked, Paul,
> With the Sabbath Prince Albert.
> I never saw more beautiful fingers
> Used to lift bootstraps.

And everywhere, the consciousness of alphabet, from the A to which the instruments are tuned, to the terminal Z, the letters B-A-C-H woven by Bach into his fugue and transformed by the poet into a laud for his wife, "*B*lest *A*rdent *C*elia..." Regarding "Eliot Square," with its high metal fence, I am reminded that it is the first poem of Zukofsky's *All*, his collected shorter poems, which sends up "The Waste Land" and its cultural vision in a cloud of bricolage, a hilarious pastiche of quotes, canon and kitsch, high and low hopelessly intertwined.

The multiple dialects of *"A"* and the pastiching of sources and citations in "Poem beginning 'The'" bring to mind the echoing and multiphonics found in sections of *X/Self*, the final volume of a trilogy by the great Caribbean poet and cultural scholar, Kamau Brathwaite. As Brathwaite sounds out his origins (European, Amerindian, African and Maroon, we are told), we experience the sound of "young Caliban howling for his tongue":

> The new man is nubile
> and has made his choice
> as priest or politician
>
> police or poet
> choirboy or cocks
> man
>
> da vinci was the last of the genies
> and he knew
>
> it
>
> though we didn't seem to believe in it
> then
>
> now the word belongs to machiavel and philip
> the second of spain
>
> and to that calculating calvin

> is them that working all night long in high
> light executive suites
>
> on all the national security commissions
> and all the full plenary sessions
>
> is them who is right what is rote in the paper
> is them the master gunners in the sweating three
>   piece suits
>
> who circumcizing caliban

Caliban cannibalized is, of course, one of the central symbols of Caribbean anti-colonial thought, representing, among other things, the dilemma of reclaiming language through the language of the colonizer, and the multiple ironies attendant to such an undertaking. It is a highly specific, other domain of "poetry at the periphery," with evident differences yet intriguing and surprising parallels to the work we have been examining from various "sites." Brathwaite's prosody is personal and exploratory, echoing at one moment European, at another African and Caribbean origins. It is generally non-metrical and cadential, and has lately drawn increasingly on indigenous, popular music forms as well as surprising graphical effects. The space of the page is taken as a site in itself, a syntactical and visual space to be expressively exploited, as was the case with the Black Mountain poets, as well as writers such as Frank O'Hara, perhaps partly in reponse to gestural abstract painting. Such work may appear arbitrary and illegible to those committed to an imagined orthodoxy. Yet one could make the case that it is the imagined Anglo-American formalist continuum, with its Arnoldean ideological underpinnings, which is largely arbitrary, given the migrations and passages of living culture. Words such as "craft" and "tradition" thus become code words for authority and orthodoxy. As the Ukrainian poet Alexei Parshchikov has stated (*Poetics Journal*, #8):

> "New poetry" has never found a place for itself against a conservative, or, as conservatism's overseers themselves continue to call it, a

"traditional" background. "New poetry" has always compared itself with previous "new poetry," and so forth.

"Make it new," of course, is a very tattered banner of the modernists, rent in part by the tragic lack of self-reflection of the figure who coined the phrase. That Pound's mind sank beneath the weight of his own intuitionism and bigotry represents a betrayal of the very means of representation he set out to renew: It is particularly tragic and ironic in light of his intention to expand the horizons of American culture, to recognize difference as a source of that renewal. "Writing reflects," states Trinh T. Minh-ha in *Woman Native Other*, "It reflects on other writings and, whenever awareness emerges, on itself as writing." It is precisely this awareness Pound came to lack, and it is this growing lack which in his mania eventually became an abyss. It is as if the periphery from which he operated, at times with great generosity and creativity, transformed itself into a lunatic fringe.[3]

In his long poem-in-progress, serendipitously (for my purposes) titled *The Alphabet*, Ron Silliman attempts to address that lack and to create a means of representation flexible enough to encompass the city in all its eruptive complexity. Silliman recognizes what our site suggests, that the city consists of intersections, crossings, foci of rapid acceleration and deceleration, all potential flashpoints of overdetermined social relations. To represent urban social space in all its complexity and contradictions, he has developed what is in effect a new form of realism (I'm tempted to say comic realism), at once caustic and ironic, and above all responsive to the city's web of differences.

He is very far from the idle dandy, yet in one respect, notebook ever in hand, he does inherit the mantle of the *flâneur*, the observer hovering at the margins of events, measuring the velocities. (I would place Reznikoff and O'Hara in this lineage as well.) Here is a passage from a section of *The Alphabet* published by The Figures Press and entitled *What*. There is a rhythm of interference between eye and ear, inner and outer, literary and popular culture:

277

Can you explain why Ezra Pound
and Ty Cobb were never,
not once, photographed
in the same room together?
The way cryotechnology
accounts for the Rolling Stones.
Heads of cauliflower
wrapped in plastic. Half moon rising
in the red dusk sky, streetlamps on
illuminating nothing. Twisting
the orange on
the glass juice squeezer.
Before dawn, alone
in the super market parkinglot,
hosing it down. Van's awning
signals catering truck. A leaf
had fallen onto damp cement,
its image sharp years after.
Old green Norton anthology
perfect for doorstop. Albino mulatto's
curiously blonde hair. Linebreak muted
says I'm a normal guy.

We begin with a joke that turns out to be serious. Two quite virulent racists, poet and ballplayer: can we prove they were not the same person? We pass then through a series of apparently random but actually linked images, the cryogenetically perserved rock band (Silliman's generation), beside the heads of cauliflower in plastic. Half moon rising and the half orange on a juice squeezer. The image of a leaf, preserved in concrete, and the superannuated Norton canon preserved or recycled as a doorstop, an ironically appropriate use for this highly problematic representation of the literary landscape. Debris—that which is generally left unremarked--accumulates to form a kind of map. The albino mulatto, figure of almost impossible difference (or is it likeness?), followed then by the ironic, distanciating comment which concludes this particular selection of lines, whereby Silliman tacitly acknowledges that his activity of recording is anything but "normal" behavior, and that the apparently relaxed and "natural" line break is nothing other than planned artifice, illusion. The flat, deaestheticized surface heightens the sense of collision, of the kind of raw juxtaposition which comprises a significant part of urban street experience. As the poem argues, such micro-events contain meaning. They are part of the field and can be read or mapped without resort to conventions of an absorptive, hypotactic narrative. Such a form of representation is prefigured in Rilke's *Malte,* if from a different social and psychic perspective:

> I have been out. I saw: hospitals. I saw a man who swayed and sank to the ground...I saw a pregnant woman. She was pushing herself cumbrously along a high, warm wall, groping for it now and again as if to convince herself it was still there. Yes, it was still there. And behind it?. I looked on a map: *Maison d'Accouchement.*

It is prefigured as well in the urban novels of the Surrealists, where "objective chance" offers the opportunity for that type of interpretation central to the Surrealist project. The sacrifice of narrative in Silliman frees writing to the flood of micro-events and elemental details which constitute the invisible, that is the often suppressed or unremarked details of life at the periphery. (It must be noted that one risk of such compulsive layering is tedium—ironically, a kind of sameness.) The work foregrounds an often farcical word-play that further emphasizes its heterogeneity and decentered focus. Micro-narratives appear and disappear like the homophones which surround them and destabilize the text. The "velocity" is that of eye and mind scanning what Victor Shklovsky termed the *byt,* the *stuff* of daily life. It is Silliman's determination to use all the letters, even the invisible ones.

Perhaps no one addresses with more creative relevance or urgency the paradoxical issues raised by "Eliot Square" than Susan Howe. A poet avowedly working at the margins, she addresses questions of disappearance and recovery, identity and absence, by means of a radical reevaluation of the space of the page and the nature of the text in relation to time. At moments her page becomes a virtual palimpsest, interrogating the notion of legibility itself. Though her acknowledged model is Olson, her perspective is explicitly female, as well as feminist, though for the latter term to make sense it must be disengaged, as she has vehemently stated, from certain institutionalized feminist critical practices that have made a place for women's work within the Anglo-American academic tradition without thoroughly critiquing many of the doxological assumptions of that tradition.

As is the case with the work of another acknowledged model, Emily Dickinson, Howe can be viewed as exploiting, with a kind of dialectical force, the paradoxes at the heart of her project. Though assuredly an outsider to contemporary mainstream New England culture, she is at the same time a pure product of that culture, an admirer of the work of the "Puritan fathers" and a self-proclaimed Calvinist by temperament. Though her work, like that of many contemporaries, interrogates the constitution of the self, it is suffused with a passionate subjectivity. As with Dickinson, her "practice of outside" (the words are Robin Blaser's, referring to Jack Spicer), takes place from within, and employs the means of critique and expression provided by that culture. She seeks out lost narratives, the words of the disapppeared, while constructing a narrative of loss. Often the result is something like the twin alphabets of the underground stone, one above the other, each carved with great clarity and care, each invisible. Peter Quatermain has written ("The Difficulties," vol.3 #2, 1989, p.75):

> Howe's work, from the very title of her first book (*Hinge Picture*) on, treads borders, boundaries, dividing lines, edges, invisible meeting points. Her language returns to such cusps again and again, for they mark extremities, turning points, limits, shifts, the nameless edge of mystery where transformations occur and where edge becomes centre. Hope Atherton, in *Articulations of Sound Forms in Time*, moves from the centre to the margin, to the wilderness, and (like Mary Rowlandson) thus marginalizes the centre.

To mine the "Pythagorean silence" is to explore the gaps in the record, the silenced witnessings, but it is also to explore the silences of the text, the space between the words into which (as with Celan) meaning erupts, the pause boundaries between larger units of utterance (the interruptions of sound by silence), perhaps even the phonemic markers of difference. Through these creases, Howe attempts to give voice to the "ghosts" of our wilderness, those who have been silenced. In an interview, Howe has stated (*Ibid.*, p.17):

> Often I think I am an interloper and an imposter.
>
> Something Nietzsche wrote I copied out because it both helps and haunts me. "People still hold the view that what is handed down to us by tradition is what in reality lies behind us—while it in fact comes toward us because we are its captives and are destined to it."
>
> Because I am a woman I am fated to read his beautiful observation as double-talk of extraordinary wisdom and rejection. *Us* and *we* are disruptions. These two small words refuse to be absorbed into proper rank in the linear sequence of his sentence. Every sentence has its end. Every day is broken by evening. A harrowing reflection is cast on meaning by gaps in grammar, aporias of historic language.

In a revealing moment, Howe both accepts and rejects Nietzsche's words. She accepts his analysis, then reveals that, if in Nietzsche's *we* remains the trace of an exclusionary tradition, then she is doubly excluded both from that tradition and from that *us*. Her poetry will then employ such disruptions, such gaps and aporias, in its interrogation of signs, texts, shifters:

> light flickers in the rigging
>
> flags   charts   maps
>
> to be read by guesswork through obliteration
>
> (from "The Liberties" in *The Europe of Trusts*, p.163)

Citation, erasure and over-writing, joined to an emotionally charged lyricism, all function simultaneously to court and question history, and to understand inheritance:

THE KEY

e n i g m a s t i f e m i a t e d c r y p t o a t h

a b c d e f g h i j k l m n o p q r s t u v w x y

z or zed

                              graphy

          reland

(*Ibid.*, p.209)

Susan Howe is of Irish descent. Ireland with the "I" removed becomes a question "re(garding) land, as geography with "geo," earth, removed (or else "bio," life, or some other prefix) becomes "writing." A famous code-machine is named "enigma." What "we" can be recovered from Nietzsche's pronoun? In the "Speeches at the Barriers" section of *Defenestration of Prague*, she writes:

For we are language Lost

in language

(*Ibid.*, p.99)

Speaking in the margins, at the barriers or boundaries, perhaps the poets I am considering might be thought of as border workers, constantly passing through checkpoints. There are, after all, guards, customs officials, official guardians of custom. Checking the papers. What deterritorialized space or page might poets be said to inhabit, what curious inside-outside, nowhere/now here? What language is (un)spoken here?

Let me attempt to address, not answer but address, such questions briefly at the final site of this talk, Leningrad, from which I recently returned[4] with four other American poets (Lyn Hejinian, Clark Coolidge, Jean Day and Kit Robinson). We were there for the last stop

282

on a tour with five Russian poets, Ivan Zhdanov, Nadezhda Kondakova, Ilya Kutik, Alexei Parshchikov and Arkadii Dragomoshchenko. The ostensible purpose of the tour was to give readings in preparation for publication of a bilingual anthology of the ten poets' work. The deeper purpose was to erode the Cold War barriers blocking the flow of cultural exchange and communication.

Leningrad, like Soviet society at large, seems virtually constituted of paradox and contradiction, external and internal, visible and invisible. There is the city of endless classical and baroque symmetries, painted in bright pastels, malachite blue and gold - a czarist fantasy. Ornate bridges, canals, onion-domed cathedrals and palaces can be seen everywhere throughout the old city. Visible everywhere as well are the grey, sullen crowds attempting to negotiate the labyrinthine difficulties of everyday life, people in endless queues for food, tobacco and clothes, scenes now well-known in the West. Rumors of right-wing coups, civil war, famine, are common. The "market," like the ruble, is a kind of free-floating signifier, a sound without a concept or a referent. Conversation is open, anticipatory, anxious and speculative.

"Poet" too is suddenly an open, free-floating term. The poet was previously defined by his or her silence and suppression, and by the refusal of that silence. Available nowhere, the work was read or recited everywhere. Stalin mandated the necessity of poetry. The poet did not exist:

> That was when the ones who smiled
> Were the dead, glad to be at rest.

(Anna Akhmatova, tr. J. Hemschemeyer)

Suppression of the subject articulated the subject and its complex encoding, truth told slant.

Strange then to be talking openly and reading in the Red Hall of the Writers' Union, the Neva's embankments beyond the windows, the KGB building with its security cameras a block away. For the American poets, the problem of the static subject of post-war culture, the pervasive "voice" not all that deep within us, and the fragility of community. For the Russians, an almost opposite problem, that of constituting a self (that self beside that X of Brathwaite) in a culture which has relentlessly devalued the individual since long before Soviet collectivism:

> Flashing teeth and flying heels in the bar. The
>   dance
> Fans out like a seine net in turtle's claws. In
>   vain
> I search for you - not even an I;
> maybe the earth reabsorbs us.

> (from "Flight II," Alexei Parshchikov, my translation)

Yet these supposed opposites are actually part of a common problem, that of articulating a language of resistance to the merely given or apparent, to hegemonic assumptions concerning self and other, voice and text, expression and form, etc. The particular "permissions" (in Robert Duncan's sense) of poetic speech offer the opportunity for an exploratory engagement with questions of voice, identity and place. What Parshchikov amusingly calls "average poetry" (which he distinguishes both from "traditional" and "new" poetry) declines such an offer, settling instead for a rehearsal of the known, the practice of the craft, the profession. Such work represents, in the words of Arkadii Dragomoschenko, "a yearning for nondifferentiation, for indifference, irresponsibility." (*Poetics Journal* 8, p.7)

　　"In poetry," writes Mandelstam, "only the executory understanding has any importance, and not the passive, the reproducing, the paraphrasing understanding" ("Conversation about Dante"). "Poetic speech," he continues, "is a most durable carpet, woven out of water." Such a figure is in itself an example of language operating in the margins. It articulates by its impossibility that space, that nowhere which allows poetry to function, to encompass the paradoxes both of sight and the site. Yet at the same time, it offers poetry no place "to be."[5] A further paradox is that, the more it achieves its goal of critique and renewal, of resistance to the rote, the more vulnerable poetry seems to become to cultural arbiters, whether official (as in the Soviet case) or designated by a somewhat unstable, even haphazard combination of established institution and market.

Since I began with photographs, let me conclude with a snapshot. In Helsinki, on the way to Leningrad, the ten poets were to read at the university's Student Hall. During a break in the reading, I stepped outside to get some air. A long, double line of large, identical black limousines was passing slowly down the avenue through the twilight and making the turn toward the airport. The entourages of Gorbachev and Bush were leaving the city after their one-day summit meeting. I had never seen a more precise physical representation of the language of power, that other syntax and alphabet, of linearity, the monotonal, the same.

Notes

1 Differing versions of this talk were first given at the State University of New York at Buffalo and at the University of Chicago in November of 1990. I have revised a few minor points for publication here.

2 A designation Celan himself understandably disavowed.

3 A significant aspect both of Pound's racism and his fascism is their unconcealedness. They are stridently declaimed. In contrast, Eliot's bigotry is, with few exceptions (such as the notorious University of Virginia address), more subtly announced and nuanced, in the style of the boardroom or gentlemen's club. As Eliot's fascist sympathies and anti-semitism come to seem increasingly ill-advised in the late thirties, he covers them over (without recantation), whereas Pound, ever the fanatic, continues to rave even after his release from St. Elizabeth's.

4 The trip took place in September of 1990, before the break-up of the Soviet Union and the restoration of the city's name, Saint Petersburg.

5 It is difficult to account for the relative avoidance, and ignorance, of new poetry by most current Western cultural and literary theorists. It may be that its very "fluidity" occasions mistrust, or that the nostalgia for grand narratives produces a stale, familiar *ressentiment*. In certain instances, a Lukácsian distaste for exploratory forms is evident; there is a reluctance to grant them a social and dialogic dimension. Many Continental philosophers (e.g., Deleuze/Guattari, Lyotard, Derrida) appropriate the means of poetry to their own pursuits "at the margins of philosophy." Among academic Marxists such as Eagleton (though many others could well be cited), form seems to be at best patent. Eagleton tends to treat exploratory work symptomatologically, as the surface evidence of some terminal social illness. He shares the nostalgia of much of the culture at large for an unproblematized, unmediated content. The irony here is that his critique of late capitalist, middle-class culture thereby ends up reflecting the prevailing assumptions and desires of that very culture. There is a further irony to this indifference, which is that the very writing they disregard is often actively exploring, by other means, the implications of the same epistemological and social issues treated dialectically in their own work.

Autobiography

All clocks are clouds.

Parts are greater than the whole.

A philosopher is starving in a rooming house, while it rains outside.

He regards the self as just another sign.

Winter roses are invisible.

Late ice sometimes sings.

A and *Not-A* are the same.

My dog does not know me.

Violins, like dreams, are suspect.

I come from Kolophon, or perhaps some small island.

The strait has frozen, and people are walking—a few skating—across it.

On the crescent beach, a drowned deer.

A woman with one hand, her thighs around your neck.

The world is all that is displaced.

Apples in a stall at the streetcorner by the Bahnhof, pale yellow to blackish red.

Memory does not speak.

Shortness of breath, accompanied by tinnitus.

The poet's stutter and the philosopher's.

The self is assigned to others.

A room from which, at all times, the moon remains visible.

Leningrad cafe: a man missing the left side of his face.

Disappearance of the sun from the sky above Odessa.

True description of that sun.

A philosopher lies in a doorway, discussing the theory of colors

with himself

the theory of self with himself, the concept of number, eternal return, the sidereal pulse

logic of types, Buridan sentences, the *lekton*.

Why now that smoke off the lake?

Word and thing are the same.

Many times white ravens have I seen.

That all planes are infinite, by extension.

She asks, Is there a map of these gates?

She asks, Is this the one called Passages, or is it that one to the west?

Thus released, the dark angels converse with the angels of light.

They are not angels.

Something else.

for Poul Borum

Far Away Near

"We link too many things together"
Agnès Rouzier

As it's said in The Fragments
I met the blind typist

inventor of words
The iris of the eye

is an inverted flower
and the essay on snow

offers no beginning
only an aspect of light

beneath a gate
only a photograph of earth

only a fold
a grammar reciting its laws

Just as the clatter
seems distant

and dies without further thought
that moment we ask

Have we reached the center yet, or
Should there be more blue do you think

or just a different shade of blue
all the while tacitly acknowledging

that by blue
she might have meant red

and by red...
As it's said

we must train our guns toward the future
where the essay on light will obviate time

and the essay on smoke
will cause the ground to open

One day I completed the final word
of a letter to my father

in what key I forget
After the ink had dried

I noticed the rain lit by a streetlamp
shaped like a conical hat

I noticed the map
of the moon you had left

half in shadow on my desk
In a city near the North Sea

white nights passed as I read
of an aviator downed

in the Barr Adjam
during the war directly after

the war to end all wars
sightless and burned across

three-fourths of his body
Listening in twin silences

his name had disappeared
from his lips

As it's said in The Fragments
There once was a language with two words

and the picture of an apple tree
As it's said

The ravens present a paradox
We learn a new gesture

utter unintelligible sounds
in a cheerful voice perhaps

pointing to the sky
where the rain continues

Joan Retallack

The Poethical Wager

Oui, mais il faut parier. Cela n'est pas volontaire, vous êtes embarqué.
Yes, but you must wager. This is not voluntary, you are embarked.
— Blaise Pascal, *Pensées*

Inserting an H in Poetics::A Slef Interview

[This interview between old friends (only sometimes at odds), Joan Retallack and Quinta Slef, took place in a short-circuited corner of cyber-space on a rainy Domingo/ Domenica/ Sunday/Sonntag/ Dimanche, etc.]

Quinta Slef: Well, how shall we begin? You've been talking and writing for the last few years about "poethics." Why? Why complicate further an already complex term by adding an accursed Aitch? (*laughter*)
Joan Retallack: Quinta, my dear friend, it's because I think a poetics can only take you so far without an "h." When complex life on earth begins for you, then you need a poethics which foregrounds all of the arts *as*, rather than *about*, forms of engaged living in *medias* mess.
QS: Ah, yes, as in Beckett's "the form must let the mess in."
JR: Yes, yes, or Cage's—to paraphrase a bit—let the mess shine in! (*laughter*) The outline of a poetics with the "h" missing delimits a style—the manner in which your experience has understood, assimilated, imprinted you. How it has transformed you in its stylistic transylvanian laboratory into something very much, actually, like an electrical transformer, focusing, even magnifying, the currents that have fed your intellectual energy, passing them on "stepped up," reenergized, but not swerving them into unforeseen collisions that produce new possibilities, that might even blow out a few old fuses. At this point, pre-swerve, but feeling a distinct surge of power, you exclaim, Ah, I have found my style! Actually your poetics has you in *its* grip.

QS: This reminds me of Sartre saying, if you don't intervene, the language will go on speaking itself. I think Sartre said that.

JR: Something like that. But, yes, you cannot breathe fully. You are in its grip. The grip of what you know you should do. Your style is identified and you are doomed to execute it, and then to reenact the fatalism of that execution over and over again. No one will dispute that you are a poet. (*pause*) Your poethical work begins when you no longer wish to shape materials (words, visual elements, sounds) into legitimate progeny of your own poetics. When you are released from filling-in the delimiting forms. This swerve, of course, comes about only as the result of a wrenching crisis. I don't mean to be dramatic, but you might not survive it. At least, not as a poet. You may at this point pick up some other line of work. If you do persist though, the patterns in your work may become flexible, permeable, conversational, exploratory. This is a radical shift. It will change your sense of the relation of your language to "the mess"—the world beyond the page, everyday life and death. And this will in turn affect the world of the page—the formal intersections of the historical fragmentation with the mess of the present, the formal intersections of space-time with linguistic forms of life, recovery and loss, silence and art. I think Francis Ponge was getting at something like this when he wrote in *Pour un Malherbe*, in 1965, "In order for a text to expect in any way to render an account of reality of the concrete world (or the spiritual one), it must first attain reality in its own world, the textual one." But before, as a poet, you can begin to attempt this you must face the fact that your present project is insufficient, that it has not moved toward the unintelligibilities of the present. You see this kind of change in the work of some poets and not others.

QS: There is a feeling of course that unintelligibility has no place in poetry, that it leads only to inaccessibility and that is *ipso facto* a form of avant-disregarde for its audience.

JR: (*laughs*) I like that, "avant-disregarde." It's a good joke because it accurately reflects a common opinion. But it's not true. The language of a time is a complex barometer of all sorts of cross-currents that are affecting us, that we are sensing, that fill us with energy and breath but which we cannot yet bring into discernible form. I once heard a scientist who loves poetry say, the language of science and the language of poetry have in common that they are both natural languages under stress. The complexity of the world in which language lives and develops and evolves forms every word into a chord, conveying many things at once. Those chords strike us on many levels. Via the neo-cortex and via the limbic system which triggers our emotions in little or no contact with the cognitive areas of our brain. And of course there's so much that we experience in the silence before, between, after, even *within* words. The poet must work with all of that.

QS: We are getting farther and farther from Aristotle's *Poetics*.

JR: Oh, you noticed! (*laughter*) Yes, Aristotle, who has cast the most enduring shadow over the course of academic poetics, quite artificially divided everything up into what he took to be thoroughly comprehensible disciplines—theory, practice, ethics, politics, poetry. Poethical poets, whether or not they have themselves used the "h," enact the complex dynamics that criss-cross through these boundaries. The model is no longer one of city or nation states of knowledge each with separate allegiances and consequences, testy about property rights and ownership, but instead the more global patterns of ecology, environmentalism, bio-realism, the complex modelings of the non-linear sciences, chaos theory. You can see this now with more and more poets using multiple languages in their work—not as quotation, but as lively intersection, conversation.

QS: Who are you thinking of?

JR: Anne Tardos who uses four languages in *Cat Licked the Garlic*. Marlene Nourbese Philip in her wonderful poem, "Universal Grammar." Kamau Brathwaite in *Middle Passages*. The Nuyorican poet, Edwin Torres's tumultous love affair between Spanish and English. I've always loved the title of Tim Dlugos' book *Je Suis Ein Americano*. What better thing for poets to do right now than to begin in one language and end up in others. This is the poethical field for a global village, don't you think?

And not so difficult. You see it in the grocery store. What used to be called "Eggplant Appetizer" is now called "Eggplant Caponata." More and more of us are healthy ethnic, cultural, racial mongrels. Our language should benefit from that, and not just in the market place.

QS: You've written about the shift that's taken place since the sixties, in which women have come into the forefront of experimentation in poetry by taking up the distinctly "feminine" experimental project that had previously been carried on almost exclusively by the male avant-garde.

JR: Yes, ironically, with appallingly few (famous) exceptions, only men until recently had the means—the wide-ranging cultural access and support, the social backing—to use what many have argued is a feminine experimental mode. Now we need no longer be in the grip of irony. Women, given our centuries of cultural training in the interrupted life in *medias* mess, in the feminine arts of making improbable connections between disparate sectors, in the service of carrying on the complexities of everyday life, are now—with fewer barriers to broad experience and study, and public agency—in a perfect position to embark on the invention of new models. To experiment with poethical, complex realisms in the arts and other humanities. So you have this wonderful array of women poets and postmodern scholars who are demonstrating new grammars and models for thinking about interrelationships. Among poets, I'm thinking of Nicole Brossard, Theresa Hak Kyung Cha, Tina Darragh, Kathleen Fraser, Carla Harryman, Lyn Hejinian, Susan Howe, Marlene Nourbese Philip, Leslie Scalapino, Anne Tardos, Rosmarie Waldrop, Anne Waldman, Diane Ward... There are many others I'm leaving out.

QS: Do you always think in alphabetical order? (*laughter*)

JR: You expose the constructed nature of this interview.

QS: OK, I confess I'm confused. One's poetics must inevitably be formed by one's personal experience—by the strange and problematic intersections of self, family, society that are unique experiences for each of us. But you claim that it is only the culture at large, and particularly the academy, that "understands" this as form.

JR: Yes, "understandards" one might awkwardly say. The form that is visible as form at any given cultural moment is what has already been assimilated into the academy. So the teaching in graduate programs of those "great innovators" of the past goes on almost entirely in an atmosphere of invisible contemporaries. And the implicit fallacy that is transmitted, say to the MFA student in "creative writing," is that if you are going to succeed in the cautious world of poetry prizes and establishment publication and professional advancement, your work must closely resemble a legitimated model. In the poetry of aboutness only what it's about changes. It's that simple. Oddly, these models, in interesting contrast with teaching in the sciences, rarely include the innovators. My impression is that the genealogy of models within most MFA programs skips right over them. But even when they are included, the modeling paradigm is off-base. They should be imitated only in their manner of operation, to once again paraphrase Cage. Each of those "great" innovators was acutely sensitive to the changing facts and forms of her or his own times and had to devise a distinct writing procedure to accommodate them. It's in this sense that their work was consciously poethical. It fully engaged with the forms of life that created its contemporary context—the science, the arts, the politics, the sounds and textures of everyday life, the urgent questions and disruptions of the times. And it was no more and no less than that lively engagement that made their work different from what had gone before. And for a time unrecognizable, by all but a few, as important extensions or trans-gressions of existing genres. (*pause*) For the work to become poethical it must go through a period of invisibility, unintelligibility. This happened with Stein, Joyce, Beckett. In other fields, Wittgenstein's *Philosophical Investigations* and Cage's music after the forties are cases in point, are poethical innovations.

QS: Unintelligibility?

JR: For a poethical development to occur, I think the language—the aural and visual forms, the grammar, the vocabulary—must precisely escape, in a radical way, the control of the poet. It must fly from the poet, like Zeno's arrow, in an imperiled, imperiling trajectory subject to cultural weather, chance, vagaries of all kinds beyond the poet's intentionality, out of zones of current intelligibility.

QS: Like Zeno's arrow! (*laughs*) This might sound rather aggressive, but Zeno's arrow didn't move. It remained motionless in the air.

JR: Quite right! Until new language—a new philosophy, a new mathematics—came along to release it. Chaos theory, fractal geometry may be helping now to release Cage's work into the culture. Of course Zeno's arrow is an unfortunate metaphor for another reason—too pointed. But I like its flimsy vulnerability in relation to the academic canon. And, quite seriously, I use it because I think when it comes to a developing poethics in relation to the canon, to the academy, to the critical establishment at any given historical moment, all of Zeno's laws against motion are likely to be in effect. It always takes a major conceptual shift—the very one we might say that the art itself previews—to release new work from that grip. It seems to happen most obviously and most widely in the visual arts. The figure-ground shift that we see in Impressionist studies of the refraction of light into color, the figure-ground shift in the study of light in quantum physics—these become received by cultural eye and brain in ways less problematic than Joyce's foregrounding of linguistic refractions in *Finnegans Wake*. Why?

QS: Yes, I don't know, but I think that's true. Thinking about the shift that occurred in the art critical world for Duchamp's "readymades" to become art brings to mind Duchamp's and Cage's belief that the work of art is completed by the viewer. For the individual viewer to make this contribution to the work, the culture must already have gone part way.

JR: Yes, or the reader, or listener.

QS: Yes, yes. So the problem of that poor stricken athlete in Zeno's paradox, who must get from one side of the stadium to the other, but must first go halfway, and half of that—

JR: The eternally transfixed conditional.

QS: —and so on in infinite regress. In the complex aesthetic condition that problem need never arise. The poet never has to go the whole way across the stadium in the first place, doesn't have to complete the transit all alone, but is met part-way by the reader.

JR: I'd put it even more strongly and say the artist *shouldn't* attempt to go the whole distance. There should always be a formally evident invitation to the reader to realize the work for her/himself. But, what you're saying immediately casts the situation out of the realm of single point perspective and progressions. There is here at least a dual perspective, that of poet and reader—two very different starting points that are of equal importance, mediated by worlds of experience between them, the vast diffusion and noise of the whole culture. Aesthetic logics always should be plural, and in the richness of their plurality you have paradoxes of other kinds, but not those that arise out of attempts to narrow the focus to a linear succession of single points.

QS: Yes. So we don't get stuck on that single track of one point following another in narrow succession. This reminds me of what Gregory Bateson said about the noise of culture--

JR: The as yet undifferentiated new.

QS: Yes. He said, in *Steps to an Ecology of Mind*, "All that is not information, not redundancy, not form and not restraints—is noise, the only possible source of new patterns."

JR: Ah yes, that's lovely. And, of course, it's the complexity of that noise that, to the extent that the artist allows it to enter the constructing consciousness, allows one to escape narrow social constructions and engage in experimental invention. This is what the narrow focus of "identity" politics and aesthetics precludes. The identified victim, is indentured by the new conceptual colonialism, cultural construction. As victims they can only raise their voices, they can only witness and shout in place, they can't invent themselves out of the single point perspective of their culturally constructed state. Awareness of cultural construction is of urgent importance, in its complexity, in its globally interconnected noise—out of which each of us must invent new life patterns. What Bateson is saying about noise involves the infinite—to return to Zeno's problems—as possibility rather than conceptual stumbling block. The medium you're using, language, has a history and a future whose potential complexity of use is infinite. Even as you're working with words they're flying away from you in all directions, into cultural logics and associations that give meaning to the intersections of language with everyday life. This is why every complex text is to one degree or another indeterminate. And its moving principle is a function of the degree of its indeterminacy. It cannot be an argument.

QS: Not an argument? Of course not. Who's saying it is!?

JR: Well there's a long-standing, very entrenched aesthetic of persuasion, isn't there? In which the reader must be *made* to feel what the author felt, must be *convinced* of the author's omniscient perspective, must come to *believe* in the characters and the point (singular) of view—at least within the microcosm of the work—and be edified and inspired (filled with the author's breath) by it. The reader's activity is not one of participatory invention but of figuring out what the author—the master creator—means. This is as true with certain kinds of poetry as it is with the novel. One of my students recently brought this to class: truth is stranger than fiction because fiction has to make sense. This is as true of the lyric fictions of the I-poem as it is of the *Ich-roman*. It all has to make internally consistent, persuasive sense.

QS: I remember you wrote somewhere that the ubiquitous three or four or five stanza lyric poem mimics those exemplar arguments in modal logic. The final epiphany equals the logical conclusion.

JR: Yes, in the sense that both are guiding the mind toward a single outburst of certitude—cognitive and/or emotional. And, of course I'm speaking of aesthetics whose guiding principle remains verisimilitude—what I think of as the unnatural realisms—they have nothing at all to do with the complexities, the multiple logics of nature, of everyday experience; they are instead highly stylized, simple and elegant conventions of "realism" or lyric "truth"—relating to the values of an earlier period in science, or of the very specialized sciences that are most removed from the conditions of everyday life. So everything depends upon the audience's suspension of disbelief—believe me, there's a lot to suspend!

(*laughter*)—coupled with a rhetoric of persuasion. Nature, the natural, is caricatured and called life-like. There is no attempt to imitate nature in her manner of operation, but rather the rhetorician in his manner of conviction. Aristotle didn't know this, so he separated the *Rhetoric* and the *Poetics* into two books even though the position of the tragic spectator is clearly the same in both instances.

QS: Surely you jest!

JR: Surely not! Not at all. The terms of the *Rhetoric*: "ethos," "logos," "pathos" are engaged in the same asymmetrical relation between writer and reader, targeting the same imaginative coefficient in the audience as "verisimilitude," the major term of the *Poetics*, don't you think? Both want to cognitively convince the audience while manipulating their emotions.

QS: And—So (*pause*) you define the terms of an art entirely in terms of the position of the audience?

JR: Yes. (*long pause.*)

QS: "Yes"? Is that it?

JR: Well, I think about the forms of life the artist brings into the work and then, thinking of the completion of the artist's part of the work as resulting in a kind of "score" for the reader or viewer, I wonder about the poethics of the kind of realization it invites. These kinds of thoughts, it seems to me, lead to the possibility of a contextual criticism based on poethical analysis, rather than judgment.

QS: What would that look like?

JR: Ah, glad you asked. I just happen to have with me a document that can be entered into the record. It came about in the course of an epistolary conversation with a young poet in which he was defending the continuing relevance of older forms like the sonnet or villanelle:

> "Poethics," as I see it, has two working uses:
>
> a) Normative: as a descriptive term denoting what one takes to be the use of a positively constructive imagination in relation to complex conditions of the society and the world in one's (or "our") current historical intersection. This relates to John Cage's

statement in his *History of Experimental Music in the United States*, "One does not then make just any experiment, but does what must be done." It's conceivable to me that a convincing case could be made that one of the experiments that "must be done" at any given moment is to bring a historical (as in "previous") form into intersection with cultural material in the present. But this clearly must be done in a mindfully poethical manner. What I mean by that is that there have always been nostalgic carryovers (e.g. the pastoral) or ideological revivals (e.g., neo-classicisms) whose effect is to mythologize or obliterate or smooth over the raw edges of both the present and the past—to avoid grappling with the noise, the unintelligibilities out of which (in large part) we must construct our future.

b) Analytical: Every form—old or new—has its poethical matrices and consequences. We can ask—after, or while, locating our questions within a value context—What are they? Are they useful to us (whichever "us" is inquiring: "world us" or me and my buddies who are charting a working poethics)? Do they seem to be constructive or damaging within the articulation of our value context?

All of the above is most importantly about investigating specific texts, not abstract declarative manifestos. That means that the ways in which language works in exemplar texts must be compared. The extent to which the analysis is comparative will, I think, determine the scope of its relevance. Manifestos are energizing perhaps because they are not about being fair. They are a call to action, not mindful exploration. The soldier doesn't question the ethical basis of the war as s/he rushes into battle. The manifesto is a festering masculinized (in the patriarchal sense) call to arms whose form of life is to end conversation, not continue it, don't you think? I think it festers in all of us (I include myself in that "us") who are passionate about what we are doing and it is difficult to redirect that passion into a useful form of exploration cum conversation.

QS: We haven't talked about the poethical implications of your own work.

JR: I'm not sure one can do that. I think of that exchange with John Cage that Rod Smith recently read in an introduction to a sort of belated publication reading for my book *A F T E R R I M A G E S*:

> Joan Retallack: You talk of artists setting examples. Is part of what artists do—in, say, using language in new ways—to change the grammar of the way we are together?
> John Cage: Are you asking this in relation to what you just read from Wittgenstein?
> JR: Yes.
> JC: Yes, isn't that beautiful? (pause) We don't know. But we can try.
> (NYC, September 6, 1990)

This exchange is from *M U S I C A G E / CAGE MUSES on Words. Art. Music.* The passage from Wittgenstein that Cage is referring to is this one from the notes gathered in the book called *Culture and Value*. Wittgenstein says, "People say again and again that philosophy doesn't really progress, that we are still occupied with the same philosophical problems as were the Greeks. But the people who say this don't understand why it has to be so. It is because our language has remained the same and keeps seducing us into asking the same questions." The same issue is addressed in the *Philosophical Investigations* (I, 132) "The confusions which occupy us arise when language is like an engine idling, not when it is doing work." About all of this in relation to my own work...I suppose I feel as Cage put it, I don't know, but I can try. That's the essence of the poethical wager.

QS: Oh, yes, that's how this conversation came about in the first place. We were going to talk about your so-called "poethical wager." How did that notion come to you? Was it directly from Cage's answer?

JR: Well, of course, it's related to Cage, to how I've been understanding his aesthetic framework for some time. But the term is something that came to me after a dinner, what we called an "experimental vegetarian barbecue," at my house with Tina Darragh and Peter Inman. The conversation was, in part, about how we could go on working in the culturally isolated field of experimental poetry when the whole world seems to be going to hell all around us. All three of us have had activist backgrounds—civil rights, anti-war. Peter is currently a labor negotiator for his union at the Library of Congress. So the question arises, given the troubles of our society in the world right now, shouldn't we be devoting ourselves entirely to direct social action, rather than the "luxury" of poetry? I think this is an intermittent question for many of us, and it's—I find it—a bracing one.

QS: Well, how do you answer it?

JR: I can't speak for Peter and Tina, of course, but my answer is poethical and related to chaos theory, and certainly a form of "we don't know, but we can try." My idea, which may be a patent rationalization, is that the world situation is so complexly interrelational—with many interconnected patterns of chaos—from weather to neural networks to economics, there are so many variables, that large-scale or even modestly scaled predictive accuracy is impossible. Certainly when you get down to the level of individual agency, the effects of any one person's actions or work, particularly from the partial and myopic perspective of that individual herself, are quite mysterious. This means, I think, that each person has to make decisions based on prescription rather than prediction. This is a common distinction in the field of ethics. They have very different logics. You might prescribe, in an aesthetic context, what your own action will be based on your conscious framework of values, knowing that you cannot predict the effect this will have on your audience, much less the world situation. You can hope that it will have a positive effect, as you construe it, but you certainly can't know. This hope would seem particularly far-fetched when the size of your readership is about a dozen people, if that! (*laughter*)

304

QS: Such considerations lead to accusations of the exclusivity and self-indulgence of the avant-garde.

JR: Exactly. So, even given that one doesn't choose to have such a small audience, how does one reply to that possibility with regard to one's own work? It strikes me that since the work of any given generation is adding to the initial conditions of the generations to come, one obviously tries to add positive, even constructive, initial conditions. We know from scientists working on complexity theory that chaotic systems, such as the ones in which culture develops, are extremely sensitive to initial conditions.

QS: The "Butterfly Effect."

JR: Yes. So we are all in effect choosing to be one kind of butterfly or another—a highly decorative, light-weight species that might seem almost like a biological whim, but of course, we know it has a very active place in nature. And that any individual member, for reasons entirely unknown qua qua qua, could shift weather patterns for the rest of the century—in ways noticeable or not by us, the "observant species." In other words, all one can do is take what is actually, in these terms, a very realistic, if improbable, chance that one's contribution might be useful, even helpful. So that's it, the long and the short of it—my view of progressive action within a paradigm of chaos. I was explaining this to Peter and Tina, and Peter said, that sounds sort of like Pascal's Wager. I hadn't thought of it that way, but of course he's right. I find it an interesting comparison. Pascal was himself trying to figure out how to proceed in the midst of potentially crippling uncertainty. And his thinking was naturally couched in terms of his involvement with probability theory—tossing the binary God coin for a 50-50 chance of heads or tails. Now we can envision many more variables and possibilities. Though I admit I always thought Pascal's Wager was somewhat cynical, related to the authoritarian nature of Catholicism, I have loved the spirit of "You must wager. This is not voluntary, you are embarked." I think that precisely describes our condition. Each era works with its own scientific and mathematical models, its own understanding of the nature of things.

The poethical wager, which is just that we do our utmost on the chance that our work will be as helpful as any other infinitesimal initial condition might be, comes out of current thinking about the intertwining trajectories of pattern and chance. There's still no certainty of course. As Cage said, you might make matters worse. But to make this wager is at least to step out into the weather of our times.

QS: (looking out window) What a good idea!

JR: Yes, enough of this, let's go for a walk.

AUTOBIOGRAPHIA LITTERARIA II

for Holly Swain

:MYSTORY: WHATS WRONG WITH THIS PICTURE:

:BEFORE: :THEN:

V.WOOLF.J.JOYCE.JELLY.ROLL.MORTON.HE.DEAD.I.HAVE.WANT
ED.TO.HAVE.THE.DRIVE.TO.KNÖW.MY.OWN.STORY.THERE.BY.
TOUCHING.THE.VIOLENCE.IN.THE.MECHANISM.ITSELF.ONLY.TO.
BE.REPLACED.WITH.ALL.AND.THEN.AND.WHERE.ALONG.THE.WA
Y.IT.[EIS].BIFURCATES.ÖEISÒ.**FROST**.IN.OLD.GERMAN.**PASSION**.
IN.GREEK.AND.LATIN.THEN.THE.FATHTHER.WAS.ARRESTED.IN.G
ERMANY.ON.THE.EVE.OF.ANOTHER.WAR.THEN.HE.SAID.HE.WAS.
THERE.TO.STUDY.THE.GERMAN.LANGUAGE.MUSIC.AND.ENGINE

307

:MYSTORY:WHATS WRONG WITH THIS PICTURE:

:BEFORE: :THEN:

ERING.THEY.COULD.NOT.BELIEVE.THE.COINCIDENCE.FACTS.AR
E.OK.HE.SAID.THEY.ARE.BETTER.THAN.LOOKING.IN.THE.MIRROR.
SEE.HOW.THE.AIR.IS.FULL.OF.AIR.A.NOTE.S.O.S.NOT.GEOMETRY.
OF.THE.EMOTIONS.MOTHER.SPOKE.SPANISH.AND.ENGLISH.AS.A.
CHILD.SHE.WAS.TEASED.BECAUSE.SHE.SAID.LOOKING-GLASS.IN
STEAD.OF.MIRROR.IS.THIS.A.PICTURE.OF.A.FACT.THE.LENS.GIVE
S.ON.A.CLEAR.BLUE.YELLOW.GREEN.MOMENT.THEN.NEI.ÖNEIÒ.
TO.BE.EXCITED.TO.SHINE.TO.LEAD.ALSO.NEIGW.ÖNEIGWÒ.OF.RI
VERS.WATERS.WASHING.THE.FATHTHER.HIMSELF.PLAYING.PIAN

:MYSTORY:WHATS WRONG WITH THIS PICTURE:

:BEFORE: :THEN:

O.FOR.SILENT.ÜjÜî.MOVIES.[DONTWORRYSAYSTHEDYINGMANI'V
EHADAGOOD86YEARSBUTDADSAYSHISDAUGHTERYOUAREONLY76]
IT.I.WANT.TO.SAY.FOLLOWS.THEN.THAT.SHOULD.BE.THE.NEXT.WO
RD.IS.IT.WORTH.USURING.METAPHOR.TO.SAY.THE.MAN.WHO.SOLD.
CANDY.AT.THE.CORNER.STORE.HAD.A.FACE.AS.OPEN.AS.A.SHUCK
ED.OYSTER.[CHILDHOODISFULLOFHORROR].MUCH.LATER.THE.DAU
GHTER.FOUND.OUT.THE.FATHTHER.HAD.NAMED.A.LOW.LEVEL.TRA
NSMITTER.AFTER.HER.DURING.ANOTHER.WAR.THE.GERMAN.ROOT.

:MYSTORY:WHATS WRONG WITH THIS PICTURE:

:BEFORE: :THEN:

WAS.**FROST**.FINALLY.INTELLIGENCE.GOT.OUT.AND.THE.WE.WO
N.THE.WAR.THEN.THERE.IS.THE.THING.IS.PLAYING.AT.THE.MOV
IES.THE.SILENT.ROOTS.OF.A.LANGUAGE.ARE.CHEMICAL.ELEME
NTS.BOPP.FOLLOWING.SANSKRIT.GRAMMARIANS.THOUGHT.TH
EY.WERE.ALL.MONOSYLLABIC.THEN.THERE.ARE.THE.STRETCH-
GRADE.VOWELS.YES.YES.I.LEARNED.ALL.THESE.THINGS.AT.THE.
SO.TO.SPEAK.KNEES.OF.MY.SPANISH.MOTHER.MY.CORNISH.FA
THTHER.MY.RUSSIAN.UNCLE.&.INTERNATIONALISTA.COMMUN

:MYSTORY:WHATS WRONG WITH THIS PICTURE:

:BEFORE: :THEN:

IST.AUNT.MY.ENGLISH.GRANDMOTHER.[THEREMAYHAVEBEENA
MOORTOO].EX.LIBRIS.CUBA.LIBRA.ONE.DAY.SHE.THREW.HER.LU
NCH.AWAY.AND.CARRIED.THE.GARBAGE.TO.WORK.[THISISANOL
DFAMILYSTORY].THINKING.OF.GREEK.MYTHS.SPANISH.TRAGED
IES.ITALIAN.OPERAS.ÖGULLÒ.ÖÒ.ÖDOLMENÒ.ÖMENHIRÒ.THE.O
NLY.CORNISH.WORDS.CITED.AS.SURVIVING.MODERN.ENGLISH.
AND.THE.LAST.TWO.JUST.BARELY.BARLEY.THE.ONLY.CELTS.WH
O.LOST.THEIR.TONGUE.DOES.THIS.ALARM.YOU.HE.ASKED.ME.[N

:MYSTORY:WHATS WRONG WITH THIS PICTURE:

:BEFORE: :THEN:

OCAUSEFORVIOLENCEORWARSHETHOUGHTINSILENCE].ÜjÜî.SO
METHING.ABOUT.A.CORNISH.LASH.FILLING.UP.ON.SUCCOTASH.TH
EN.LATER.MOTHER.CONFESSED.SHE.NEVER.LIKED.LIVER.AND.SHE.
DIDN'T.BELIEVE.IN.GOD.DID.SHE.SAY.THE.HIDDEN.FAT.OR.FACT.OF
DOUBT.HER. *TOPIARY. GAZE*.HER. *CONVEX. VOCABULARIES*.HER.CONCA
VE.SMILE.[YOUDON'TPERSUADESOMEONETOSMILE].THE.CHILD.CO
MES.BRINGING.SOUND.AND.LIGHT.THERE.ARE.A.LOT.OF.ÖSHEÒS.IN.
THIS.STORY.ÖSHEÒ.WANTS.TO.PERFECT.THE.GRAPPLING.ARTS.ÖSH

:MYSTORY:WHATS WRONG WITH THIS PICTURE:

:BEFORE: :THEN:

EÒ.SAY.SHE.WANTS.SPIRITUALITY.TO.CHANGE.THE.DIRECTION.OF.
HER.POWER.ÖSHEÒ.ÖSHEÒ.SAY.ALL.THESE.THINGS.ARE.THE.THIN
GS.THAT.I.TRULY.LOVE.IN.THE.MS.OF.THE.FIFTEENTH.CENTURY.M
ISSA.NOTES.BLEED.THROUGH.FROM.THE.OTHER.SIDE.OF.THE.PAGE.
FILLING.IN.BLANKS.ON.THE.STAVES.AND.COMPLICATING.THE.MU
SIC.

310

Intersperse entries & numerals from notebooks
(back to Chicago (Chinese story in tact (quotes
from assordid pm sages
= Manual text ?

She is captive in China
  "   "   "   " a moment in history
  "   "   "   to a sense of history

but in the way a wordswerve could turn a century's prose for a second
or two away from history first from property then ideas then property as
idea then idea as property

creating parallel texts left and right full of opposing forces in a sad space
of alternating dire lexical black and white squares

the flat degraded feeling in telling the story or describing the passage
and/but they are very proud of this Searle says suppose that unknown to
you the symbols passed into the room are called questions by the people
outside the room and the symbols you pass back out of the room are
called answers to the questions

She-?.
how do you know the person locked for all those years in the Chinese
room is a woman there are few if any signs if she exists at all she is the
content of a thought experiment begun in a man's mind this is nothing
knew and perhaps more complicated

She-1.
now that we think we know that the world is not all that is the case the
case in question the space of the case sad but fierce with light upholds

the dark it seems to utter itself must there be subtitles must there be translation she thinks she knows but doesn't want to accept that in order to write or read or speak there must be a division between light and dark

imagine that you are locked in a room and in this room are several baskets full of Chinese characters she is glad they are Chinese of course glad to continue Pound's Orientalism there will be no punctuated vanishing points she is given only rules of syntax not semantic rules she is relieved of the burden of making meaning she need only make sense for the food to be pushed through the slot in the door it is thought that these are situations more familiar than we would like to think them to be in the new technologies and to men more than to women but it oddly feels quite normal

She-2.
what's to keep her from responding to their cues with syntactically correct non sequiturs in effect surrendering they might ask does the past tense give you vertigo she might reply there's no sense in knowing what day or night it is they're always changing

She-3.
yes it gives me vertigo knowing they've all been locked in that prose for centuries by comparison this makes the Chinese room feel full of breath of fresh air the point has been made that this prose has justified the violence and then it's been made and they can say oh that point has already been made

She-4.
is being too careful not exploring the other possibilities but this could be serious it might not be the thought experiment he thought it was or it might be irreversible once set in motion vert-I-go not abject advert to yes Duchamp turns out all along to all along have been all along Fred Astaire and Kate Smith coming over the mountain is Gertrude Stein

312

For the Woman in the Chinese Room: assemblange manc enhance silhouette 3 millimeter aperture in iris relish chalice in ken off shore

vegetables were being smashed hard to find dotted lines and arrows from aesthetic to ethical to spiritual to penthouse level the woman with four shopping bags said I don't want your money I just want to tell you that I dreamed I went to the Hilton Hotel because I knew God was there I knew He was in the penthouse I tried to find the elevator but they stopped me they wouldn't let me past the lobby

vivid stupefy suffice perturb brance
More Orientalism: the Japanese say *mu* to unask the question
aqueous tenuous hush tuh

in this story to describe roundness you may have to think about a square you may have to retreat from decorum or just spell it out phonetically you may have to find an Oriental Jesus with a vertical smile you may have to calculate the rectilinear coordinates of a blue duskless mountain with the distance of a female Faust

excessive evil nonsense Agamemnon lemon mythos ethos logos pathos fauxed yes/no nothing no thing to be gained do not reach out do not attempt to grasp let it slip by

mbers shoul ha gn
uides
e
ity
f
ected

ultra horizon breaking either/or parapet

blank dark returns new page tilted

speaking blank strange northern apple

in stant pivot sigh then of (blank)

toward 13 squares 13 syllables 3

points blank clear between bracket

asked light light 20 thin flips blank socket

ancient coil's pro's cunt's critique's pure reason's

blank erosore blanke paw thrumb Hegel

blank remedy beard agenda dramb

fraucht ergle gloss remainder squat

in history's twitter rut she blank

twi-lips pensive grim reminder mirg mirror

blanck trace there pocket vox map

thing I ness inging hind able isible erved

protentending crack blank fast air cont'd

quiet putt rusted civet beast or breast

Nicole Brossard

FLUID ARGUMENTS

BRIEF CASE: A PLACE OF ONE'S OWN

Comme autrefois hier et demain simultanément. Aujourd'hui, ciel bleu, odeurs de Montréal. Devant la maison, le Parc de Vimy, l'automne. Ma table dite de travail et mes stylos nombreux avec lesquels je fais alterner les images et le silence en pensant que toujours je n'aurai qu'un seul corps pour comparer les livres, les couchers de soleil, discourir sur le monde, les idées et les objets produits au fil des siècles. Un seul corps pour m'émerveiller, pour m'adapter. Pour comprendre la vaste entreprise du délire, de la raison et de la création, un seul corps pour décider de la présence et du futur.

Il y a les livres. Les musées. Des endroits: Venise, Santorini, le Grand canyon, Kyoto, les pavillons. Il y a la multitude des images, un nombre effarant de crânes; masses humaines allongées dans l'herbe fétide. Il y a ça, bien sûr, qui persiste: la croyance en quelques valeurs humanistes puisque croire en l'espèce fascine, oblige à des performances hautement morales, gages d'espoir ou tout simplement croyances qui rassurent nos gènes, l'écho de nos voix décalées dans le temps.

Aussi y a-t-il plusieurs façons de refaire la phrase, de l'entourer pour qu'elle fasse bonne impression, toute la différence. Petite ou grande émotion en poésie se calcule au mot à bout de bras, l'horizon ou deep down dans la poitrine comme une certitude.

Ecrivant ces pages, une fois de plus me plonger dans l'inédit. Ce texte, je le voudrais en action, plein de feu, d'images et de questions comme une mouvance de la pensée en train de gagner du terrain sur l'inquiétude contemporaine ou de s'éclater dans l'acuité des sens et des questions nées du changement et du sens en accéléré.

L'inédit. Voilà qu'à mon insu, je viens de témoigner de l'obsession qui traverse tous mes livres. Produire de l'inédit, m'aventurer dans l'inconnu, naviguer parmi le nombre effarant des permutations sémantiques. Explorer, toujours intriguée, révoltée by the non-sense of violence et fascinée by the full meaning of being alive, catching up with virtual dimension of the self and its nervous system. Produire des objets de pensée et d'émotion qui puissent être partagés. Vivre les bras chargés de métaphores, allant à la rencontre d'un second moi épris de spectacles, de vertige et de lucidité.

Réalité: on dit fiction issue du bord des pensées qui la recomposent. Plus tard, les grands symboles nous collent à la peau: il faut recommencer au milieu des questions surprenantes, la joie de vivre et autres sentiments angoissants qui multiplient la possibilité de collision. Recommencer car c'est prématurément qu'on a levé les yeux

de la page ne sachant pas exactement jusqu'où l'obsession de l'écriture pouvait nous entraîner. Alors on déplace les roses, les autoroutes, l'horizon s'il le faut la mer dans une autre dimension. Et tout est à recommencer puisque que pendant le temps court et irréversible de l'instant on a fermé les yeux de plaisir

tell me more about you how you shape your dreams what you think about *la littérature québécoise* how language crosses your mind night and day in order for you to believe that the nature of language is to be enjoyable. Tell me why you approve so loudly when a woman puts words in your mouth with her warm voice. Explain yourself can you go on with **writing** as a key word for processing the living and its enigmas. Why don't you simply answer by beauty. Extra/vagance. Suppleness of the mind or consciousness or syntax or simply passion.

tell me if

tell me why

tell me: are you really serious when you engage in such a thing as narrative?

Do you like repeating **I believe**, **I think** every two or three sentences? Wouldn't you rather start by *there was a time when* or *for the moment*? Sure you can find some words to translate your relation with prose and poetry,

I am a woman of the present, of the instant, and this no doubt explains my reluctance in regards to prose. I like to feel that the world can converge, come apart and be reconstituted inside me in the moment of a poem. I seek that tension, and prose leads me away from it. Prose dilutes tension, excitement, the effect of synthesis which is what dazzles us in the poem intrigues, so that even the body worries and is astonished by what suddenly is making it so feverish. A poem is a product of desiring energy, here and now, word by word. Prose dims the present, projects it into several temporal dimensions, builds slowly, sentence by sentence, slows down desire, even though every act of writing forces us to slow down and because of this, remains a precious warrant of renewal for thinking and for feeling. Prose works like a game of patience in the midst of chance and memory. Its urgency lies in its diversion of the real despite the real. Prose works where dreams are checkmated, poetry works in the vivid torment of the dream. Prose investigates, fantasizes, speculates on the relations that form between people, where we would like to make them more alive than we are, or more troubling than our desires, more inclined to express our ambivalence and the identity crises that unsettle us. In prose there is always someone who resembles us, who escapes us. In the poem, I takes care of everything, alone among the planets or in mid-ocean like a swimmer who, breathless and all-of-a-breath appears, disappears, resurfaces with her wet muscles between the blue folds, the vast grey wave of the faraway.

I see. Now tell me where you start from in order to fill the page with explicit contradictions.

still and the challenge meets excessfully
the new surfaces
trace and obscure phrases
this gesture or the overflow of the code spilled out
prefigures the text permutes it
horizontal and fragment   1974

To write *I am a woman* is full of consequences
                                   1977

I said, with a taste of salt in the mouth, on the subject of
Utopia beginning with the word woman that Utopia was not
going to ensure our insertion into reality but that a Utopian
testimony on our part could stimulate in us a quality of
emotion favourable for our insertion into history
                          1982

Subjectivity is not to be found in pr   in content
and strategies, that is, in the   we use to
accommodate our subjectiv

the poem does not have   of proof that
meaning, informed   en two women
envisaging a sexual   rasure of the lie
and its thrusts sc   d the imaginary.
The poem is desir   elters a soul said
to be sensitive to th   oving   Without the poem,
neither the one, wo   r the other   rable, would have
in the depths of   eyes that expr   ssion that ignites
metaphors, that i   es pleasure and recognition, that
expression where li   within the so-called flow o
take stock of its v

Body: fait partie du trio texte/corps/cortex. "All bodies carry within themselves a project of sensual high technology; writing is its hologram."

Dawn: "Dawn attracts, this is certain, dawn fascinates. She is at the edge of night, at the edge of the soul a quiet certitude, an appeasement of the eyes smitten with changes and utopias." Revient chaque fois que l'espoir et la nostalgie s'affrontent. Le mot apparaît dans le titre du premier recueil *Aube à la saison* (1965) et le dernier livre *Baroque d'aube* (1995) de l'auteure.

Death: mot tabou mais fréquemment utilisé particulièrement dans les oeuvres inédites. Apparaît dès 1970 avec la parution du recueil *Le Centre blanc (1970)*.

Délire: Voir *Lovhers*. Délire amoureux. Jouissance. A parfois été utilisé pour rendre compte du flot de paroles qui jaillit des femmes lorsqu'elles prennent conscience de l'ampleur de la violence et des mensonges patriarcaux.

Dé/lire: employé pour traduire une méthode d'analyse du texte partriarcal.

Desire: s'emploie au sens de projet, de fébrilité et d'intensité. Semble à l'origine de l'acte d'écriture. Remplace parfois le mot énergie.

Energy: apparaît dans la suite lesbienne que composent les livres *Lovhers, Picture Theory, The Aerial Letter* et *Under tongue*. Par la suite, utilisé pour analyser les forces en présence dans le processus de création littéraire. "L'imagination passe par la peau la peau est énergie."

Eye: mot-clé apparaissant dans la plupart des textes. Associé à l'écriture et à la lecture. Regard-désir-horizon. Autre regroupement: hologramme, écran, réalité virtuelle. Voir: Act of the eye in *These our Mothers* et le recueil *Double impression* (1984).

Horizon: traduit un besoin d'espace, de liberté. Peut être rattaché à la définition que l'auteur donne parfois d'elle-même comme exploratrice. A mettre en relation avec la mer et le désert. Voir au mot dawn.

Light: doit être associé à l'intensité, à la beauté, à l'aveuglement et paradoxalement à la lucidité. "Sur fil de lumière je suspends la poésie" in *Aube à la saison* (1965). "For in full light our whole body rears up, aura of being or fabulous animal, gifted with splendor and ingenuity." *Mauve Desert* (1990)

Lucidity: sert parfois de synonyme au mot conscience. Est étroitement associé au sens de l'honneur, à la morale, à l'honnêteté, à l'intégrité ainsi qu'aux valeurs humanistes. Etre lucide est une preuve d'humanité.

Mauve: employé pour le plaisir des sons et pour la couleur à laquelle le mot revoie. Associé à l'amour lesbien, à l'aube.

Montréal: ville natale. Prononcer en français. Ne pas oublier l'accent qui fait la différence. Apparaît surtout dans le roman *French kiss*. Constitue un point d'ancrage pour les thèmes de la ville et de la modernité. Parmi les noms de rue qui reviennent fréquemment: rue Cherrier, rue Saint-Laurent, rue Saint-Denis, rue Sherbrooke; autres endroits: le Carré Saint-Louis, le Parc Lafontaine, le Vieux-Montréal.

Shadow: certainement un mot-clé dans ma poésie. Interrogée à cet effet, je n'ai jamais su justifier ou expliquer la fréquence du mot dans mes écrits. Première hypothèse: la douceur et la gravité des sons qui composent le mot. Deuxième hypothèse: la question du double. Le trio Ombre/Sombre/Tombe apparaît dans un recueil de 1968.

Sex: emploi rare. Remplacé par les mots corps, peau et langue. Parfois par clitoris. Tantôt utilisé pour provoquer, tantôt comme méthode de connaissance.

Transgression: appartient à la période 1968-1974. Transgression sociale, sémantique, syntaxique et sexuelle. Sera par la suite remplacé par les mots marginalité et vision.

Text: "The text, the notion of text, has been, as we well know, subjected in the past few decades to several transformations; most have been a response to the necessity for politico-sexual subversion. The textual site has become the repository for the body, sex, the city, and rupture, as well as the theory that it generates, which in turn regenerates text." *The Aerial Letter*.

Utopia: "I said with a taste of salt in the mouth, on the subject of Utopia beginning with the word woman that Utopia was not going to ensure our insertion into reality but that a Utopian testimony on our part could stimulate in us a quality of emotion favourable for our insertion into history." *Picture Theory*.

W   o   m   a   n   :

....

26 janvier 1983. Neuf heures vingt-quatre. Assise à ma table de travail, je cherche à éviter le quotidien, ce continu durable qui n'a de cesse qu'au moment où l'on ne parvient plus adéquatement à le nommer réalité. Autour de moi, la réalité. J'essaie d'être concrète. Tout ressemble à ce que j'imagine. Ma vie n'est qu'un tissu de mots. Aujourd'hui, j'ai relu quelques pages de ce que d'autres appellerai

jamais eu de journal intime. Tout au plu

lesquels j'inscris une fois ou deux par anne

année à l'autre, le texte varie peu. En gén

sans plus, je referme le cahier. Il m'arriv

D'avoir à écrire j'existe est une preuve qui

C'est la moindre des choses que de ne pas

preuve qu'on existe. Sans doute quoique de

en faire chaque jour la preuve. Certaines

d'autres se tordent de rire, d'autres se frott

faire jaillir le feu, d'autres se penchent su:

qu'une existence remplie de mots c'est c

cosmos; d'autres disent qu'exister c'est par

qu'exister c'est tracer un chemin avec sa

l'infini recommencé de la matière. *Dix heures vingt et une secondes*. Chaque instant a son importance pour ce qui s'éveille en moi du seul fait de penser à l'instant. Si la vie est faite d'instants précieux, on ne peut pas en dire autant du quotidien. Aussi, d'un instant à l'autre suis-je en train de m'inventer comme ce matin, un avant-midi ensoleillé, glacial, blanc. Aveuglant. Terriblement blanc. C'est le temps qu'il fait: blanc et

324

lumière. La lumière prend toute la place, s'infiltre dans l'avant-midi silencieux. Toute la chambre est envahie de mille structures qui comblent l'espace et le vide rapidement laissant ainsi les objets familiers sans ombre. Il n'y a d'ailleurs dans cette chambre que l'indispensable: le papier, le stylo, la table et moi. Et le givre m'aveugle, c'est le givre; ne

ma vie, ne me demandez pas ce qu'elle

rnal m'aveugle. Quelle étrange matinée

s cinquante. Qu'y a-t-il de si intime dans

partagé, entamé par la lecture d'autrui?

nt l'expression Mono no aware pour

des choses". 19 mars 1983. Tout cela:

p d'énergie et de désespoir. Mais j'avais

vant, ralentir l'acte d'écriture. Je l'avais

sant entre chaque mot que j'ai appris à

aussi appris à voir venir les blancs, à les

en faire tout à fait l'écho. Les blancs que

: en fait tellement remplis de pensées, de

ıs et d'audaces qu'on ne peut traduire tout

'est-à-dire par un autre blanc, celui-là

visuel. C'est dans le blanc que quiconque écrit, tremble, meurt et renaît. Avant et après le blanc tout va bien puisqu'il y a le texte. Et ça remplit bien la vie, un texte! Tout texte est un échantillon, c'est-à-dire une petite quantité que l'on montre pour donner une idée de l'ensemble. Tout texte est exemplaire parce qu'il témoigne du processus de la pensée, dans sa plus simple expression comme dans sa plus exploréenne trajectoire. Montréal, lundi 27 novembre 1995. Un autre projet de livre. Soleil.

Books are from the past. No need to panic.

Yale: Debout les yeux levés vers une **si** immense colonne de livres, j'observe les jeux d'ocre et de bourgogne, la lumière sur l'épine des ouvrages. Les murs de la bibliothèque sont en marbre transparent et les livres je les imagine dégageant une odeur de cuir et de poussière. Plus loin, la Bible de Gutenberg, ouverte comme les ailes déployées d'un grand **SILENCE** oiseau messager. Premier livre imprimé. Emotion. From copying to printing. La Bible, dit-on, fut vendue par des moines durant la dépression qui suivit la première guerre mondiale. Only money could bring the book in New Haven. A quelques trois mille kilomètres de là, la bibliothèque du troisième millénaire abritera onze millions de volumes. Les tours de 80 mètres de haut encadreront un jardin des délices où personne ne pourra SILENCE entrer. Il faudra lire et apprendre à faire du jardin un objet de désir au milieu de Paris. *S I L E N C E* Université de New York à Buffalo: entre les étagères pleines d'archives, je m'amuse pleine de vie avec la canne de James Joyce. Plus tard en me penchant sur les manuscrits, je remarquerai qu'il soulignait en rouge et vert ou jaune ne sais plus s'il raturait. Aperçu aussi "Another manuscript of "The Cyclops" episode. A late draft of the text from the end of 1919 consisting of two large sheets of paper." One day Beth Miller from San Diego went à la Bibliothèque nationale du Québec pour y consulter le manuscrit de *These our mothers*. Elle y trouva des traces de biscuits et d'eau répandue ainsi que la page d'un livre à colorier. Je donnai mon consentement et elle fit des photos. Dans mon dernier roman, deux femmes

et si une image valait mille mots

l'écriture avait agrandi le fossé entre la réalité et les pensées. Puis, elle l'avait comblé patiemment partiellement avec un choeur de *je* inquiets, propulsés têtes chercheuses, dans l'aventure de la "chose" écrite, aujourd'hui si énorme que la pensée pour résumer passait directement par l'image de synthèse.

la langue qui agite le plexus, serre le coeur, la gorge et
autres muscles habiles à se manifester soudain comme
des traits d'esprit dans le corps, cette même langue s'en
remet à l'oeil pour étaler sa toute-puissante turbulence
pendant que *ma* main. Elle trace à deux pas de là de moi
des signes et des oscillations entre mots et mort signés
ignés se détachant soudain sur fond blanc, se détachent
les uns des autres, certains allant à la dérive, à contre-
sens, d'autres revenant sur leur chemin, aptes à rattraper
le temps perdu ou à signaler quelques contradictions
entre les hémisphères du cerveau. Encore elle témoigne
résolument de la grande variété de sensations qui
fissurent le temps de notre présence.
Le manuscrit est sans doute un palimpseste de l'identité
je veux dire qu'il est toujours réécrit sur les traces de
quelques associations libres alimentées dans l'enfance par
on ne sait quel hasard sémantique. Le manuscrit donne
à penser que la nature de nos désirs est de nous associer
en permanence à l'idée de recommencement. Toujours
menacé par le temps, l'humidité, la poussière et le feu,
le manuscrit témoigne de notre passage dans le temps
quotidien de la faute et de la rature, de notre inénarrable
vulnérabilité au contact de l'air et de la langue
maternelle. Le manuscrit est preuve à l'appui que dans
l'écriture, mot effacé n'attend pas l'autre.

"D'une main la femme rapproche le dictionnaire. Pendant un moment, sa main reste appuyée sur la couverture comme si on allait l'assermenter." *Baroque d'aube (1995)*

Tous ces textes écrits en tournant les pages du dictionnaire pour échapper à la banalité du sens commun. Ce sont les textes écrits avec le trésor (1050; du latin thesaurus, du grec Thêsauros) qui m'ont procuré le plus de plaisir. Avec le dictionnaire, il m'était facile de mettre de côté le petit moi de vertige. Je pouvais alors naviguer des heures entières allant d'homonyme en synonyme, scrutant l'étymologie, amoureuse des verbes réfléchis et réciproques. Fascinée par les pluriels difficiles, les familles de mots et les traits d'union inopportuns, je déployais les mots, les ouvrais en éventail comme un jeu de cartes. Toujours un sens nouveau apparaissait, atout de hasard ou libre association fructueuse qui me donnait simultanément plaisir et matière à réflexion. J'ai souvent affirmé ne pas avoir d'imagination mais une aptitude à imaginer entre les mots, dans l'interstice du sens la matière énergisante qui permet au sens de faire des boucles, laminaires gracieux qui font tourner la tête d'une ivresse sans nom.

Fouillant dans le dictionnaire comme d'autres creusent le sol pour y chercher des preuves de vie ancienne, j'ai toujours senti le besoin de comprendre jusqu'à la racine comment chaque mot pouvait sortir de son lit comme une rivière ou, soudainement attiré par une source lumineuse, bifurquer et tromper toutes les attentes.

A tort ou à raison, nous associons la liberté au futur comme si les deux mots formaient un couple moralement compatible. A l'épreuve du temps. Le futur est une rumeur continue qui intoxique l'énergie du présent, nous tient constamment sur nos gardes. Au futur, la diversité d'autrui revient au même: le caractère effrayant de notre aptitude au voyage et au vertige des grands espaces et de la promiscuité. Le futur nous enracine dans la fiction.

*

Can we develop new datas while arguing on the basis of a meaningful ludic behavior in language?

*

The future is all over the place. Should I relax? In one moment I still exist. Full speed: ratrapper le sujet aérien et bien respirer une main sur mon sexe, l'autre rapprochée du siècle virtuel.

*

Pouvoir faire dans la langue commerce d'émotions et change de valeurs avec des figures de style qui tiennent mal dans nos mains. Au bout de nos doigts: un peu de libido, de détresse et d'autrui, parfois colère, avant-garde et fragments mais au bout des doigts encore la limite est un silence recommencé. Virtual breathing among the alphabet as an expension of time.

*

Caught between existence, exit and extension of the brain, the voice and the self, what's next if I move slowly toward a poetic and the wild urban crowd trying to reach beyond the beyond of language and the multitude of *I for one*.

Quelle étrange sensation! Empreinte d'une légèreté coupable car sortir précipitamment du langage et de son ventre riche en appétit et fureur incite à transformer chose dense du sujet en jeux et sauts cursifs sur la surface jeune du futur.

Quelle étrange sensation! Tenir dans sa main le sens du mot érosion en pensant que quelque part une femme me donne encore envie d'écrire à cause des syllabes qui tombent à la renverse en frôlant le rose éros de nos lèvres.

Il y a toujours dans nos gènes une lueur d'émotion qui finit par déplacer le sens et nous faire traverser le quotidien, les tempes imprégnées de poésie, de sons et de ferveur. De toute manière, il faudra frôler l'abstraction puisque l'âme du poète est ainsi composée d'organes si sensibles qu'ils s'éveillent au moindre contact de l'air et des voyelles qui entrent dans la composition des soupirs.

Honestly! I have a humanist sense of vertigo which provides for a manic I can't get rid off. I was trained to believe in the future as a proof *de la supériorité des êtres pensants*. I got a free ride from Renaissance to the Enlightenments. Then stopped over Mallarmé's pages where I spent a great deal of time indulging in my natural inclination for figures and abstraction. Then I flew over surrealism landscape enjoying the perfect match between images and the colours of desire, later on landing in the pages of Maurice Blanchot and Roland Barthes as well as in my own literature where I eventually became a poet. From there I kept moving from books to books until I encountered essays written by feminists. I started meeting with women and dating with those I could feel in real time with a lesbian body full of utopian ideas.

Kept moving, exploring. From one city to the other. Nights were full of discussions and excitement. Kept moving until recently when suddenly I was caught in a turbulence for which I had no written explanation nor experience of. Gradually I could feel that I was developing a strange inability to convey my ideas with certitude or should I say to connect properly with time. Felt as if I had entered another space another present. Life went on as usual. People were walking on the street, talking on terraces about their poetics. Reality was going on as history. Reality was from the past and my head full of electricity.

This explains why for the moment phrasing a poetics seems an impossible task. I need time to figure out things. Need to see if my humanist realm of values can translate into an electronicscape. Isn't it ironic that such values as present, sensations, synchrony, perfect matching between the senses and the mind which have always been at the core of my poetics as natural resources for consciousness have been transformed into technico-cultural devices allowing the body to escape the burden of emotion and memory.

332

Polir son texte, ses phrases, sa vie.
Danger de faire pâlir la réalité. Des gens
ont parlé de la mode, d'autres s'en sont
tenus au phénomène des générations,
affirmant que certaines époques plus que
d'autres facilitaient l'émergence de
nouveaux cris. Une femme a déclaré ne
pas savoir distinguer entre le cri et le si
d'une époque.

Absurde cette idée qu'il existe des
époques faciles en écriture. Comme si le
sens n'était pas toujours à recommencer
au milieu de questions chargées de
mythes et d'électricité. La connaissance
innée que nous avons de la mort, de la
beauté ne peut qu'éprouver nos
croyances, raviver en nous l'ivresse des
sens. Non, il n'y a jamais eu d'époques
faciles. La mort et la violence, la
science sont toujours contemporaines,
cerceaux de feu qui fascinent les fauves
pleins d'entrain que nous sommes,
enclins à refuser les temps morts et les
bouts faciles.

they say who are you they mean
we need a story I never answer
how could I repeat sorry I won't
slip the taken for granted of sorrow snow or sky
into my life as if I could
make a real story out of
flurries and flying glasses over continents
so the reader can absorb the next war
get excited about the many layers
of meaning on my shoulders in my eyes
next year I promise to recapitulate

shadows on my shoulders shelter an unknown
meaning
I always pay attention to the raw version of today
before I answer
with a story one should never start
the next war at night before falling asleep

poems can go on as long as we
long for images or say: look
another narrative coming this way
the next war is on time

say darkness for example say it twice
so you can feel it on your shoulders
thinking: should I write this down
or simply write till morning blue sky
matches the colour of ink on my page
lights it
enough for me to get excited

BRIEF CASE: A PLACE OF ONE'S OWN

As if long ago yesterday and tomorrow simultaneously. Today, blue sky, smells of Montréal. In front of the house, Vimy Park, autumn. My so-called work table and my numerous pens with which I alternate images and silence while thinking that for all time I will only have a single body to compare books, sunsets, to speak about the world, ideas and objects produced down through the centuries. A single body to delight myself, to adapt myself. For understanding the vast undertaking of madness, of reason and of creation, a single body to decide on the present and on the future.

There are books. Museums. Places: Venice, Santorini, the Grand Canyon, Kyoto, pavillions. There are the multitude of images, a frightening number of skulls, masses of humanity, spread out in the stinking grass. There is that, of course, which persists: the belief in certain humanist values because it is fascinating to believe in the species, it requires highly moral performances, demonstrations of hope or simply beliefs that reassure our genes, the echo of our voices let loose in time.

Also there are various ways to remake the sentence, to manage it so that it makes a good impression, all the difference. Small or strong emotion in poetry is calculated by the word at the end of the arm, the horizon or *deep down* in the chest like a certainty.

The author wishes to make clear that the reason she wrote the original in French and English was that it was destined for an English-language publication.

Writing these pages, again to dive into the unedited. This text, that I would like to be in action, full of fire, of images and of questions like a movement of thought in the process of gaining ground on the contemporary disquiet or to explode in the acuity of the senses and those questions born of change and of accelerated sense.

The unedited. Notice how without my knowing, I just testified to the obsession that marks all of my books. To produce the unedited, to venture into the unknown, navigate among the frightening number of semantic permutations. To explore, always intrigued, revolted by the *nonsense of violence* and fascinated *by the full meaning of being alive, catching up with the virtual dimensions of the self and its nervous system.* To produce objects of thought and emotion that can be shared. To live with arms filled with metaphors, going towards an encounter with a second self hooked on shows, on dizziness and on lucidity.

Reality: we say that fiction emerges from the border of thoughts that recompose it. Later, great symbols stick to our skin: we must begin in the middle of surprising questions, the joy of living and other anguishing feelings that multiply the possibility of collisions. To begin again because we raised our eyes prematurely

of the page not knowing exactly where the obsession of writing might take us. So we move roses, highways, the horizon if necessary the sea in another dimension. And everything remains to be begun again because during the brief time and irreversibility of the instant we closed our eyes from pleasure

MY PRIVATE VOCABULARY

Body: takes part in the trio text/body/cortex. "All bodies carry within themselves a project of sensual high technology; writing is its hologram."

Dawn: "Dawn attracts, this is certain, dawn fascinates. She is at the edge of night, at the edge of the soul a quiet certitude, an appeasement of the eyes smitten with changes and utopias." Returns each time that hope and nostalgia come together. The word appears in the title of the first collection *Dawn at the season* (1965) and the most recent book *Baroque at dawn* (1995) by the author.

Death: forbidden word yet used frequently especially in unpublished works. Appears as early as 1970 with the publication of the collection *The White Center (1970)*.

Délire: See *Lovhers. Délire amoureux. Jouissance.* Has sometimes been used to register the flood of words that spring forth from women once they become aware of the vast extent of patriarchal violence and lies.

Dé/lire (Un/read): used to translate one method for analyzing patriarchal texts.

Desire: used in the sense of project, feverishness and intensity. Appears at the origin of the writing act. Sometimes replaces the word energy.

Energy: appears in the lesbian sequence constituted by the books *Lovhers, Picture Theory, The Aerial Letter* and *Under tongue*. Afterwards, used to analyze those forces present in the process of literary creation. "Imagination goes through the skin the skin is energy."

Eye: key word appearing in most texts. Associated with writing and with reading. Gaze-desire-horizon. Another grouping: hologram, screen, virtual reality. See: Act of the eye in *These our Mothers* (1983) and the collection *Double impression* (1984).

Horizon: translates a need for space, for freedom. Could be associated with the definition the author sometimes gives of herself as an explorer. To be seen in relation to the sea and the desert. See also the word dawn.

Light: must be associated with intensity, with beauty, with blindness and paradoxically with lucidity. "On the thread of light I suspend poetry" in *Dawn at the season* (1965). "For in full light our whole body rears up, aura of being or fabulous animal, gifted with splendor and ingenuity." *Mauve Desert* (1990)

Lucidity: serves sometimes as a synonym for the word consciousness. Is strictly associated with honor, with morality, with honesty, with integrity, as well as humanist values. To be lucid is a proof of humanity.

Mauve: used for the pleasure of its sounds and for the color to which the word refers. Associated with lesbian love, with the dawn.

Montréal: birthplace. Pronounce in French. Don't forget the accent that makes the difference. Appears above all in the novel *French kiss*. Constitutes a ground for the themes of the city and of modernity. Among the street names that recur frequently: rue Cherrier, rue Saint-Laurent, rue Saint-Denis, rue Sherbrooke; other places: le Carré Saint-Louis, le Parc Lafontaine, le Vieux-Montréal

Shadow: certainly a key word in my poetry. Asked about this, I've never known how to justify or explain the frequency of the word in my writings. First hypothesis: the sweetness and the gravity of the sounds that make up the word. Second hypothesis: the question of the double.

The trio *Ombre* (Shadow) /*Sombre* (Somber) /*Tombe* (Tomb) appears in a collection from 1968.

Sex: rarely used. Replaced by the words body, skin and tongue. Sometimes by clitoris. Sometimes used to provoke, sometimes as a method of knowledge.

Transgression: belongs the period 1968-1974. Social, semantic, syntatic and sexual transgression. Will be replaced later by the words marginality and vision.

Text: "The text, the notion of text, has been, as we well know, subjected in the past few decades to several transformations; most have been a response to the necessity for politico-sexual subversion. The textual site has become the repository for the body, sex, the city, and rupture, as well as the theory that it generates, which in turn regenerates text." *The Aerial Letter* (1988).

Utopia: "I said with a taste of salt in the mouth, on the subject of Utopia beginning with the word woman that Utopia was not going to ensure our insertion into reality but that a Utopian testimony on our part could stimulate in us a quality of emotion favourable for our insertion into history." *Picture Theory* (1991).

W   o   m   a   n   :
....

January 26, 1983. 9:45. Seated at my work table, I seek to avoid the quotidian, that durable continuum without end except at the moment when one no longer is able to adequately call it reality. All around me, reality. I try to be concrete. Everything appears as I imagine. My life is nothing but a fabric of words. Today, I reread a few pages of what others would call my diary. But I've never had a *journal intime*. At most, three black notebooks in which I write some short sentences once or twice a year. From one year to the next, the text varies little. Generally, I write "I am suffering" and, no more, I close the notebook. Sometimes I find that I write: I exist. Being able to write I exist is a proof of sorts that is sufficient in times of crisis. It is the smallest little thing not having every day to make something that proves one exists. Certainly however millions of women must make that attempt (*faire la preuve*) every day. Some cry, others grimace, others convulse with laughter, others rub their hands together as if trying to start a fire, others wrap themselves around a child, others think that an existence filled with words is like a black hole in the cosmos; others say that existence is to speak within matter or even that existence is tracing a path with her mouth and her breath in the always renewing infinity of matter. *Ten o'clock and twenty-one seconds.* Each instant has its importance in what arises in me from the simple act of thinking about the instant. If life is made of precious instants, one cannot say the same thing about the quotidian. Also, from one instant to another I'm in the process of inventing myself like this morning, a time before noon that is sunny, glacial, white. Blinding. Terribly white. It's the weather: white and light.

The light takes up all the space, infiltrates into the silent morning. The entire room is invaded by a thousand structures that fill the space and the void quickly leaving even familiar objects without a shadow. Otherwise there is nothing in this room except what is indispensable; paper, pen, table and me. And the frost blinds me, it is the frost, don't ask what will become of my life, don't ask what it has been. I won't speak about it. This journal blinds me. What a strange morning has passed for someone who loves to write. *Ten fifty*. What is there so intimate about a journal that could not be shared, engaged with by a reader? Intimate. The Japanese use the expression *Mono no aware* to signify "the emotional intimacy of things." *March 19, 1983*. All of that: understanding has cost me enormous energy and despair. But I had one advantage: I was able, by writing, to slow down the act of writing. I've always done this. It is by slowing down between each word that I learned how to identify, to compare. To laugh. I also learned to see the whites coming, to hear them without ever being completely able to sound their echo. The whites that one calls white spaces are in fact so filled with thoughts, with words, with sensations, with hesitations and with chances to be taken that it is impossible to translate all that by a tautology, that is, another white, this one visual. It is in the white that whoever writes, trembles, dies and is reborn. Before and after the white everything's fine because there's the text. And that fills up a life so well, a text! Each text is a sample, that is, a little bit that one shows to give an idea of the whole. Each text is exemplary because it bears witness to the process of thinking, in its simplest expression as in its most exploratory trajectory.

Montréal, Monday November 27, 1995. Another book project. Sun.

342

the tongue/language that agitates the plexus, constricts
the heart, the throat and other muscles able to manifest
itself suddenly like features of spirit in the body, the
same tongue/language turns back on the eye to stage its
all powerful turbulence while *my* hand. It traces at two
steps from there from me signs and oscillations between
words and dead igneous signs coming loose suddenly
the white background, coming loose one from the other
some of them reaching the limit, against the sense,
others retracing their path, apt to recapture lost time, or
to signal those contradictions between the hemispheres of
the brain. Again it bears resolute witness to the great
variety of sensations that fissure the time of our
presence.

The manuscript is undoubtedly a palimpsest of identity,
I mean that it is always rewritten over the traces of those
free associations fed during childhood by who knows
what semantic chance. The manuscript allows one to
think that the nature of our desires is to associate
ourselves permanently with the idea of new beginning.
Always threatened by time, humidity, dust and fire, the
manuscript bears witness to our passage through the
quotidian time of error and erasure, but also our
unerring vulnerability in contact with the air and the
maternal tongue. The manuscript is final proof (*preuve
à l'appui*) that in writing, the effaced word doesn't wait
for another.

343

"With her hand a woman nears the dictionary. For a moment, her hand rests poised on the cover as though ready to testify." *Baroque at dawn (1995)*

All these texts written by turning the pages of the dictionary in order to escape the banality of common knowledge. The texts written with the thesaurus (French *trésor,* 1050; from Latin *thesaurus,* from Greek *Thêsauros*) are those that have given me the most pleasure. With the dictionary, it was easy for me to put aside the little vertiginous I. I could navigate for hours on end going from homonym to synonym, inspecting etymologies, in love with reflexive and reciprocal verbs. Fascinated by difficult plurals, word families and unexpected hyphens, I unfurled the words, fanned them open as in a game of cards. Always a new sense appeared, the summit of chance or free fructifying association that simultaneously gave me pleasure and material for reflection. I have often affirmed having no imagination but rather an aptitude to imagine between the words, in the interstice of sense the energizing matter that permits sense to make the links, graceful laminaries that make the head spin with a nameless rapture.

Digging in the dictionary as others turn the soil to find evidence there of ancient lives, I always felt the need to understand down to the root how each word could emerge from its bed like a river or suddenly be drawn to a luminous source to split in two and confound all expectations.

What a strange sensation! Imprinted with a culpable lightness since to leave suddenly from language and from its womb rich in appetite and fury incites a transformation from the dense thing of the subject into games and cursive leaps on the young surface of the future.

What a strange sensation! To hold in one's hand the sense of the word erosion while thinking that somewhere a woman gives me once more the desire to write because of the syllables falling in reverse while lightly touching the rosy eros of our lips.

There is always in our genes a spark of emotion that ends up displacing sense and making us cross the quotidian, temples impregnated with poetry, with sounds and with fervor. In any event, it's necessary to touch abstraction lightly because the soul of the poet is in this way composed of organs so sensible that they awaken at the slightest contact with the air and the vowels that enter into the composition of sighs.

Polish her text, her sentences, her life. Danger of causing reality to fade. Some spoke of fashion, others were concerned with the phenomenon of generations, affirming that certain eras more than others facilitated the emergence of new cries. One woman announced she was incapable of distinguishing between the cry and the what if (*si*) of an era.

How absurd the idea that there are some easy eras for writing. As if sense were not always to begin again surrounded by questions charged with myth and electricity. The innate knowledge that we have of death, and of beauty can't help but test our beliefs, revitalize in us the intoxication of sense. No, there have never been any easy eras. Death and violence, science are always contemporary, circles of fire that fascinate the beasts full of energy that we are, inclined to refuse dead times and easy endings.

French texts translated by Peter Baker

Carolyn Forché

On Subjectivity

The difference between the living and the dead is that the living talk while the dead do not.

Our body decays when it is suddenly robbed of its language, no longer conversant with itself, unable to form, to inform, to confirm.

We speak to the dead in order to bring them back to life. All we manage is the illusion of a general resurrection.

Light also is a word which begets other, explosive words.

Night, reign of respite after the explosion. Blind regrouping of our lights.

(Edmond Jabès, *El*, p. 11)

We speak to sustain the body: our texts are life-forms summoning the haunted and haunting particular. But this is not a fatal restriction for the powers of speech and the rigors of writing—this is Walter Benjamin's "weak Messianism"—the dream of the redemption of the past in and through history and historiography—at its best, because most demystified. Words on words on words—a vast begetting away from the past in all its painful particulars. *Pathos* here belongs to the present in its blind and necessary orientation towards speech. This pathos is not pity, but a sadness born of the knowledge of its task: that of knowledge and remembrance.

I was hurt into poetry by pathos and while I respect and read for it in others, in the course of my work, I have come to suspect that pathos might well be suspect, a relic of pre-modernist nostalgia, banished by writers as diverse as Flaubert, Eliot, Mallarmé, Valéry, and the Surrealists. For a poet and a reader in the late twentieth century, the problem with pathos is that it seems irredeemably subject-centered.

The classical rhetoricians locate *Pathos* in the speaking voice, as one of the three graces of persuasion, accompanied by *Ethos,* the credibility of the speaker, and *Logos,* the truth of the speech. In a century where blank appeals have become normative, where *Logos* might be as much an enemy as its opposite, where conviction comes more from the listener's position than the speaker's stance, *Pathos* seems a dangerous attitude. For this reason a fierce demystifier of ideology, Paul de Man, was particularly harsh on the humanistic pieties of pathos in literary criticism. However, to sacrifice pathos in the name of a demystified anti-humanism might have humanly dangerous consequences. How can we divorce pathos from the burdens of the subject? Can the after-image of the voice be saved while jettisoning the narcissistic rage of the ego? What is the subject, what the object, of pathos for us, at the end of the twentieth century?

My sense of discomfort with the monologic first-person seems to be shared by many of my colleagues and contemporaries, especially those who have an affinity for French poetry, German theory, and Gallic philosophy. My allegiances and my difficulties are signaled by the title of my third book—*The Angel of History*—derived from Benjamin's "Theses on The Philosophy of History." Benjamin, as Theodor Adorno noted, was a committed opponent of bourgeois subjectivity and the false immanence of modernity, and I have found myself drawn to this idea in his writing, as well as toward the thought of Maurice Blanchot, Edmond Jabès and Emmanuel Levinas—those so infused with Heideggerian thought that they wish to dissolve the speaker, the fiction(s) of the speaking voice, into the play of Being, of Language, of Differance (at least as a first critical step of their project). The pathos of these writers seems to inhere in their own asceticism, in their determination to give up the illusion of the self, of knowledge, of centeredness, of control. They are willing to forgo the urgent fiction(s) of undistorted communication. There are counter-pleasures, of course, to be found in such writers—in the thematics of play, slippage; in the sense of liberation Nietzsche celebrates as the Dionysian in *The Birth of Tragedy* before he falls into the Wagnerian hyperbole underwriting that book. Similarly, Blanchot locates an important, deeply ethical moment in the act of writing. It is an moment of affirmation:

348

> The work requires of the writer that he [sic] lose everything
> he might construe as his own "nature, that he lose all character and
> that...he becomes an empty place where the impersonal affirmation
> emerges."

The affirmation of *what does not cease speaking*, the voice of Language, of the Other, requires the effacement of the self, whose presence, if we can call it that, is only legible in its silence, in its rupture of the stream of language.

While I am inclined toward what could be called the "pathos of the Absolute Other," and willing to give up the imperialism of the self, the controlling eye and the terrified because illusionary mouth, I am also disturbed by the submission of the space the *I* fills to the external authority of a complete alterity. I am bothered by Blanchot's merely structural affirmations, those *yeses* that are—by his insistence—devoid of content. This effacement of content, especially in regard to time, disturbs me as well.

Karen Mills-Courts' account of John Ashbery's poetics, of his acceptance of *chronos*, "time as endless succession," and his rejection of *kairos*, the dream of transcendence, is disturbing. The pathos of Ashbery's authenticity thus lies in its ineluctable sense of loss, in the concession that poetry serves as the epitaph of the illusionary self. Mills-Courts seems to return us to a nostalgia for the self, to a "longing to join with the selves distributed into the acts that have been left behind."

I wonder if this longing for the self alienated by time is not the reverse of the deliberate effacement of the self by the writer in the face of the impersonalities of language and time: both place the writer's self at the center of their endeavor, both care more for their inscriptions, their divagations, than for the calls of the Other. The sheer abstractness of the OTHER should be a suggestive: it is alterity devoid of content, devoid of feeling.

Such a criticism, of course, would be Benjamin's view: the empty time of "chronicity" is nothing less than the destruction of experience, of happiness. Empty time is reified time, made abstract and interchangeable by the exchange principle itself. The modern world of routinized wage-labor has emptied out the filled spaces of life: the *Jetztzeiten,* the *Nowtimes,* of messianic time. If this would seem a nostalgia for presence, it is worth remembering that De Man derived his defense of allegory from Benjamin's first book. Benjamin, no less than Derrida, is deeply worried by Representation, by the conquering reach of the inflated, narcissistic ego. He attacks that ego and tries to circumscribe its reach from the end of the First World War to his last work, "Theses on the Philosophy of History," written at the beginning of World War II. That hint of nostalgia serves an important function. Benjamin does not want to sacrifice alterity to random Otherness: he retains the pathos of truth (as Nietzsche calls it [*Beyond Good and Evil*]) to counteract reification, to redeem the other in its concrete particularity. As Adorno noted, Benjamin was the philosopher of happiness and was therefore the philosopher of suffering. The radical aspect of Benjamin's thought is that it not only seeks to succor suffering nature, as in Adorno's *Negative Dialectics,* but also the deep suffering of Second Nature, the pathos of outdated commodities. In his work, *kairos* entails the redemption of each particular from the forgetfulness of the pseudo-progress of global commodification: as Benjamin says in one of his notes, "the frill on the dress will lead us to eternity." For Benjamin, the truth of the particular should burn through the negligence imposed by a falsified experience of time itself.

Benjaminian pathos—and his work is thick with pain—does not depend on the narcissistic self-projections of the perceiving self, but it does not get rid of selves: the particular is just that, particular, peculiar, one-of-a-kind. Against the plains of phenomenology, he posits the concrete minutiae of the everyday, of the world, of the suffering of other people and other things. A work of quotations—Benjamin's dream— would not efface the voice, but allow other voices to speak, would re-situate the so-called author of the text as the organizer of the montage— a high modernist notion, but still worthwhile, for it grants identity, albeit fractured and unfulfilled, to others, *real* others. It entails neither a grandiose self-effacement nor an equally grandiose nostalgia for a never-quite-existent self. It locates pathos in the object itself, and does not register that pathos in terms of the subject's own language (as if the subject could *own* language), but rather in the language that surrounds the object. (This might sound like a deeply metaphysical strain of thought and it is. One might want, however, to see in it a similarity to Ludwig Wittgenstein's philosophy, both early and late: the philosophical despair of the *Tractatus* and the commitment to the everyday of the *Investigations*.)

It is for these reasons that I have found Benjamin a source of sustenance, a provocation, and for these that I have found myself addressing more and more the illuminating translations of Edmond Jabès by Rosmarie Waldrop.

Jabès gives us a text profound in its diversities, in its beautiful tailoring of words to names, of names to the world beyond us. There might be a danger in Jabès's play with the notion of the Word, his Kabbalistic/Mallarméan insistence on silence and the letter, if it served nothing but the narcissistic regard of Representation with itself. But Jabès' monumental *Book of Questions* bears with it the threat of another silence, real and illimitable: the silence that threatened to attend the *Shoah*. At the silent center of the work stands the woman who is already dead, Sarah, whose pathos inheres less in her suffering (she is remarkably affirmative for one deceased) than in her absence. If Death is the horizon within which Jabès's text is written, the text imagines itself as the necessary illusion of Life itself.

The rupturing silence of the Shoah hurls us into its aftermath, and demands a turn toward *Ethos*, and one's infinite responsibility to the other one (*l'autrui*). The question of subjectivity might then be: to whom or what, if anything, am I subject? Pre-Shoah thinkers might say *to the object of consciousness or knowledge, to Being*. Derrida and the deconstructionists might say *to nothing, an illusion of my own power or force, a play of linguistic signfiers*. Levinas, Buber, and Blanchot might say *to the other one, and my infinite responsibility for, the unlimited nature of my obligation for, the life of the other one, even for her death*. Franz

Rosenzweig in this connection might say *to the creation of the universe,* which may be the same thing.

My preoccupation with questions of ethics and aesthetics (which are, for Wittgenstein, conflated), has been nurtured by the thought of Wittgenstein, who believed ethics beyond the realm of language, and Mikhail Bakhtin, whose dialogics attempt to hold open the meaning of ethical utterance. Wittgenstein and Bakhtin both oppose any theoreticism which might diminish the rich complexity of life in its experiential particularity, or determine creativity as a mode of mere discovery. Bakhtin foregrounds the cacophony of voices, the polyphonic and dialogic heteroglossia of human languages, interacting whether they are contentious or parodic. It is in concrete particularity that the world is apprehended, and by poets, encoded in the "language game" of literary-poetical performance and inscription, against what Wittgenstein perceived as the cage of language and its limits, to be decoded dialogically by the reader/audience. In this practice, I am only and always beginning to test the world-boundary of subjectivity.

"Nothing conclusive has yet taken place in the world, the ultimate word of the world and about the world has not yet been spoken, the world is open and free, everything is still in the future and will always be in the future."

"What the poem translates, I propose we call experience, on condition that this word be taken literally—from Latin, *experiri*: the risky crossing…, and this is why one can refer, strictly speaking, to a poetic existence, if existence it is that perforates a life and tears it, at times putting us beside ourselves."

"…in the poem, where the poet writes himself, he does not recognize himself, for he does not become conscious of himself. He is excluded from the facile, humanistic hope that by writing, or 'creating,' he would transform his dark experience into greater consciousness. On the contrary: dismissed, excluded from what is written—unable even to be present by virtue of the non-presence of his very death—he has to renounce all conceivable relations of a self (either living or dying) to the poem which henceforth belongs to the other, or else will remain without any belonging at all. The poet is Narcissus to the extent that Narcissus is an anti-Narcissus: he who, turned away from himself—causing the detour of which he is the effect, dying of not recognizing himself—leaves the trace of what has not occurred."

"Writing leaves the trace of an original disaster which was not experienced in the first person precisely since it ruined this first person, reduced it to a ghostlike status, to being a 'me without me.'"

"Spellbound, the living have a choice between involuntary ataraxy—an esthetic life due to weakness—and the bestiality of the involved. Both are wrong ways of living. But some of both would be required for the right *désinvolture* and sympathy. Once overcome, the culpable self-preservation urge has been confirmed, confirmed precisely, perhaps, by the threat that has come to be ceaselessly present. The only trouble with self-preservation is that we cannot help suspecting the life to which it attaches us of turning into something that makes us shudder: into a specter, a piece of the world of ghosts, which our waking consciousness perceives to be nonexistent."

"In what extreme delicacy, at what slight and singular point, could a language come together in an attempt to recapture itself in the stripped-down form, 'I speak?' Unless, of course, the void...of 'I speak'...were an absolute opening through which language endlessly spreads forth, while the subject—the 'I' who speaks—fragments, disperses, scatters, disappearing in that naked space."

"Listening, not to the words, but to the suffering that endlessly, from one word to the next, runs through words."

"Anything we say must, a priori, be only nonsense. Nevertheless, we thrust against the limits of language.... This thrust against the limits of language is ethics."

"We were aware that the visible earth is made of ashes, and that ashes signify something.... And we see now that the abyss of history is deep enough to hold us all. We are aware that a civilization has the same fragility as a life.... Everything has not been lost, but everything has sensed that it might perish."

"The writer, it is said, gives up saying 'I'."
—Carolyn Forché

Mikhail Bakhtin, Philippe Lacoue-Labarthe, Maurice Blanchot, Claire Nouvet, Theodor W. Adorno, Michel Foucault, Maurice Blanchot, Ludwig Wittgenstein, Paul Valéry, Michel Foucault.

Hive

                                                    the spirit
executed prodigious labors in the darkness whose writings are lost
into most unexpected light the glass hives
live only in the midst however abundant

as a society organizes itself and rises so does a shrinkage enter
so crowded does the too prosperous city become
the era of revolutions may close and work become the barricade
suddenly abandoning the generations to come
the abode of the future wrapped in a kind of shroud

inaudible to them the murmur that comes to us
not without prescience their summoning
as though nothing is happening will come back
and prefer what is not yet visible to that which is

Book Codes: I

We must know *whether*
And *if not*: then what is the task
very much on the surface
by means of finite signs
when one is frightened of the truth
"Are there simple things?"
    What depends on my life?
would be possible for me to write
like the film on deep water
over too wide chasms of thought
the world does not change
the visiual field has not a form like this
so many graces of fate
the boundary (not a part) of the world
mirrored in its use
nothing except what can be said

Book Codes: II

a field tunneled by mice the same thought continually
like two hands indissolubly clasped to begin
as if in a coffin and can therefore think of nothing else
how incomplete a moment is human life

fragments together into a story before the shape of the whole
like a madman—time and again torn from my mouth
out of a nearby chimney each child's hand was taken
though this is not a fairy tale explained in advance

the sign of the cross on an invisible face with the calm of a butcher
as if it bore witness to some truth
with whom every connection had been severed
as if in a coffin and can therefore think of nothing else

an afternoon swallowing down whole years its every hour
troops marching by in the snow until they are transparent
from the woods through tall firs a wood with no apparent end
cathedrals at the tips of our tongues with countries not yet seen

whoever can cry should come here

Book Codes: III

stories no more substantial than the clouds or what had been his face
the view, the wind, the light disposing of the bodies
who walked in the realm of dreams but like everything else

for our having tried to cross the river caught between walls,
one could hear a voice "Bear the unbearable"
and the broadcast was at an end

you might relay the message the rivers and mountains remained
the unseen figure of the enemy entirely covered
the central portion of their visual fields this blindness for names

the bone became black with flies again hatching in ruins
here were the black, burnt ceilings and boxes of flags
the walls covered with soot like a kitchen

smaller clouds spread out a golden screen
give the task of painting wounds
through the darkened town as though it had been light

at the moment of the birth of this cloud

Bob Perelman

Statement

I've been working in word-counted couplets for a few years now (from *Virtual Reality* to the current present: 96), and the form continues to strike me as interestingly unstable and usable. Couplets are the smallest stanzas and they show, as compactly as possible, the spatial extravagance of poetry on the page. Counting words to make couplets might strike some readers as mechanical, and thus as unpoetic. But the mechanization of these couplets is far removed from the phrase and sound balancing of Pope or the semiotic unbalancing, or say doppel-ganger mimicry, of lines in Michael Palmer's work. It's a process applied to something larger: each couplet is clearly part, a foreign part, of ongoing passage. I often reline passages, changing them back and forth between poetry and prose (thanks to computer macros), and between 6 word-, 7 word-, 6/7 combination-, and uncounted couplets. I'll skip the particulars, but they're abacus-like dealings with hard returns and word spaces. Here my aggressive defensiveness wants to write: "If that's not mechanical, anti-transcendent, anti-inspiration, what is?" but that's not the whole story. This lining strategy, simultaneously elemental and artificial, casts odd effects (from my vantage anyway) on the most expository passages. I won't say a 'poetic' effect, because half the time I do feel like I'm signifying on poetry. But all the time I feel like I'm calling attention to the technical, material, external side of words without leading things into what is beginning to feel like the cul-de-sac of revolutionary textuality. That's a rather polemical way of putting it. Say that the couplets, with their dual vantage onto ordinary language and onto enumerative, spatial estrangement of that language, allow me to make capacious pieces. Messing around with the lines is now an integral part of my writing-rewriting process. I'm not trying to undo the social, cultural, epistemological category of poetry: I'm trying to make it larger, more in touch with the cacophonous, harmonic, good-faith, faithless, interesting rhetorics that surround it.

The Marginalization of Poetry

If poems are eternal occasions, then
the pre-eternal context for the following

was a panel on "The Marginalization
of Poetry" at the American Comparative

Literature Conference in San Diego, on
February 8, 1991, at 2:30 P.M.:

―――――――――

"The Marginalization of Poetry"—it almost
goes without saying. Jack Spicer wrote,

"No one listens to poetry," but
the question then becomes, who is

Jack Spicer? Poets for whom he
matters would know, and their poems

would be written in a world
in which that line was heard,

though they'd scarcely refer to it.
Quoting or imitating another poet's line

is not benign, though at times
the practice can look like flattery.

In the regions of academic discourse,
the patterns of production and circulation

are different. There, it—again—goes
without saying that words, names, terms

are repeatable: citation is the prime
index of power. Strikingly original language

is not the point; the degree
to which a phrase or sentence

fits into a multiplicity of contexts
determines how influential it will be.

"The Marginalization of Poetry": the words
themselves display the dominant *lingua franca*

of the academic disciplines and, conversely,
the abject object status of poetry:

it's hard to think of any
poem where the word "marginalization" occurs.

It is being used here, but
this may or may not be

a poem: the couplets of six
word lines don't establish an audible

rhythm; perhaps they aren't, to use
the Calvinist mercantile metaphor, "earning" their

right to exist in their present
form—is this a line break

or am I simply chopping up
ineradicable prose? But to defend this

(poem) from its own attack, I'll
say that both the flush left

and irregular right margins constantly loom
as significant events, often interrupting what

I thought I was about to
write and making me write something

else entirely. Even though I'm going
back and rewriting, the problem still

reappears every six words. So this,
and every poem, is a marginal

work in a quite literal sense.
Prose poems are another matter: but

since they identify themselves as poems
through style and publication context, they

become a marginal subset of poetry,
in other words, doubly marginal. Now

of course I'm slipping back into
the metaphorical sense of marginal which,

however, in an academic context is
the standard sense. The growing mass

of writing on "marginalization" is not
concerned with margins, left or right

—and certainly not with its own.
Yet doesn't the word "marginalization" assume

the existence of some master page
beyond whose justified (and hence invisible)

margins the panoplies of themes, authors,
movements, objects of study exist in

all their colorful, authentic, handlettered marginality?
This master page reflects the functioning

of the profession, where the units
of currency are variously denominated prose:

the paper, the article, the book.
All critical prose can be seen

as elongated, smooth-edged rectangles of writing,
the sequences of words chopped into

arbitrary lines by the typesetter (Ruth
in tears amid the alien corn),

and into pages by publishing processes.
This violent smoothness is the visible

sign of the writer's submission to
norms of technological reproduction. "Submission" is

not quite the right word, though:
the finesse of the printing indicates

that the author has shares in
the power of the technocratic grid;

just as the citations and footnotes
in articles and university press books

are emblems of professional inclusion. But
hasn't the picture become a bit

binary? Aren't there some distinctions to
be drawn? Do I really want

to invoke Lukács's "antinomies of bourgeois
thought" where, rather than a conceptually

pure science that purchases its purity
at the cost of an irrational

and hence foul subject matter, we
have the analogous odd couple of

a centralized, professionalized, cross-referenced criticism studying
marginalized, inspired (i.e., amateur), singular poetries?

Do I really want to lump
The Closing of the American Mind,

Walter Jackson Bate's biography of Keats,
and *Anti-Oedipus* together and oppose them

to any poem which happens to
be written in lines? Doesn't this

essentialize poetry in a big way?
Certainly some poetry is thoroughly opposed

to prose and does depend on
the precise way it's scored onto

the page: beyond their eccentric margins,
both Olson's *Maximus Poems* and Pound's

Cantos tend, as they progress, toward
the pictoral and gestural: in Pound

the Chinese ideograms, musical scores, hieroglyphs,
heart, diamond, club, and spade emblems,

little drawings of the moon and
of the winnowing tray of fate;

or those pages late in *Maximus*
where the orientation of the lines

spirals more than 360 degrees—one
spiralling page is reproduced in holograph.

These sections are immune to standardizing
media: to quote them you need

a photocopier not a word processor.
In a similar vein, the work

of some contemporary writers associated more
or less closely with the language

movement avoids standardized typographical grids and
is as self-specific as possible: Robert

Grenier's *Sentences*, a box of 500
poems printed on 5 by 8

notecards, or his recent work in
holograph, often scrawled; the variable leading

and irregular margins of Larry Eigner's
poems; Susan Howe's writing which uses

the page like a canvas—from
these one could extrapolate a poetry

where publication would be a demonstration
of private singularity approximating a neo-Platonic

vanishing point, anticipated by Klebnikov's handcolored,
single-copy books produced in the twenties.

Such an extrapolation would be inaccurate
as regards the writers I've mentioned,

and certainly creates a false picture
of the language movement, some of

whose members write very much for
a if not the public. But

still there's another grain of false
truth to my Manichean model of

a prosy command-center of criticism and
unique bivouacs on the poetic margins

so I'll keep this binary in
focus for another spate of couplets.

Parallel to such self-defined poetry, there's
been a tendency in some criticism

to valorize if not fetishize the
unrepeatable writing processes of the masters

—Gabler's *Ulysses* where the drama of
Joyce's writing mind becomes the shrine

of a critical edition; the facsimile
of Pound's editing-creation of what became

Eliot's *Waste Land*; the packets into
which Dickinson sewed her poems, where

the sequences possibly embody a higher
order; the notebooks in which Stein

and Toklas conversed in pencil: these
can make works like "Lifting Belly"

seem like an interchange between bodily
writers or writerly bodies in bed.

The feeling that three's a crowd
there is called up and cancelled

by the print's intimacy and tact.
In all these cases, the unfathomable

particularity of the author's mind, body,
and writing situation is the illegible

icon of reading. But it's time
to dissolve this binary. What about

a work like *Glas*?—hardly a
smooth critical monolith. Doesn't it use

the avant-garde (ancient poetic adjective!) device
of collage more extensively than most

poems? Is it really that different
from, say, *The Cantos*? (Yes. *The*

Cantos's growing incoherence reflects Pound's free-fall
writing situation; Derrida's institutional address is

central. Unlike Pound's, Derrida's cut threads
always reappear farther along.) Nevertheless *Glas*

easily outstrips most contemporary poems in
such "marginal" qualities as undecidability and

indecipherability—not to mention the 4
to 10 margins per page. Compared

to it, these poems look like
samplers upon which are stitched the

hoariest platitudes. Not to wax polemical:
there've been numerous attacks on the

voice poem, the experience poem, the
mostly free verse descendants of Wordsworth's

spots of time: first person meditations
where the meaning of life becomes

visible after 30 lines. In its
own world, this poetry is far

from marginal: widely published and taught,
it has established substantial means of

reproducing itself. But with its distrust
of intellectuality (apparently synonymous with overintellectuality)

and its reliance on authenticity as
its basic category of judgment (and

the poems exist primarily to be
judged) (with the award having replaced

aura in the post-canonical era of
literary reproduction), it has become marginal

with respect to the theory-oriented sectors
of the university, the sectors which

have produced such concepts as "marginalization."
As an antidote, let me quote

Glas: "One has to understand that
he is not *himself* before being

Medusa to himself. . . . To be oneself
is to-be-Medusa'd . . . . Dead sure of self. . . .

Self's dead sure biting (death)." Whatever
this might mean, and it's possibly

aggrandizingly post-feminist, man swallowing woman, nevertheless
in its complication of identity it

seems a step toward a more
communal and critical reading and writing

and thus useful. The puns and
citations lubricating Derrida's path, making it

too slippery for all but experienced
cake walkers, are not the point.

What I am proposing in these
anti-generic, over-genred couplets is not some

genreless, authorless writing, but a physically
and socially located writing where margins

are not metaphors, and where readers
are not simply there, waiting to

be liberated. Despite its transgression of
local critical decorum, *Glas* is, in

its treatment of the philosophical tradition,
decorous; it is *marginalia*, and the

master page of Hegel is still
Hegel, and Genet is Hegel too.

But a self-critical poetry, minus the
short-circuiting rhetoric of vatic privilege, might

dissolve the antinomies of marginality that
broke Jack Spicer into broken lines.

The Manchurian Candidate: A Remake

1st shot (for the trailer, also)

Bang we see the crosshairs targeting
the spineless forehead

2nd shot

Didn't you hear me the first time?
We know you know what we're saying to you.

3rd shot

They have such power over me
but Frank isn't bothered by them all that much.

Ulysses lies there on his floor
a closed block with a big name.

4th shot

Closeup of the duskjacket: words.
They have power over me.

The dustjacket is orange & black
but this is black and white so I just say it.

The cover isn't part of the book—obviously.
I'm not in the movie—obviously.

5th shot (for the trailer)

A harpsichord on the soundtrack signals
something's false—this is the 50s remember.

On top they're hearty, fussy old ladies;
underneath they're murderous cold war hypnotists.

On top they're discussing hydrangeas; underneath
they make soldiers strangle each other.

On top it's a movie;
on top the frozen war.

Underneath markets wither; underneath
pleasure, all its eggs in one basket, explodes at the sound of shots.

Underneath you have to follow these words to the letter.
You're on top.

6th shot

At last the truth can be told.
Let all the spies stand naked.

I was sitting in the den
watching a tape of *The Manchurian Candidate*,

secular, married, legible, American,
looking at what's showing.

Let all the words be sold at cost.
Let all the words be read at cost.

I was playing solitaire because of Korea.
The deck contained 52 diamond queens.

7th shot

That was in the movie,
but a picture is exactly where I don't want to live.

PANDA—Where would you like to live? China?

KOALA—I'd love to visit. The food, the umbrellas, the bicycles. Where
would you like to live? Australia?

373

PANDA—Australia's too ironic for my taste. I'd love to visit, though.
I've never seen a kangaroo. Their leg muscles must be remarkable.

It looked as if I was
coming out ahead. Not quite victory, perhaps,

but what have we been fighting
for all our lives if not a

New York where you can go into
a bar in the fifties, order

a beer and read *Ulysses*? I saw
paradise the other night. It was

as easy to read as breathing
and writing one's invitation to the world

in progress, frank, surprised, very amused.
It was a dream I can't remember

—obviously—in a phrase not this one:
this is just an assertive shielding

echo, a deeply loved surface. Then
I woke up. I was watching television.

8th shot

The clicker and a right hand above grey couch material.

9th shot

The grey voice never transgressing word boundaries,
the plate compartmentalized, the carrot section

filled precisely, never a spatter of
pureed orange slopping into the section for

374

desire, which was filled with a
clear layering of deeply loved picture: the

beautiful blonde biking by tearing off
her blouse to bandage his leg where

the snake had conveniently just sunk
his admittedly abstract, offscreen fangs, but narrative

homeruns over the abyss of incoherence
are America's ice cream, I saw leaden

geo-toy Raymond Shaw murder mother and father
in the snap of the plot;

10th shot

while I was waiting for the kids to go to sleep
so you could nicely slip your underwear off.

Oops you went to sleep.
I never meant any of this.

I have not done these things. Any of these things.
I write for you and strangers.

11th shot

in her bra, outside. Summer. Some
are others. Not her. Friendly. Filmy.

12th shot

I place myself in the position of the viewer, then I view.
On the night in question I was home all evening, viewing.

13th shot

Frank Sinatra's had it. The social
cardboard's not worth the sweat he

constantly carries around on his face.
Wherever he looks: locked American lives.

No writing the great book. Might
as well read the ashtray. No

loving the great smile, no riding
the city down to bodies that

can be yours for the right
song, the instant aria just before

the light changes. Too many cigarettes,
too many buddies strangling each other.

Why? Because. Why? Because the smiling
Chinese totalizing science sentencer of history

pronounced the words, just the pleasantest
trace of accent, "With the hands."

14th shot (for the trailer)

I Chinese view duty-free writing strangle experience
you Amerikansi mister irony door plenty WD-40 but no key poly-sci
      thinker figure out later-never.

15th shot

Frank wasn't strangled but now he can't read *Ulysses*.
It means nothing to him, just another big brick of paper named after itself.

When the world is weird,
being bounced around on a word trampoline won't get you any rest.

From in front of the VCR field in the psychic past of the Cold War,
this is Bob Perelman.

16th shot

Yes, mother, every word must count: 6
Yes, father, I will count each word: 7

If any one of them gets away
then I will be alone in

a locked mess. The warm curves
the grassy hills and the actual caves

I will want to write myself.
Please I'll write it myself. The way

streets look from inside the house,
at night, either end blocked or shielded

by maple leaves lit black green
by streetlights, stating my feelings of home,

mouth & ear and leading them
out to the attentive spark. I read

Jack Kerouac who is free to drive
a Ford in the specific direction

of heaven where art is a very
good investment, although you only should

say that well after the fact.
In 1955 the many love the few

or at least the few are free
to think that they do and

"it was a very good year,"
the present recording its pleasure in being

recorded. Frank Sinatra is rewarded with
a stage full of underwear and keys

while standing up and swaying, his
inward light spotlit smokily, his throat open

to extort every sung syllable, the bedroom
board meeting smoldering, shareholders on fire,

humming along. In 1955, art is
as exciting as the perfect bid, the

sunsoaked homerun, the victory over the others
that they like too, acknowledge, buy,

put on the wall. Kids wait, but
the early offscreen doors don't reopen.

17th shot (voiceover)

The Manchurian Candidate stars Frank Sinatra as Benny Marco, Lawrence
Harvey as the horrible Raymond Shaw, Janet Leigh as Benny's girlfriend,
Angela Lansbury as Raymond's mastermind mother. American soldiers
are betrayed in Korea, and captured by the Chinese Communists. After
offscreen brainwashing, they are shown to the Russians. Both groups are
intellectuals, quoting conflicting studies as the commonsense Americans
sit there patiently, in alternate shots, brainwashed into thinking they're at
a horticultural meeting in New Jersey where matrons in white dresses and
broad flowery hats are attending a lecture extolling scientific gardening.
"Another modern discovery which we owe to the hydrangea concerns the
influence of air drainage upon plant climate." Slow modern harpsichord
jangles the soundtrack. The film is racially progressive: when the onscreen

378

American soldier is black, his hallucinated matrons are uppermiddleclass black; there's no plantation subtext. When Shaw is ordered to strangle another soldier, he's almost too polite, saying "Excuse me" as he brushes another's chair; the soldier to be strangled is polite, too. It's a liberal utopia: good manners have triumphed over competition. The Chinese are jovial and authoritative—they've perfected the procedure. They can make the Americans believe anything: the Camels they're smoking turn out to be yak dung. It is to laugh, for the Chinese mastermind at least. The Russians are surly and badly in need of dental work. You can't believe what you see. But you have to look. Finally, the poem is beginning to focus. We know you know what we're saying to you.

KOALA—I hit my head; I had a dream. Isn't that how it always starts?

PANDA—Maybe that's the way it starts in the West. It's not a collective form; there's no rhetorical place for people to come together. That's the way you've started, but that's not the way it's supposed to start. Hitting your head is personal.

KOALA—I was cutting the grass and I hit my head on the branch of an apple tree. An old one, twenty-five feet tall with two live quarters sprouting north and south, two dead ones east and west. It was not symbolism, only matter. If you don't believe me, you can feel the ridge of healing flesh on my head, under the fur here. It's as real as history.

PANDA—Cutting the grass is a fairly trivial instance upon which to balance the non-concentric circles of history. Go in, I would have said, have a little lemonade, & read Whitman or the Misty poets. Particulars only exist by being collective.

KOALA—So audience—fuzzy little me in the case of your remarks—becomes crucial.

PANDA—When you're a nation, being cute is not enough any more. No, an audience is a serious, collective enterprise. The ironic single writer in a cage, treasonous, or loyal, or mad, riven by pathos, unfamiliar tears...it doesn't really matter much to the words or the world. Once the hypnosis of the singular is snapped, that is. Before, one can think that anything might happen on the page.

KOALA—I'm willing to bob for very small favors, balls of hard candy swimming almost ethically in the sweat of irony's personal furnace around which individuals are gathered into gendered masses in lieu of lives for all lived under the changeable blue fields of utopia otherwise known as international justice!

PANDA—International justice! I think we might as well the subject, don't you?

KOALA—Fine. Which do you hate more, symbolic poetry, or poetry that's all language?

PANDA—Easy: poetry that's symbolic.

KOALA—But what about poetry that's all language?

PANDA—Poetry that's all language makes me cry when I'm asleep and can't hear the tears hitting the pillow, I mean the top of the page.

KOALA—I actually hit my head: that means something. It was hot, I was inside one body for the duration, cutting the leaves of grass and I saw myself walking on air on cloud stilts of biological perpetuity and sweat of the word. I was not a nation, I was not a species, I was a speaker, fully alive just because I like the sound of that the noisome hiss of this making a made world under me undergo twisting birth and destruction just to keep me saying what I was going to say anyway! Or anything else! Or nothing so what black hole blank! An apple an unoriginal sin a day goes astray into the many minds of the many many others who don't think this! And neither do I! neither we nor me! I say it! Where was I? Where are we? Don't you love the intrusion of speech where no speech can be, life where sounds are the slippery start to never finish but get there already anyway...

PANDA—Did you show that to your trainer before you turned it loose on me?

KOALA—My teacher?

PANDA—I'm assuming your teacher was your trainer before he was your teacher.

KOALA—My teacher trained in the finest zoos of Europe.

18th shot

I can't remember the movie anymore.
Art means throwing scraps of code

to the bodies as appetite supplements.
The screen is softwired so the bars disappear.

after the primal shot

I can see eyes painted open on
the death mask of that lovely arrangement

I used to call the world, America,
my life, the page, the academy of

the future, which as it turns out
is in the past. They even move.

They're mine: that was home. It's plain
that there was time and that it

took place but its quick pleasures are
now words in a language with only

scattered survivors. A single word means nothing.
Or a line without a world. The

381

present is full of survivors' sentences. With
disoriented conviction and memory too deep for

instrumental speech swimming sinkingly toward pre-owned futures
hosed down the hyperspace of capital where

freedom spells the rampant logos turning attractively
bemused typefaces and bodies toward the traffic.

Or language it for yourself. Make your
own recipes: ironize, experiment, write wrong, but

don't forget the old pleasures: skies, turkeys,
playgrounds. We know you know. Meanwhile, one

drives, an open lane a paycheck of
sorts, leading to the biography glimpsed in

the gas station john mirror. Until the
war's over there's nothing to eat but

information, and the new mixes with the
old down through all the details. Taste.

19th shot

Who folded my clothes? You did! I did!
Who watered my tears? You did! I did!
Who batted an eye each word I woke? You did! I did!
Who waited for me to sleep so I could wake one step further inside the
        world? You did! I did!
KOALA—To survive you have to be willing to do anything. Anthologies!
That's where the money really is, or might be. At least so I imagine from
my fuzzy animal distance. Reprint the material! Dominate the gene pool!
Rise like Godzilla and make them read you for fucking ever!

PANDA—If you use language like that, you'll have a hard time even
making it into the La Brea tar pits.

20th shot

To be free and to be
Frank Sinatra the pinnacle artist but

to be pictured as *homo ordinarius*
keeping the public world private by

visible quotidian heroism: that's the lesson
scorching the director's desire in every

shot. If you feel like arguing
with the movies, then step outside.

21st shot

The Chinese mastermind has the one
successful marriage in the movie. Of

course it's offscreen: you can't have
everything. He's really a most happy

fella. He leaves the Russian doctor-spy's
so-called clinic in NY after making it

clear that Raymond has to murder
his would-have-been father-in-law, the honest muckraking

journalist, as well as the love-of-his-life
blonde. Don't fall asleep, this is

plot. Everyone has to sacrifice. Except
for perhaps the mastermind, jauntily tugging

his gloves tight, saying now he
has to get off to Macy's

for some Xmas shopping. Smiles the
happy social smile sans dissonance: the

wife gave him a list yea
long, shrugs: what are you gonna

do? He knows how to get
in bed with capital and let

it charm his pants off. Having
them "tight enough so everyone will

want to go to bed with
you," as Frank O'Hara writes, is

a youthful gesture under the dappled
shade of capital's frond-like pleasances. That's

one thing. But to live as
a large system of control is

quite another. As the mastermind leaves,
the Russian stares. He just doesn't

get it: he believes in history
not Macy's, inextricable direction, totality, the

concrete-translucent materiality of class truth, one
world one history at the end!

Meanwhile one's provisional oneness stands with
oblique conviction against the waterfall of

happily pregnant wage-slaves—that buoyant rainbowy
spray is guilty as Sunday! those

sunny lakes, those caves of ice,
those miracles of rare device forced

from the deep romantic chasm of
bourgeois pastoral-pornographic shopping, which that fucking

crypto-individualist Chinese mastermind indulges with his
credit flowing past the respectful cashier

like vodka down a mule's throat!
or whatever! Thus the Russian revolutionary-bureaucrat

murderer actor placed on the verbal
screen by the all-too-human history of

this shot. He never gets time
off. His face is a burden.

closing shot

Raymond's gunsight targets Communist McCarthyite foster
father's forehead, as said before, though

in a novel continuum. The movie
wants to reach the new world

and, in the same gesture, conclude.
A well-formed narrative should hold you

with concern, intimacy, but not too
close because you'll be heading out

one day, pegged, looking back for
the recognizable trees, the known cars,

glad animal movements traded in for
manageable novelty... It's become a habit,

you might say. Here is America,
with the generative one repeated in

each pillar and bar. Underneath the
place names, the flags of private

longing fluttering against the vistas, molecular
revolutionaries dream of taking all desires

to court and setting them loose
beneath the robes of judgment. To

pull the gown from knowledge, to
pull the eye from noon, and

not see the catered wants of
Tom, Dick, and Harry navagating the

street, the mall, the clicker and
the dust. And Jane, Ketisha, and

those tender technocratic shoots & stumps,
you & me? On screen, nations

personify the pursuit of happiness. Beyond
the blinds: rain, the end. Days

regular as sprocket holes, while decades
slide with unevenly layered minds of

their own. Which makes for tangled
gaps in all the word screens.

Barrett Watten

Nonnarrative / History

I

While narrative is conventionally thought to be both the implicit goal and explict norm of art's temporal organization,[1] time in modernist and postmodernist art and writing often is organized in ways not dependent on narrative as formal guarantee of meaning or as necessary horizon of understanding. Further, there have been particular historical frames for the development of nonnarrative aesthetic forms. Individual practitioners of nonnarrative, of course, have assured places in literary history, from Sterne and Blake to Walt Whitman, Lautréamont, and Gertrude Stein. In the 1920s there took place, for however brief a time and with whatever instability, a culturally productive moment of nonnarrative writing among a group of American expatriate writers that was represented as a "revolution of the word."[2] This movement had notable descendants in the postwar period, particularly in the abstraction of the New York School (both poets and painters) and in the aleatorical methods of John Cage and Jackson Mac Low. About 1975 new conditions for the social reproduction of nonnarrative forms emerged—during a period of national crisis at about the time of the Fall of Saigon—for a number of writers. This literary phenomenon has been related to the crisis of historical narrative in postmodernism;[3] a rejection of narrative for other forms of temporal organization took place, and was culturally productive, at a given historical time.

If nonnarrative is at once a form of temporal organization and a form of historical self-consciousness, it will be necessary to say what nonnarrative is, both in works of art and as a kind of history. In a defining sentence written by a historian wanting to pose the nonnarrative against what he sees as a positive and stultifying narrative among historians, it is a moment of negative totality that cannot be told: "A culture is reactive when it continues to narrativize itself despite, at any moment, being six minutes away (by missile) from its own nonnarrative obliteration."[4] If narrative for Sande Cohen is a species of ideology, nonnarrative must be the real that can only undermine it. Such a negative notion of nonnarrative must have ideological investments of its own, as are evident in Cohen's fantasy of self-destruction in retribution for the denial encoding a fearful reactivity to historical events. Negative notions of nonnarrative owe their formulations as well to linguistic models, in which, for example, a paradigmatic break in syntagmatic progression yields an atemporal moment in a temporal sequence presumed to be narrative. The distinction between synchronic structure and diachronic development has, of course, many consequences, some of which have contributed to the sense that nonnarrative can only be imagined as an impossible, self-undoing moment of negative totality.[5]

In works of art, however, nonnarrative is not simply an undoing, interruption, or denial of narrative; it is a positive form of temporal organization. As narrative comprises a number of forms of discourse, from oral epic to *Swann's Way*, that can be seen as a "discursive mode" in Gerard Genette's sense, nonnarrative comprises a "discursive mode" but not a single form of discourse. While set apart from narrative by the prefix *non-*, nonnarrative includes a number of forms of discourse that are not simply negating of narrative. Nonnarratives are forms of discursive presentation in which both linear and contextual syntax exist but where univocal motivation, retrospective closure, and transcendent perspective are suspended, deferred, or do not exist.[6] Nonnarratives range from a pure formalism of temporal accretion to the complex immediacies of modes of expression that would not be possible within the confines of narrative form. Sequential lists such as a ticker tape or a grocery bill are, in minimally formal terms, nonnarrative, as is the voice announcing times of departure and arrival at a train station—even if stocks and prices rise and fall or trains traverse a beginning, middle, and end. More complex forms of nonnarrative involve "immediacies" of presentation whose force would be lost if subsumed within narrative. The temporal *dilation* of Abstract Expressionism is an affectively motivated form of nonnarration realized in the form of the temporal *condensation* of its "all-over" mode of presentation. A minimalist sculpture such as Richard Serra's *Tilted Arc* is likewise nonnarrative, even if it has been inserted into narrative debates about the politics of authority and community. Nonnarrative forms, in their affective immediacy, certainly engage, rescript, and displace narratives in this way, even as they may not be reducible to species of narrative. The fifty random numbers I used to begin my poem "The Word" are nonnarrative, even as they serve as a "disorienting" device in a poem that has many features of oral narrative. Experimental writers often, in the words of Carla Harryman, "prefer to distribute narrative rather than to deny it."[7] Nonnarratives may subtend, deform, or even enable narrative, while leaving open questions of motivation, transcendence, and closure.

While it is useful to imagine minimal paradigms for nonnarrative such as a work of sculpture or a list, and while there has been a wide range of aesthetic use of just such forms, much nonnarrative art poses questions of motivation, transcendence, and closure in more complex ways. A "family resemblance" between minimally formal and more expressive instances of nonnarrative still remains in the way both are organized in terms of a single temporal moment or an open sequence of events. Both aspects of temporal organization structure the affective complexity of the following poem by Lyn Hejinian:

EXIT

Patience is laid out on my paper
is floodlit. Everything's simile.
The cadence is detected, the cipher is broken, "resolved
the sky bears the enjambments, heavy clouds
the measure of one with a number block
changes shade. The flow of thoughts—impossible!
with which we are so familiar. The river
its visuals are gainful and equably square
in an automatic writing. Self-consciousness
to reclaim imagination...to rise early
that is, logic exaggerates the visible

to oppose laziness." Unto itself, built of bricks
is a cumbersome monument on whom motion
is bent over, having sunk a fork into the ground.[8]

This poem is nonnarrative. The way its discursive form is organized in a temporal series is basic to its intended effects. These effects are created by the positive and negative (and neutral) valences of the poem's progression from one increment to the next. The poem argues a particular form of self-consciousness, an intensified and disjunct present that will "reclaim imagination" in recognizing the discontinuities of thought. A virtually embodied sense of what the Russian Formalists called *ostranenie* (defamiliarization) is distributed here between the poem's thematization of self-consciousness and its techniques of discontinuity; the question of whether the poem is arguing the priority of one or the other clearly has been left open. It would be impossible to decide whether the poem's thematicization of self-consciousness presents moments of linguistic discontinuity, or whether its discontinuity demands a specific kind of self-consciousness. While the dissociation of thematization and technique is clearly central to the poem's affective presentation, it is also evident that these effects depend, in a number of ways, on a re-presentation of narrative. For example, there are thematically resonant but disjunct narrative framing devices at the beginning and end of the poem; "Patience is laid out on my paper" takes the place of an orienting moment of oral narrative, while "having sunk a fork into the ground" marks a moment of finality much like Walter Cronkite's "And that's the way it is!"[9] But these narrative frames are skewed, as are many more that are engaged in the course of the poem; it would be futile to go through it to prove that a single organizing perspective motivates the unfolding of the verbal material, however constitutive of narrative Viktor Shklovsky thought such discontinuities to be. The poem alternates the ironization of narrative effects with a nonironic materiality of language in its claim to self-consciousness; lines such as "a measure of one with a number block" are not simply negative obstructions to a hidden narrative but moments where language presents itself in its mode of

390

signification. Hejinian's nonnarrative insists that the affective consequences of such a materiality of language be taken into account as a form of self-consciousness.

There may be disagreement with the notion that thematization is possible in a nonnarrative form, and this would be one explanation for the "folk theory" of such work that its meaning is completed by the reader.[10] Clearly, the poem's engagement of a range of narrative frames creates a field of referents for its explicitly stated theme of self-consciousness, even if the poem's gaps and discontinuities, as well as its moments of linguistic materiality, are as important to achieving these effects. Hejinian moves between transcendental and immanent (as well as impossible!) self-consciousness in the poem, all three of which possibilities can be read in the poem's title. "Exit" may indicate a narrative closure by which the conflicting frames of the poem are resolved; it may be a resistant exit sign that is the locus of a deferred question about meaning; or it may be a solution to a dilemma unstated elsewhere that motivates the poem's ephemeral form. But while a narrative reading of the poem would see its negative moments as simply aesthetic interference setting up a desire for transcendent closure, a nonnarrative reading keeps the entire range of meanings in play—such an allowance for material, contingent effects being exactly what Hejinian wants as a redeemed imagination. While there is no denying narrative in the poem, or the possibility of framing a narrative reading, nonnarrative organizes the poem's narratives for a range of possible effects—which may change in time as different frames are brought to the poem for historical reasons.

A reading of the poem's moment of false closure shows how its total form tries to engage these effects. "Having sunk a fork into the ground" is a condition of finality for the poem's material "bricks" that could either precede (having sunk a fork, all this came about) or follow from (this happened, and then a fork was sunk) the moment when "motion / is bent over" the "cumbersome monument." Split grammatical predication makes it impossible to find a retrospective moment outside the poem from which the prospective fork being sunk into the ground always would have been determinate of its total form. Not possessing narrative closure, the poem provokes historical retrospection into a series of positions from which to draw out the implications of that fatal fork. As with this moment of finality, time throughout the poem—in narrative tags, shifts and dislocations, orders of tense, disjunct predication, and resolutely immanent language—is organized to engage historical rereadings, beginning with its point of production.

It may be responded that if there is a potential for thematization here, it resides solely in the narrative elements being deployed by nonnarrative forms. In that case, it is instructive to look at a poem that is even more "language-centered," less provocative of overlapping interpretive frames, than Hejinian's. Jackson Mac Low's work reaches a certain limit of material effects—paradoxically based in a linearity of technique quite different from Hejinian's ephemerality—that produce an even more radical temporality. For instance, Mac Low has composed poems based on computer selections of Basic English word lists. The following poem, however, engages its formal implications in a more than simply aleatorical way:

WALL REV

A line is a crack
is an entrance furrow
distracting between thighs

Attracting between sighs
a parallel cataclysm
cannot tell its name

Active well of flame
tense entrance clues
obligate avoidance[11]

More reduced in its construction than Hejinian's poem, this poem also moves between thematization and technique as it creates an affect of generalized eros in the structured displacements of language. In its opening and closing lines, "A line is a crack" and "obligate avoidance," the materiality of language evokes sexual tension and denial; between them, a sequence of definitional moments creates a semantic field in which the play of positive and negative attractions becomes a condition of equivalence that "cannot tell its name." The movement from approach to avoidance is dispersed among equivalent lines in a parallel structure, while the semantic distance between lines is so rigidly measured as to be virtually syllogistic. The poem presents the condition of linguistic equivalence that Roman Jakobson described as characteristic of poetic language, but nonnarration goes farther than Jakobson's poetic "message for its own sake" in structuring effects that both invoke and withhold provisional closure.[14] Presented as an immanent effect of language, the poem's material displacements evoke both attraction and repulsion in a sequence of ambivalent moments within a bounded temporality. The experience of language from line to line may demand closure, but no retrospective motivation can be inferred. Mac Low's poem links the materiality of language to the representation of desire, but it is not given to desire, it seems, to know how things are going to turn out.

Seeing Mac Low's poem as a temporal series of parallel oppositions may resolve thematic readings (such as the surplus eros that makes most sense of the poem) into a formal immanence. But the sexual reading shows exactly how the equivalences staged in the poem, in a highly condensed manner, produce self-consciousness (one that may not yet be historical) in their form of "parallel cataclysm." The equivalences Jakobson found as the basis of the "poetic function," strictly observed in Mac Low's argument of parallel increments, find another value here in the relation between representation and event. Equivalence constitutes parallelism for Jakobson; for Mac Low, it invokes cataclysm—the devolution of negative totality that Cohen fantasized as nonnarrative. But this cataclysm, in a reversal not unlike Hejinian's forked closure, splits into two registers. Language and event must be brought together *as event* in order that the "parallel cataclysm" of representation resolve, but it cannot within the temporal duration of Mac Low's poem—a parallel series predicated on the dissociation of "the line is a crack." This notion of an event presented as a "parallel cataclysm" that at the same time exceeds the language of representation will have consequences for an account of art at once dissociated from but "parallel" to moments of historical crisis.

II

A poetics of "parallel cataclysm" may seem literally "the end of history" if imagined as taking place in a history rather than in a poem. But the creation, in a nonnarrative text, of a formal distance between narration (*fabula*) and event (*syuzhet*)—the one presentable, the other not fully representable—has critical force when applied to the construction of history itself, whose narrative form has been discussed by philosophers of history from Arthur Danto to Louis O. Mink, Hayden White, and Sande Cohen. Such a rupture foregrounds temporal sequence in dissociating the transparency between narration and event, severing transcendental organization from the progression of subordinated events toward discursive closure. Nonnarratives call into question the transparency of history toward event.

Several recent discussions have taken up what I am calling the ethical dilemmas of historical transparency, but without being able to conceive an alternative to narrative form. A critically modified narrativity, for example, seems to resolve the question of historical transparency in Joel Fineman's claim that "the anecdote...as the narration of a singular event, is the literary form or genre that uniquely refers to the real."[13] Fineman's sense of the "real" splits here between a commonsense notion of "real events" and an exalted one of the "real" as inaccessible substrate to events that can be known only through their failed representations; one of these registers refers to local, containable events and the other to grand narratives that subordinate them. Uniting both, the anecdote then would be a form of historical monad that Fineman terms the "*historeme*... the smallest minimal unit of the historiographic fact"

(57). As history, the anecdote asserts a unified temporal frame that is distinctly lacking in the incremental sequences of the poems discussed above. Even so, as Fineman observes, the notion that it takes such a foregrounded literary form to conjoin registers of narration and event "is not as trivial an observation as might at first appear" (56). That the anecdote works as an *exemplary* form for the renewal of history argues, it seems, against discursive transparency—the theory that narrative fully captures the reality of an event, with the corollary claim that events can be represented only in narrative terms.

It is the exemplary position of the anecdote within larger, not so easily narrated history that leads to the undoing of its transparency. In a skeptical discussion of fully narrative history, Louis O. Mink proposes the following test: if a given narrative can be said to refer uniquely to an event, as with Fineman's anecdote, it should follow "that historical narratives can be *added* to others, as in the periodization of political history by reigns."[14] In order to do so, however, there would have to be an underlying substrate of narrated events that would make such accretions possible; such a substrate could on no account be considered exemplary. There are two levels of narrative at issue—*petits récits*, which "*should* aggregate*," and the *grands récits* of Universal History, in which "past actuality is an untold story" (142). But by virtue of the formal properties of narratives—minimally, that each has the beginning, middle, and end proper to narrative unity—such a subordination cannot occur; the best that can be said for the objective continuity of Universal History is that it organizes the *petits récits* contained within it in the form of a chronicle that is not fully narrative. As a result, "narrative histories should be aggregative, insofar as they are histories, but cannot be, insofar as they are narratives" (143).

With this distinction in mind, the identity of narration and event in Fineman's anecdote and in the theory of narrative transparency may appear as overdetermined in their quests for history. That the anecdote is a literary form, for Fineman, means that it works to renew history by defamiliarizing an already automatized narration (such as the one he offers later to support a historiographical progression from Thucydides to the Renaissance to his own critical moment): "The anecdote produces the effect of the real, the occurrence of contingency, by establishing an event as an event within and yet without the framing context of historical successivity" (61). Fineman's solution to Mink's dilemma of narrative history is thus that the anecdote need not worry about its aggregation with other anecdotes but instead may open a unique and individual "hole" that dilates temporal succession precisely by means of its formal opposition to teleological history. This is a distinctly antinarrative moment.

The opening anecdotes of New Historicist exposition, seen as formally analogous to the more general agency of the anecdote in Universal History, thus work to dissociate and thus renew history by creating a disjunct moment of transparency between narration and event (which would not be sustainable through an entire text).[15] This moment, which often takes the form of proposing an eruptive, miraculous, or horrific event narrated to determine a given historical date, is valued precisely for creating an "effect of the real" which it then transfers to the total argument. History by that act will be renewed in the determination of an event as formally distinct from its narrative. The contingency of this eruption (and vice versa), however, leads from Fineman's analogy between anecdote and historical period to Mink's skeptical question concerning the status of retrospective periodization—"Is the Renaissance an event?" (145); if an anecdotal event is an exemplary narration, what are the limits of its form?—from the transcendental position invoked by these transparent effects. Perhaps such a summoning of narrative would be accomplished just as well by a nonnarrative moment of expository orientation, such as the fifty random numbers referred to earlier, to establish an indexical substrate as much determining of the total form of narrative history as the anecdotal date. So in the discursive openings of oral narrative, if the listener's attention is both grounded and perplexed—indexically defamiliarized—the anecdote has done its job.[16]

The notion of an exemplary anecdote that renews history by

creating an "effect of the real" provides an analogy for the ways in which transparent narratives are organized in everyday forms of historical representation. Raymond Williams has described the discursive accretion of seemingly isolated, reified, and often anecdotal narratives in larger narrative structures as a basis for mass communication, understood as reproducing beliefs about events more generally.[17] We see this mechanism on the nightly news, where for reasons of both ideology and economy events are packaged into short narrative units that can be assembled at any future date into larger narratives. The upper limit of this discursive totality would be an accretive horizon of continuous dates, to which the media in its historicizing capacity often refers (at moments of crisis, identification of narrative units with historical date is particularly marked, as in the Iran Hostage Crisis or during the Persian Gulf War). Such indexing of narrative to event demands a transparency whereby accretion is not only unproblematic but immanent in the structure of narrated events. But it is exactly the eruptive discrepancy of the anecdote that renews an overarching discursive field; thus, paradoxically, the commercials interrupting war footage segued between sound bites Williams saw as guaranteeing the formal totality of mass communication create overdetermining effects whereby discontinuity just is the guarantee of narrative. Any history of the present will have to take this paradox of interrupted, overdetermined, and undermotivated narrative into account. That this assembly line of events is discontinuous with a larger historical narrative is, however, clear.

A reconsideration of processes of historical accretion and subordination, in Mink's sense, is the point of the distinctions between annal, chronicle, and history which Hayden White sees as revealing the gaps that separate events as such from their narrative organization.[18] Annals are simply events with dates organized on a time line; chronicles provide a necessity of sequence such as "and then, and then" but come to no retrospective conclusion about why these events had to occur in this sequence. The chronicle "is usually marked by a failure to achieve narrative closure.... It starts out to tell a story but breaks off *in medias res*, in the chronicler's own present" (5). A realist might find that, in the end, an objective time line unifies—by analogy with material causation— these provisional historical forms with historical narrative per se, thus making chronicle a species of narrative. But for historians with other ontological commitments, it has fallen to history seen as continuous with narrative to organize these events in a unified frame. White quotes Hegel to motivate this elevation of historical event to narrative in desire, "in the same way as love and the religious emotions provoke imagination to give shape to previously formless impulse" (12), and asks, "What wish is enacted, what desire is gratified, by the fantasy that real events are properly represented when they can be shown to display the formal coherence of a story?" (6). History takes place as narrative equally because consequent events are narratable and because we desire them to be narrative. But is narrative the only form that desire takes, in organizing events, "to give shape to the previously formless impulse" that is the mere succession of events in time? Could other forms of temporal organization, analogous to the sequence of dates or chronicle in the schema proposed by White, also make history?[19]

History in this larger sense may be constructed by a wider range of formal relations between narrative and event than has been supposed. Mink's notion that narrative fails to accrete in a Universal History creates a kind of "open form," a semantic field in Umberto Eco's sense, where specific narratives compete in the determination of events.[20] Oppositely, Fineman's defense of Universal History through the anti-narrative formal moment of the anecdote restricts the range of such a semantic field by overdetermining the value of contingent effects. But the performative value of such a strategy may also be seen in nonnarrative forms that, while leaving the larger historical horizon open, specify a historical date within a total form. For example, in San Francisco artist Seyed Alavi's 1991 installation *Blueprint for the Times*, blueprints of the front pages of major international newspapers are mounted in groups of three in stainless steel frames. The pages are all from the same date, 31 December 1989, but the only alteration of any of the blueprints from their originals is that the dates have been removed. This barely perceptible deletion causes the time-valued materials displayed on each page—stories of many levels of implication held in a kind of referential suspension—to be read in entirely different ways than if they were fixed in time by their dates. This removal of the date, as a device, is the formal opposite of the establishment of the date in the anecdote, but its negativity equally creates a hole in presumed historical time (the redundant sequence of dates that makes "yesterday's papers" old news). What results is a situation in which the viewer may create new narratives from the stories and images to be seen in a field of meanings; but this reading is bounded at an upper limit precisely in its determination of the historical date that had been removed. The entire form of Alavi's installation is a nonnarrative that by means of a specific form of displacement and reintegration constructs, in both senses of the word, history. Desire begins with the removal of the date and ends in a bounded field.[21]

Alavi's *Blueprints* comprise a kind of annal that, in its total form, presents world events to self-consciousness in a form of historical nonnarration. For Fredric Jameson, however, it is clear that nonnarrative can be thought of only as a deformation, incompletion, or deferral of narrative. Narrative is "an all-informing process" that Jameson takes to be "the central function or *instance* of the human mind," while it is inescapably historical in its revealing "a single great collective *story*... the collective struggle to wrest a realm of Freedom from the realm of necessity."[23] One test of such a story is in its encounter with the nonnarratives of postmodernism; so in his notably disjunct reading of Bob Perelman's nonnarrative poem "China," Jameson finds its discontinuity to be an example of the postmodern dilemma in which "the subject has lost its capacity actively to extend its pro-tensions and re-tensions across the temporal manifold and to organize its past and future into coherent experience."[24] At the same time, the poem's oblique reference in its title to China is an appeal to grand narrative, in which "it does seem to capture something of the excitement of the immense, unfinished social experiment of the New China" (29). The latter reading is centrally thematic for Jameson, if somewhat ancillary to Perelman, in Jameson's identification of the postmodern condition as coincident with the end of the era of "wars of national liberation" (xx-xxi). Jameson assumes that the negativity of Perelman's poem (as species of the genus post-modernism) reinforces the narrative he imposes on it from the position of History (but which may, in fact, be called up as much as denied by the poem itself). What follows, as from the evidence of Perelman's poem, is that "the breakdown of narrativity in a culture, group, or social class is a symptom of its having entered into a state of crisis" (149). But a paradox emerges when Jameson identifies History as being itself non-narrative: "It is fundamentally non-narrative and nonrepresentational," and it is on the foundation of this inaccessible nonnarrativity that History "can be approached only by way of a prior (re)textualization."[25] If "history is what hurts," Perelman's poem is historical precisely because, appearing in the form it does, it makes Jameson account for its non-narrative. Even so, such a historical presentation must relate to narrative or else lapse into an inchoate ground, for which Jameson invokes a narrative of "necessity" as "the inexorable *form* of events; it is therefore a narrative category in the enlarged sense of some properly narrative political unconscious" (102). Sande Cohen's fundamental criticism of narrative history, his sense that "historical thought is located, intellectually considered, near its suppression of the nonnarrated," is here demonstrated in the way that postmodernism (aligned with a political unconscious) makes History happen for Jameson.[26]

Nonnarrative exists—demonstrably in the work of contemporary artists and writers but also in temporal forms that construct history. A critical account of nonnarrativity, as well as aesthetic strategies for its use, thus may proceed not simply in terms of the negation of cultural narratives (as with Jameson's postmodernism) but in a discussion of the historical agency of its forms. Jerome McGann discusses nonnarrative in this sense as a construction of history, distinguishing "antinarratives" as "problematic, ironical, and fundamentally a satiric discursive procedure" from nonnarratives, which "do not issue calls for change and alterity

[but] embody in themselves some form of cultural difference. [Their] antithesis to narrative is but one dimension of a more comprehensively imagined program based in the codes of an alternative set of solidarities." These senses allow for particular forms of organization as proper to nonnarrative per se; even so, both are read against narrative "as a form of continuity; as such, its deployment in discourse is a way of legitimating established forms of social order."[27]

The historical meaning of nonnarrative, however, will not only be given in its opposition to narrative. There is more history to nonnarrative than in McGann's view, as is evident in the development of the modern American epic poem, which in many ways qualified or even abandoned narrative as its primary vehicle after Ezra Pound's disjunct appropriations of Ovid, Browning, and contemporary history in *The Cantos*.[28] The self-canceling millenarianism of Pound's moral conclusion in the Fascist state led, at least in the formal possibilities of epic, to the identification of events with the allegorized but open-ended subject as history in Charles Olson's *The Maximus Poems*, as well as to an often nonnarrative linguistic subjectivity in Louis Zukofsky's *"A."* Olson's maxim as an epic poet indicated just what kind of problem he faced in his identificatory poetics: "It is very difficult to be both a poet, and, a historian."[29] The poet's dilemma here is similar to the problem of narration faced by the transcendental historian in Cohen's sense: "If... narration is the core of historical autonomy...the cultural-intellectual organization of this 'doing' is linked to its cognitive severing, which has to preclude thinking from appearing in the same scene or space as the told."[30] Olson's solution to the problem of transcendental position, the dilemma of "where to stand" in his epic, was to see himself, like any poet, in two places at once—for example, both in his body and outside it ("Offshore / by islands in the blood")—even if this solution led to a gradual devolution of narrative that is at the same time the argument of his poem. Olson raised the possibility of a nonnarrative history in his refusal to transcend or close his epic, even if his ultimate horizon in a tragic self—which inevitably must disintegrate to prove the discursive truth of history—qualifies his poem's inclusion of events that are not only to be subjectively identified, events within a present social horizon, for example. As a kind of "parallel cataclysm," the *Maximus Poems* substituted its own undoing for an account of such incommensurate events.

Notes

This essay was originally written for a presentation on "The Narrative Construction of History" organized by Laura Brun at the Southern Exposure Gallery in San Francisco, March 1990; it was given in revised versions at a conference on "The Ends of Theory," Wayne State University, Detroit, April 1990; at the Unit for Theory and Critical Interpretation, University of Illinois, Champaign-Urbana, October 1992; and at the University of California, San Diego, March 1993. Thanks to all those who commented on earlier versions, in particular Randy Starn. The present version comprises two opening sections excerpted from "Nonnarrative and the Construction of History," in Jerry Herron, Dorothy Huson, Ross Pudaloff, and Robert Strozier, eds., *The Ends of Theory* (Detroit: Wayne State University Press, 1995), 209-45.

    1 Paul Ricoeur's *Time and Narrative*, 3 vols. (Chicago: University of Chicago Press, 1984-88), forcefully argues the necessary reinforcements between the two.

    2 See Jerome Rothenberg, *Revolution of the Word: A New Gathering of American Avant-Garde Poetry, 1914-1945* (New York: Seabury Press, 1974).

    3 Jean-Francois Lyotard, *The Postmodern Condition: A Report on Knowledge* (Minneapolis: University of Minnesota Press, 1984); Fredric Jameson, *Postmodernism, or, The Cultural Logic of Late Capitalism* (Durham, N.C.: Duke University Press, 1991); Fred Pfeil, *Another Tale to Tell: Politics and Narrative in Postmodern Culture* (London: Verso, 1990).

    4 Sande Cohen, *Historical Culture: On the Recoding of an Academic Discipline* (Berkeley: University of California Press, 1986), 1.

    5 Claude Levi-Strauss, *The Savage Mind* (Chicago: University of Chicago Press, 1962), originates a series of positions in which "there is thus a sort of fundamental antipathy between history and systems of classification" seen as synchronic (242); cf. Seymour Chatman, *Coming to Terms: The Rhetoric of Narrative in Fiction and Film* (Ithaca, N.Y.: Cornell University Press, 1990: "Non-narrative text-types do not have an internal time sequence, even though, obviously, they take time to read, view, or hear. Their underlying structures are static or atemporal—synchronic not diachronic" (9).

6 In Hayden White's summary of the Lacanian view in "The Question of Narrative in Contemporary Historical Theory," *The Content of the Form* (Chicago: University of Chicago Press, 1987), 36, "What is 'imaginary' about any narrative representation is the illusion of a centered consciousness capable of looking out on the world, apprehending its structure and processes, and representing them to itself as having all the formal coherency of narrativity itself." Such imaginary coherence—be it fictional, millennial, or simply transparent—constitutes and is constituted by the specific transcendental overview.

7 Barrett Watten, "The Word," in *Conduit* (San Francisco: Gaz Press, 1988), 39; Carla Harryman, "Toy Boats," in *Animal Instincts* (Berkeley: This Press, 1989), 107.

8 Lyn Hejinian, "Exit," *This* 12 (1982).

9 Mary Louise Pratt synthesizes the work of William Labov on oral narratives with the notion of the "cooperative principle" in Paul Grice's pragmatics in *Toward a Speech Act Theory of Literary Discourse* (Bloomington: Indiana University Press, 1977).

10 Theories of open reading practices as in Umberto Eco, Wolfgang Iser, and others have been assimilated to the reading of language-centered writing; see, e.g., Linda Reinfeld, *Language Poetry: Writing as Rescue* (Baton Rouge: Louisiana University Press, 1992).

11 Jackson Mac Low, "Wall Rev," *This* 12 (1982). See also Mac Low, *Representative Works, 1938-85* (New York: Roof Books, 1985).

12 Roman Jakobson, "Linguistics and Poetics," in *Language in Literature* (Cambridge, Mass.: Harvard University Press, 1987).

13 Joel Fineman, "The History of the Anecdote: Fiction and Fiction," in *The New Historicism*, ed. Aram Veeser (New York: Routledge, 1989), 49-76.

14 Louis O. Mink, "Narrative Form as Cognitive Instrument," in *The Writing of History: Literary Form and Historical Understanding*, ed. Robert H. Canary and Henry Kozicki (Madison: University of Wisconsin Press, 1978), 129-49; 140.

15 An example of a New Historicist anecdote that makes an argument out of the performative value of its disjunct date is to be found in Simon During, "The Strange Case of Monomania: Patriarchy in Literature, Murder in *Middlemarch*, Drowning in *Daniel Deronda*," *Representations* 23 (Summer 1988): 86-104.

16 Pratt, *Speech Act Theory*, 45-46.

17 Raymond Williams, *Television: Technology and Cultural Form* (New York: Schocken Books, 1975), esp. 96-108.

18 White, "The Value of Narrativity in the Representation of Reality," in *Content of the Form*.

19 "Desire" as a concept is here an admitted placeholder for negative motivations of ideological effects, as indicated by Slavoj Zizek, *The Sublime*

Object of Ideology (London: Verso, 1989): "What is missed by the...idea of an external causal chain of communication through which reference is transmitted is...the fact that naming itself retroactively constitutes its reference" (95).

20 Umberto Eco, *The Open Work* (Cambridge, Mass.: Harvard University Press, 1989).

21 Barrett Watten, "Seyed Alavi," *Artweek* (San Jose, Calif.), 14 March 1991.

22 Fredric Jameson, *The Political Unconscious: Narrative as a Socially Symbolic Act* (Ithaca, N.Y.: Cornell University Press, 1981), 13, 19-20.

23 Jameson, *Postmodernism*, 25. George Hartley sums up the presuppositions in Jameson's periodization of this and other instances of post-modern culture in "Jameson's Perelman," *Textual Politics and the Language Poets* (Bloomington: Indiana University Press, 1989), 42-52; and Perelman responds in "Exchangeable Frames," in *Non/Narrative, Poetics Journal* 5 (May 1985): 168-76.

24 Jameson, *Political Unconscious*, 82.

25 Cohen, *Historical Culture*, 69.

27 Jerome McGann, "Contemporary Poetry, Alternate Routes," in *Politics and Poetic Value*, ed. Robert von Hallberg (Chicago: University of Chicago Press, 1987), 253-76; see also responses by Charles Altieri and Jed Rasula. For statements by a number of contemporary writers on the question of narrative and nonnarrative in their work, see *Non/Narrative, Poetics Journal* 5.

28 Michael André Bernstein discusses the American epic tradition in *The Tale of the Tribe: Ezra Pound and the Modern Verse Epic* (Princeton, N.J.: Princeton University Press, 1980); Joseph Conte, *Unending Design: The Forms of Postmodern Poetry* (Ithaca, N.Y.: Cornell University Press, 1991), treats a range of "serial" forms that reject the epic vocation but insist on an experience of temporality.

29 Charles Olson, *Selected Writings*, ed. Robert Creeley (New York: New Directions, 1966); Olson, *The Maximus Poems*, ed. George F. Butterick (Berkeley: University of California Press, 1983); Butterick, *A Guide to the Maximus Poems of Charles Olson* (Berkeley: University of California Press, 1978); Barrett Watten, "Olson in Language: The Politics of Style," in *Total Syntax* (Carbondale, Ill.: Southern Illinois University Press, 1985), 115-39.

30 Cohen, *Historical Culture*, 105.

Position

The monument speaks correctly.
To get results
that all might disappear. As
extreme. The words themselves
reversed, "going
forward." The apex settles on

Tones in surrounding heads.
A test case, or
exile. No wires account for
failure of specific response.
A triangle gives,
circles branch out. Forced

Exposure to limit distorts.
Accumulation of
artifacts in identical tombs.
Any view appears as a hole.
Each is a unit,
and all else. Corrosive air,

Hit by something. Spot-lit
on center stage.
Correction, a large boulder.
The parts avoid being seen.
Portraits of
witnesses other than oneself,

Pasted, stacked. White clouds
and blank tape.
Architects bury their careers,

survived by their mistakes.
 Mirrors tension
of surfaces at work. Lies,

Extension of screen. Grammar
 signifies refusal
to correspond. Multiple cracks
spread out. A sequence of
 obstacles blocks
the memory of facts. Voice of

The word it approximates.
 The foundation
floats without opposing tides.
Into the center of potential,
 stop. The road
decaying into frame. This

Impression turns inside out.
 In perspective,
feeding on industrial waste.
The endless text manipulates
 by fatigue. Street
where no one lives. Pressing,

Yielding to the arguments of
 mass. The hawk
tears the sparrow to pieces.
Coded sparks, holding patterns.
 The privilege
of vanishing speech. All else

Diminished to expanding scale.
Shifted in
the order by which it occurs.
Identity is the cause of war.
The point both
pans and zooms. "Our father

Would be bored to sickness."
The shadow of
difference predicting retreats.
Water follows in its steps.
Ironic index
of what seen. Further claims

Of shape built into line.
The spectator
hiding his uncertain springs.
The story holding the man in.
A series of
reductions. Suppressed end

Where nothing is explained.
The town dissolves,
its factories work at night.
Signals in neutral terrain.
Fog explodes into
perfect control. A spasm of

Zig-zags of mannered sweeps.
The type of prose
departs in ascending steps.

The perfectly natural figure's
tight orange face.
Exits take down signs. Obvious

Fragment. Wandering through
the static list.
A fluorescent toy depicting a
miniature solar system. Inert
metaphysic of
effect. At the same time

Everyone is aware of distance.
The irritant spins,
without any help from them.
A method to invent disbelief.
No one decides
not to notice. He would die

Resisting total thus achieved.
A record of
all that remains. Museum tour
conducted by mutes. Language
palpable as
continuum over shape. "Substitute"

Not equal to stand for itself.
Progress into
retreating barriers makes sense.
Return to the beginning and note.
Ends in a heap,
exhausted. Branches touch cloud

At the bottom of the well.
        Print monitors
illusion of depth. Counter to
river stones, mineral samples.
        The moment of
mixed lots. The skeleton at

The border instructs. Spread
        of the fingers
between keys. Telephone poles
standing on disputed ground.
        The fountain gels.
Blinks in the sun, intuitive

Technique. Rocks fill the eye
        at the corners.
Sleeping man walks into house,
turns on the light. Rolling
        over hills to
concretize plains. "Because,

It can say that." Threat of
        motion from stills.
A statue surrounded by priests,
lying face down on the ground.
        A puffy rope,
gathered manfully. Wish for

Invulnerable sentence, walking
        in air. Thought
mechanics of emphasis places in

reach. Decapitated mannequin
            takes a few steps.
Inherent strain. Unlocatable

Entrance at odds with address.
            Window glass
obscures the intended effect.
Ventilation furnished with keys.
            Thereafter fused,
heated to an improbable degree.

[from *1–10*, 1980]

from *Bad History*

The evident irritation expressed with a concept of event which does not measure up to its canons of evidence, the shock expressed at a practice whose interpretations refer to events which 'historically' may not have happened.... Imagine a practice of interpretation which prefers secondary sources, and unreliable witnesses!

—Mark Cousins, "The Practice
of Historical Investigation"

I

A bad event happened to me, but its having occurred became more complicated even in my thinking of it. Even if this event had happened only to me, it was only until recently available for retrospection; it had to be proved as taking place in every other event. Take the War for example; I no longer know for certain which war is meant. When people say, "After the war," I no longer know which war—there are three wars at least, each antedating, following, and confirming the others. It is always "the era between two wars." So there was a very long war before a period of time in which that war had just been over for a very long time—even though it took its place as immediately preceding that time. Then a very short war called that very long time into question because suddenly time became something that had happened to me—only happening so directly that I could say, "This war is different from that other war, or even from the long duration that followed it." All those times even now seem very much of a piece—as having taken place in order to guarantee each other, as part of an assertion of the reality of the first and only war. That war in which we certainly could not believe, because we meant not to believe in it. And consequently, for a long time, our having decided not to believe in that war returned to us willingly to confirm our disbelief. A bad event had happened to me, but I could not talk about it until recently. And when I did talk about it, there was a return to the sense that, in recognizing what I had chosen not to believe in as really having happened, I was responsible for disbelieving it all along. That war, which was very long, never seemed to be on the verge of ending. It was always on the verge of not ending, of giving more justification for there being no reason it should not continue indefinitely. And we had to agree with its assumptions, because they held in place our disbelief (which we willed). So we willed ourselves into a kind of suspension, until in a decisive moment an event occurred which was the collapse of that untenable state of always believing in the necessity of our disbelief. Because the war was an event of very long duration, a short event like the end of the war could only reinforce the effects of our having willed to cancel it out. Do you see what kind of effect this always willing a disbelief in what we did not want to continue had on us, when time pulled the rug from under our feet and the very long war started to end? So a separation and a caesura became the truth of any event—having happened in that state of suspension between our willing disbelief and need to know that it had happened (so we could continue our disbelief). Take the war, for instance—immediately it is unclear of which war I speak. I must mean the war that ended yesterday at 4 o'clock that Robert Creeley wrote about, and the subsequent tigers that sprang at him from imaginary jungles. In any case the war ended and it was a relief—I always doubted the extent to which Creeley could just by writing think that he could keep it going, even for the space of a lyric poem. Perhaps he really meant that other war, the one we won and that sent him around the world in a pacifying mission, a victory so reassuring in its scepticisms that the whole world was unleashed to reimagine its self-identifications. Think of Kwame Nkruma in Ghana. He could only have come to power after such a war. Think of Patrice Lumumba in Zaire—a case where all of that unleashed skepticism failed to provide any stable identity and history just began to drift as some overloaded barge down the interminable river. Creeley wasn't talking about Nkruma and Lumumba; Creeley was talking about some reassuring but freakish monstrosity that would rivet us in our seats, as in a Stephen King movie. But isn't it enough to have been responsible for one's own disbelief not to have to go out and bring in some sentimental figures to stand in for one's loss of control? We could make a game out of this. Something bad happened to me and I started thinking about it intensely in the period between two wars. Which one ended which? The former certainly was the condition of possibility of the latter, so that we knew that we would, in the end, go through with it. Each new war being the culmination of our old belief in the supersession of a new technology, so that time must pass before the technical conditions for a war can be reinvented. Only later did we find out that the success rate for Patriot missiles was only 6 percent. How can we so thoroughly be taught to disbelieve the evidence of our senses? Didn't I see an incoming missile come down through the sky from the vantage point of a TV crew in Dharan, Saudi Arabia? Most of the crew huddled in the basement while one cameraman tracked the outgoing Patriot to an explosion that was visible proof of its success? Segue to cheering workers at the missile plant in Massachusetts? To be reassured by lines of Patriots identified as "ours" brought in for the defense of Israel? Consider the etymology of invented words such as *Patriot* and *Scud—Scud* not an acronym for anything (like *SAM* is an acronym for "Surface-to-Air Missile") but a kind of media-initiated synthetic image that combines its self-evident scudding over the surface of the water toward a heat-blistered target with a racial characterizing of the kind of agent person it is—scum of the cracked earth spitting up to erupt over and come back to thud. To the same ground where we were sitting still and waiting for it? Creeley didn't want to think about that ground, so pleased he was with the spectacle of a disbelief that would call into question any criterion for an historical event. Imagine the shock we would express when encountering the report of an event that never happened, by an unreliable witness! Let's put an end to that and call it "the Vietnam Syndrome" as helicopters circle in around the Capitol Dome. A bad event happened to me and now I understand that it occurred only there and then. But it was the continuous, circling treadmill of its displacement for a very long time brought to a single image—obscured, interfered with, reprocessed at a third remove over remote-control channels of communicative links—that got me here to say this.

[1992]

John Ashbery

In Conversation
with David Herd

The interview took place in John Ashbery's New York apartment on Thursday, 17 February, 1994. We spoke for some three hours on a range of subjects. This is an edited transcript of the conversation.

David Herd: *Your poetry is associated with the city but frequently incorporates rural terms and references. Do you feel that the landscapes you encountered as a child have found a way into your poetry?*

John Ashbery: Yes. When I was very small I lived with my grandparents much of the time, in the city, in Rochester, New York, where my grandfather was professor at the university. But when I was seven years old he retired and left that house and moved to the country to a little village where he had grown up, on the edge of Lake Ontario. My parents lived a few miles away on a farm. I always felt a great nostalgia for living in the city, and for that house in particular and for the fact that there were lots of kids to play with, and when I was taken back to the farm I was really quite solitary and lonely for much of the time, except during the summer when I spent much of the time at my grandfather's house. The village was a summer resort and I had a lot of friends there; mostly children whose parents lived in Rochester. I enjoyed very much the lake and the countryside. Somehow the lake which was also close to where my parents lived, which I could see from my window, was a kind of soothing presence. And even though I wasn't very happy living at home, sometimes those landscapes do turn up in my poetry. I probably appreciate it more now than I did then.

So it was the fact of being alone that made the landscape important to you.

Well, it was not only that. I didn't get along with my father. My grandfather was very kind and a very learned man as well; my father was a farmer. He was a good person, but he had a very violent temper. It was mainly that. Also I didn't really have any friends in the local school. I was sort of an outcast because I liked poetry and art. It was very rural.

At what age was this?

From the age of about eight until sixteen. I went away to a private school in Massachusetts for my last year, but ended up staying there two years because they thought I was too young to go to college. I had skipped one grade when I was younger.

When did you first read poetry?

When I was small I had this children's encyclopedia called *The Book of Knowledge* which had a lot of poems in it, mostly Victorian narrative poems suitable for children. It was published in England in fact. So much of the poetry I read as a child came from there. Also my grandfather had the poems of Browning and Shelley, and other nineteenth-century poets.

The private school you mention was the Deerfield Academy wasn't it? Didn't you have poems published while you were there?

Yes. They actually appeared after I had left.

You were writing a lot while at Deerfield?

Quite a lot.

Was it a literary school?

No, not at all. It was a sort of jock, upper-class WASP school which I didn't fit into at all. But I did have a friend who wrote poetry, and he actually stole my poems and submitted them through a local poet, a minor Robert Frost type poet, who sent them on to *Poetry* magazine as his. Meanwhile, I had submitted some of the same poems to *Poetry* magazine and I got back a very curt reply. Then when the poems came out I thought they would think I had been plagiarizing and so I thought I would never be published in *Poetry*, which was about the only place to publish then.

In his recent biography of Frank O'Hara, Brad Gooch writes: 'At Harvard in the late 40s, among the young poets a civil war had developed between those who favored Yeats and those who favored Auden.' Were you aware of being involved in a civil war?

No. I don't remember anything of this sort going on, and a lot of that book is quite inaccurate. It has got very mixed reviews, although it seems to have done better than I would have expected since 'O'Hara' is not a household word, except in households that read poetry, which is not that many. I suppose it's successful because he somewhat distorted the picture of Frank putting in a lot of gossip and sex. In the case of the latter really it's not a very accurate picture of O'Hara. Passionately interested, as he was, in relationships, sex was an afterthought... I didn't know very many poets at Harvard. I was friendly with Kenneth Koch. I didn't get to know O'Hara till a month before I graduated from Harvard. We published his work in *The Advocate*, and I used to see him around college but he had a very sort of pugnacious or pugilistic look. He had a broken nose. He didn't look like a very cordial person. That of course turned out to be completely misleading.

While at Harvard you wrote your senior thesis on Auden. What sparked your interest in Auden?

Auden was the first modern poet I read, at the suggestion of woman professor of English at the University of Rochester, our neighbor over the summer. I found it very difficult, although now Auden's poetry seems very easy. But of course this was at a time before he had written his late poetry and besides the early poetry can be quite knotty. At any rate after a while I was completely smitten with his work and tended to write like him. I think he played a much more important role in my formation as a poet than other poets I have been associated with, such as Stevens, who I didn't read for a while. I found him too hard to understand. Of course after I got to know and like his poetry I was strongly influenced by him, but I think it is always the first literary crush that is the important one.

Have you remained more interested in the early rather than the late Auden?

Yes. I like "The Sea and the Mirror" which he wrote in America, but after that I began to lose interest.

Who else were you reading at this time?

The English poets of the thirties: Spender, Day Lewis, Thomas. One of my favorites was Nicholas Moore, who was very popular for a while but then kind of disappeared. F. T. Prince was also a favorite of mine. And among American poets I liked Marianne Moore, Elizabeth Bishop, Stevens, William Carlos Williams, Delmore Schwartz.

Shortly after leaving Harvard you went through a period of relative poetic inactivity. Why was that?

Well, it was very discouraging to get out of college and think about getting on with one's life, and then suddenly the Korean War came along and it looked as though I might be called up for it. In fact, I was called up for a medical examination but I managed to convince them that I was hopelessly insane. The everpresent McCarthy and his disciples was a very depressing feature of American life... I'm not sure if that was why I stopped writing or not. I have noticed a lot of people in their early twenties have a kind of reaction to the initial thrust and pause to wonder, 'What am I going to write about, what am I doing here?' It takes a while to reinvent sometimes. When I started writing again I was trying all kinds of things to see if they would work out.

When were the poems that made up the Some Trees *volume written?*

They were written at that time, but there were some of them that I wrote even when I was at Harvard. The title poem, and one called 'The Painter,' I wrote when I was still an undergraduate. The others I had written up until I was 26 or 27. I had lots more that I didn't use in that volume.

I wonder if we might talk a little about the associations and collaborations that constituted the so-called 'New York School.' In a letter to Jane Freilicher, O'Hara commented, 'you could fit the people I write for into your john, all at the same time without raising an eyebrow.' Was this reciprocal, were you also writing for O'Hara?

Well yes and also for Kenneth Koch and James Schuyler. We would get together and show each other our poems. We had no other audience at the time. I can't say that I wrote for him, although I did write hoping he would like what I had written. I didn't tailor them to what I thought he would like.

Did you have them in mind as readers?

Yes, I suppose so.

O'Hara's poem 'Memorial Day 1950' survives because you copied it out and sent it to Kenneth Koch...

Yes. Kenneth at that time was spending a year in France on a Fulbright. When I first met him he had decided that we were this circle of poetry of two people. He was very reluctant to admit that anybody else would qualify. What I was doing in the letter was saying that he really should take Frank's poetry more seriously. So I typed out several poems and sent them to him, which actually had the desired effect. He was converted to Frank's poetry. That was one I was particularly fond of. Frank was a year older than I, but he stayed on a year after me at Harvard because he had been in the Navy for two years in the war. I had gone up to visit him in Boston where he was spending the summer in a

419

friend's house. It was there that he showed me his recent poems.

You collaborated with Koch and Schuyler. Kenneth Koch has said that one of the reasons for collaborating was the fact of being so unrecognized, and of only having each other as an audience. Was that how you saw it?

If we had had an audience we probably wouldn't have written most of these things. It was a kind of game. There was also a feeling in the air about collaborations that it was a good thing to do because then you couldn't take sole credit for producing a work of art. This is still hanging around. We did them mainly for fun, never dreaming—since our own works were unknown and unpublishable at the time, and with which frankly we were just amusing ourselves—that our collaborations would ever see the light of day. Especially *A Nest of Ninnies*.

How did that come about?

Well, I was with Schuyler and we were driving back from Long Island to New York and in order to pass the time he said, 'How about we write a novel?' I said, 'So how do we do that?' and he said, 'Well you write the first line.' So I did and we continued to write alternate lines. Then we passed a house along the way; a typical American house where we decided we'd have the characters live. And then we'd get together and write it about once a week or so. But we never thought that it would be published. We suspended work on it during most of the time that I was in France except for one winter I spent in New York, '57-'58, when Schuyler and I roomed together. But we found that we couldn't do it by correspondence. We attempted that, but it didn't work out. We really had to be together. Then when I moved back, I had become known as a poet and my editor, as editors always do, said, 'Why don't you write a novel?' hoping to get back a little of their investment. He said, 'Did you ever try it?' And I remembered *A Nest of Ninnies* and said that Schuyler and I had been doing some work on this playful novel, but that it was really just a private joke. But he said, 'Oh no, it sounds interesting,' so when we started working on it very intensively; I think we'd only written about a third of it at that time.

You said that the feeling was abroad that collaboration was a good thing. Who was that coming from?

Probably from John Cage, although I can't think of any collaborations he did at the time. Later on I know he collaborated with a composer named Lejaren Hiller. But since he was collaborating with the I Ching he didn't take the credit for his music.

Paul Violi has written that the subject of collaborative art is its own occasion. Does that meet with your experience?

Probably in the poems that Kenneth Koch and I wrote together which had no other raison d'être other than our being in the same room together.

You also worked with Alex Katz.

That was not exactly a collaboration. I was still living in Paris and rather out of touch with what artists were doing over here. When I came over once I met Alex. I'd actually met him years before but never looked at his work. I thought it was very intriguing. At that time I was working on the poem 'Fragment' and I thought it would be interesting to do a book with Alex because his images were so concrete and this poem was turning out to be very abstract. So what happened was, when I finished the poem I then went back to see him again. He had done a number of gouaches in shades of grey and white, but they were themes he had taken from paintings he had already done. So I thought it would be interesting if he used a mix of pictures of scenes to illustrate the text, some that had no connection at all and some that might or might have had any connection, as a way of curtailing the abstractness of the poetry and the concreteness of the images.

You have suggested of Gertrude Stein's Paris experience that the foreign language that surrounded her was a necessary insulation in the writing of 'The Making of Americans.' How similar or different was your own experience of Paris?

I felt inhibited at first by not having my own language, by not hearing it spoken around me. Lots of my poems have their origin in what I hear people saying in the street in New York, in the American vernacular, which I guess is what American is. So I felt insulated not in a good sense, for quite a long time. It was not so much a question of not being able to understand French, which I did after a year or so, but not being able to use it. I still think French is much too clear a language for poetry. The exception to the rule being Rimbaud of course; I don't know how he managed to cloud the language the way he did and still keep to the rules of French.

Is American dirty then?

The English language in general lends itself to chiaroscuro in a way that French doesn't.

Were you happy in Paris?

I was very happy in Paris. I would have liked to have been able to visit America, but I didn't have enough money to do so. I was quite poor at the time I was living there. My parents were unhappy about my staying there, and would have paid my passage home, but not my return. Finally, there was a period of five years when I didn't go back at all and much as I enjoyed my life there, I was feeling that I would like to see New York, see my parents, my friends. So actually Jane Freilicher sent me money to buy a ticket and that was the first time I went home in five years.

During this period you were producing cut-up poems: cutting up magazines and newspapers...

Yes. I used to buy American magazines in Paris, things like *Esquire* and *Life*. Those were the ones I cut up. I didn't actually cut them up but looked at them and picked lines at random. It helped me at the time to get over my writer's block but I don't feel that those poems were successful. They were successful in helping me to move on to something else which was really all I expected. I didn't think I would ever have another book published after the lack of success of the first one and it was John Hollander whom I had never met, who liked *Some Trees* and wrote to me asking me to submit to the Wesleyan University Press. So I put in what I had, including a lot of poems I probably would have left out if I had had enough that I liked better.

The L=A=N=G=U=A=G=E poets have championed your early work, citing The Tennis Court Oath *as a key influence on their practice. Do you feel any affinity with L=A=N=G=U=A=G=E poetry?*

I like some of them. I have always liked Clark Coolidge's work, although he was around long before there was such a thing as L=A=N=G=U=A=G=E poetry and is wont to way that he doesn't consider himself to be a part of it, but I don't think he minds the added attention. I like Leslie Scalapino's work very much; much of Charles Bernstein's work. And then there are a lot of people who seem to be on the fringe of L=A=N=G=U=A=G=E poetry, like Anne Lauterbach and Stephen Ratcliffe. And I think in the same way that surrealism was more effective as it's become more diluted and appeared in more unexpected places, so L=A=N=G=U=A=G=E poetry will probably develop in unexpected ways.

Were you enclosing the poems that went to make up The Tennis Court Oath *in letters home, and were you receiving comments and criticisms in return?*

Well, I never seemed to get enough. Actually Frank and Kenneth praised those poems, but I was never quite sure whether they were doing that just because we were pals.

Who were you reading when you were in Paris?

I was reading French poets, particularly the poets of the Pléiade, and
Maurice Scève. Also nineteenth-century French poetry and the surrealists
once I became proficent enough to be able to read them: Max Jacob,
Breton, Eluard, Reverdy. And Raymond Roussel. When I had come back
to spend the winter of '57 and '58 in New York I took some graduate
courses in French at New York University with the idea of going back
to France and doing a dissertation on Raymond Roussel and I was able
to persuade my parents to finance this. So then in the summer of '58 I
went back. I read all of Roussel and did quite a lot of research, which
was rather fun because no one had really done any before. He was
completely neglected. People thought I was crazy to be interested in him
but it worked to my advantage in the case of his surviving heir, his
nephew, who had always refused to speak to anybody about his uncle,
who was the black sheep of the family. But since I was American he
fancied that he might be able to make some money from him and his first
question was, did I think his uncle's work might be as successful as
Françoise Sagan's, and I assured him that this would be possible. So he
was helpful, although he had no papers or anything really, except a
family photograph album.

Do you count Roussel as an influence?

For a long time I thought that I wasn't influenced by him, though I was
perhaps more interested in him than in any other writer. He boasted that
there was absolutely nothing real in his work, that everything was completely invented. I think that perhaps could be said of my work as well.
I have never used his famous procedure. I can't think of an example of
how I have been directly influenced by him, although one occurred to me
not long ago, but now I can't remember it.

Is 'The Instruction Manual' an example perhaps?

Oh, actually that is true. I wrote that before I went to France when I still didn't read French very well, but just glancing at the poem *La Vue* (it was actually Kenneth who discovered Roussel and brought the poems back) I could figure out what he was doing in the poem and I did in fact get the idea of writing the poem from Roussel. It was one of the last poems in the book, a rather paint-by-numbers poem written in '55 just before I submitted the manuscript.

You have said that at the time of writing The Tennis Court Oath *you felt the reader had turned his back on you. When do you feel the reader came back to you?*

Not until *Rivers and Moutains* which got somewhat more attention. I think *The Double Dream of Spring* was perhaps the first book of mine that seemed to register with the audience for poetry. I think one is rewarded for just hanging around long enough and perhaps it was a more substantial piece of work. A lot of people liked 'The Skaters' from *Rivers and Mountains*. I received an award that year, or the following year, from the American National Institute of Arts and Letters, and they specifically cited 'The Skaters.'

In the poetry you wrote during the late sixties and early seventies, I'm thinking in particular of The Double Dream of Spring *and* Three Poems, *you seemed to make considerable use of the political idiom. What was your interest in this idiom?*

I'm interested in all kinds of idioms, or rather in tones of voice; or one might say discourse (a word that should be banished from the language). I don't think that any subject ought to be excluded a priori from poetry, and politics is one of them. Politics is something we think about and talk about, so it gets into my poetry. But with few exceptions political poetry has the effect of turning me off. Whereas unpolitical poetry, if it is good, makes one want to behave politically and on other levels as well. Usually political poetry is preaching to the converted, since the only people who are going to read it are probably going to be already convinced that war is bad and capitalism is evil. Senators and presidents will probably not come into contact with it. So it will mainly serve to enhance the political wholesomeness of the writer.

Your poetry is often described as philosophical, in mood at least. Does that term seem appropriate?

No. I took a beginning course in philosophy and did miserably in it. I've never been able to understand the language of philosophy. The professor was always stressing the importance of a clear and distinct idea, and I never could determine what that was. I suppose I'm a kind of bricoleur as far as philosophy goes.

Your poetry has given extended attention to the problems of subjectivity and self-expression, most famously of course in Self-Portrait in a Convex Mirror. *Recently, however, the 'I' has, on occasion, seemed a less problematic pronoun for you. For instance the seventh part of 'And the Stars Were Shining' opens with the remark, 'Rummaging through some old poems / for ideas—surely I must have had some / once?' This would seem to be you speaking?*

Yes, it is and there are some other examples too, like 'my own shoes have scarred the walk I've taken.' But I'm not aware of these things until after I've written them. I don't sit down and think, now I'm going to write about 'I' and really mean me. It's only, well sometimes a long time afterwards that I sense that I was talking of myself rather than through a persona.

Is editing an important part of the poetic process for you?

That question is often asked of me by students because they are encouraged to edit their poetry as much as possible. I did when I was young but as I'm older I have done it less and less, probably because I have grown

426

more practiced at writing poetry. What I usually do is when I have finished writing a poem I go over it once or twice and make what changes I think seem necessary and then I put it away, and then eventually I type up a final version which is usually unchanged. If I write something I don't like I tend to discard it. Rather than try to improve on it I write something else.

Much of the pleasure and uncertainty of your poetry is, for me, generated at the line-break. Is the location of the line-break particularly important for you?

Yes, it is. Sometimes, especially when I'm writing a long poem, I get really intoxicated by the idea of the line break. It's exciting to see where it will happen, or where I will unconsciously make it happen. I always used to get bored listening to painters talk about the edge, as they are wont to do. But I sort of see it now. The line break is something of the same importance; it has a mysterious thrill. In one of my poems in *And the Stars Were Shining* I broke the line in the middle of back-scratcher; 'the back- / scratcher vendors.' I was wondering why I did this, but it seemed to have something with the gesture of scratching your back with a back-scratcher.

Have you sensed, over the years, a difference between your American and your British audiences?

Well, lately I've wondered if any of my poems suit a British readership. The reviews I have received in England have been negative. There was a sort of brief honeymoon with the British press. I think that one problem is that the British always expect American writers to be certifiably American and I don't think my poetry is. Although on the other hand it does use American language and subject matter, but it is also influenced by English poetry which I think on the whole is less imaginative than English poetry before the war. Then the most brilliant poet was obviously Auden, and it was the early experimental Auden. After the war it was Larkin. A similar thing actually had happened in the United States when Lowell came to prominence at the same time as Larkin, and the kind of dreamlike more imaginative poetry of the thirties such as that of Delmore Schwartz and Randall Jarrell was replaced by their later work, and by Lowell and confessional poetry... In America the reviews have been pretty evenly divided between negative and positive. With *Flow Chart* there were a number of enthusiastic reviews. Helen Vendler reviewed it in a long piece in *The New Yorker* which is one of my favorite reviews of me that I have seen. It seemed to me that at one point I was more esteemed in England than I was here, but now it's the other way round. In fact, poetry doesn't get reviewed much over here, much less than in England. I have to subscribe to the *TLS* to find out about what books are being published in America. The *New York Times* Book Review is allied with the book industry and they almost never review poetry. About once every four months, perhaps, they will have a club-sandwich review of three poets and that's it. In fact I've just added my name to a list of writers who are protesting this situation. Not that it will be having any effect because the *Times* seems to be going more and more in the direction of 'dumbing down' as we call it. And for that matter the *New York Review of Books* hardly ever reviews poetry either. So there you have the two major outlets for book reviews, unless you count *Publishers' Weekly*. I usually get a nice review there, but nobody ever sees it. But I don't think it really matters very much in America whether something has been reviewed or not. People who want to read poetry will find out about it, and others won't.

Does it puzzle you that your poetry seems to alienate reviewers?

I can understand how it would puzzle and mystify readers. Especially readers who had neglected to read the modernist poets of this century. But I am puzzled that it makes people so angry; the 'Oh, not another book by him, again' attitude. I've noticed that critics get very annoyed if they have settled your hash, and then you have the temerity to publish

428

another book, despite what they thought of the last one. I don't want to discourage readers. I suppose I try to write from the point of view of the unconscious mind of 'l'homme or femme moyen sensuel,' but perhaps this creature has no unconscious. My early work which completely mystified people is now accepted as rather traditional, and my later work is criticized in relation to it. I think it is also a question of something being around long enough. I remember when I was young Stevens was a highly controversial poet but I don't think he is anymore.

You said earlier that you felt that British poetry is less imaginative than it was before the war. Are there any contemporary British poets you would choose to read?

Well let's see. W. S. Graham, Lee Harwood, Peter Didsbury, Peter Robinson. Another is Anthony Howell and some of the poets who are his friends: John Welsh, Deborah Evans. Another is Mark Ford. He is somebody whose poetry I read when I am trying to put myself in the mood for writing poetry. It is playful and improvisational, it doesn't preach. It doesn't have any political content, which is a good thing. And it's funny, and mysterious, and melancholy.

Do you sense your influence on his poetry?

No not really. It's more in the same hemisphere as my poetry, in the sense that it's improvisational, and non-didactic. But I don't see much resemblance.

Inclusive as it is your poetry has been described as accommodating, and you have continued to be interested in types of accommodation. Recently, for instance, you, and for that matter Kenneth Koch, took a hotel as a title for your book. What attracted you to the image of the hotel?

We didn't know about each other's plans for these titles. But suddenly a whole raft of books appeared called hotel this or that. Actually hotels have always been popular as book titles, *The Haunted Hotel* by Wilkie

Collins, for example, and Elizabeth Bowen's *The Hotel*, and of course *Grand Hotel*. Anyway, there is something very attractive about a hotel because it has got so many rooms, and so many different kinds of people doing different things. In my case I wrote the poem 'Hotel Lautréamont' because I found a photograph of Lautréamont. I think I'd never seen one before, it may well be the only photograph of him. I misplaced it too; I cut it out of a magazine. He seemed to be in a hotel room, and of course he lived in small hotels during his brief career, and the photograph of him kind of haunted me. And of course Joseph Cornell did a series of boxes called hotels. And the fact that his collage, which I chose for the book jacket, seemed to be looking out of a window—or into a window, you can't tell which—had a hotel-like feel. And then I thought of the four sections of four stanzas each as being like four floors of a hotel, like the boxes behind the desk where the keys are hung. I've always been fascinated by the idea of houses, and I think hotels would come under the same general category. Especially houses in America in older parts of cities. They seem to have a commanding presence somehow. They're telling you something.

In 'Ghost Riders of the Moon' in And the Stars Were Shining, *you write: 'We collected / them after all for their unique / indifference to each other and to the circus / that houses us all, and for their collectability.' Do you think there is any sense in which your poetry is engaged in the act of collecting?*

Yes, I think it is a kind of cabinet of curios. Collectability is a relatively recent concept, I think. A collectable is something that doesn't have the same status of an antique, yet. But people collect them for mysterious reasons. In 'The Skaters' there is a part about collecting. I collect a lot of things, including the vomit bags from airplanes; unused. I did it because I thought, 'I never heard of anyone collecting these.' People collect matchbooks, which are gradually disappearing, but not these. I did it because I was trying to have something that nobody else collected. I already had this idea a number of years ago when I started collecting aquarium ornaments: chests of treasure, and sunken ships, and pagodas. Then I discovered shortly afterwards that these had become the latest collectable.

So you were ahead of the trend.

Yes; as always.

Your poetry takes a pleasure in listing, which seems to be a collector's habit.

Yes. That's probably a Rousselian trait, although I think I did it before I became aware of his lists, which are principally in *Nouvelles Impressions d'Afrique*, which I wasn't able to read for a long time. There's an anthology of list poems in England, and I'm in it. It's fun to make lists. Whitman of course was someone who liked to do that, and that's one of the reasons I like his poetry. That anthology has a couple of lists of mine in it, including one from 'Daffy Duck in Hollywood' which they title 'An American Evening.'

How important has New York been as an occasion and setting for your poetry?

It certainly isn't in the Frank O'Hara sense. I find it a good place to write poetry in because it is such a large space. There is not too much to distract the eye, and yet there are many tall buildings which are always drawing one's mind upwards, perhaps to a spiritual realm, perhaps not. It's sort of a benignly neutral place to write in. Everything one needs can be found here. People are always passing through. One's friends, one's books, one's toys are all here. And it's always changing. Just in the years that I have lived in New York it's changed enormously. When I was first here the Third Avenue elevated railroad went up Third Avenue, and as a result nobody wanted to live there and there were cheap tenements and rowhouses, and then after that was torn down it became a hot piece of real-estate, and now there are skyscrapers. People are always bemoaning the fact that everything in New York is so transitory, and in Europe they care for their monuments. Which is true and it's unfortunate also that they don't do it here, but on the other hand that's the way life is, and poetry has to keep changing. It must change, according to Wallace Stevens. It's a sort of disposable environment... I think if I lived in Europe I would be too much in awe of the history that had gone before me. Of course people tend to see that as a fatal flaw in America, but the artist Joan Mitchell once said 'I don't want to have to look at a thirteenth-century church every day' and I can sort of see what she meant. Although of course she spent most of her adult life in France.

Wooden Buildings

The tests are good. You need a million of them.
You'd die laughing as I write to you
Through leaves and articulations, yes, laughing
Myself silly too. The funniest little thing...

That's how it all began. Looking back on it,
I wonder now if it could have been on some day
Findable in an old calendar? But no,
It wasn't out of history, but inside it.
That's the thing. On whatever day we came
To a small house built just above the water,
You had to step over to see inside the attic window.
Someone had judged the height to be just right
The way the light came in, and they are
Giving that party, to turn on that dishwasher
And we may be led, then, upward through more
Powerful forms of poetry, past columns
With peeling posters on them, to the country of indifference.
Meanwhile if the swell diapasons, blooms
Unhappily and too soon, the little people are nonetheless real.

And *Ut Pictura Poesis* Is Her Name

You can't say it that way any more.
Bothered about beauty you have to
Come out into the open, into a clearing,
And rest. Certainly whatever funny happens to you
Is OK. To demand more than this would be strange
Of you, you who have so many lovers,
People who look up to you and are willing
To do things for you, but you think
It's not right, that if they really knew you...
So much for self-analysis. Now,
About what to put in your poem-painting:
Flowers are always nice, particularly delphinium.
Names of boys you once knew and their sleds,
Skyrockets are good—do they still exist?
There are a lot of other things of the same quality
As those I've mentioned. Now one must
Find a few important words, and a lot of low-keyed,
Dull-sounding ones. She approached me
About buying her desk. Suddenly the street was
Bananas and the clangor of Japanese instruments.
Humdrum testaments were scattered around. His head
Locked into mine. We were a seesaw. Something
Ought to be written about how this affects
You when you write poetry:
The extreme austerity of an almost empty mind
Colliding with the lush, Rousseau-like foliage of its desire to
    communicate
Something between breaths, if only for the sake
Of others and their desire to understand you and desert you
For other centers of communication, so that understanding
May begin, and in doing so be undone.

What is Poetry

The medieval town, with frieze
Of boy scouts from Nagoya? The snow

That came when we wanted it to snow?
Beautiful images? Trying to avoid

Ideas, as in this poem? But we
Go back to them as to a wife, leaving

The mistress we desire? Now they
Will have to believe it

As we believe it. In school
All the thought got combed out:

What was left was like a field.
Shut your eyes, and you can feel it for miles around.

Now open them on a thin vertical path.
It might give us—what?—some flowers soon?

Contributors Notes

Peter Baker is the author of *Obdurate Brilliance: Exteriority and the Modern Long Poem* (1991) and *Deconstruction and the Ethical Turn* (1995). He is Professor of English at Towson State University in Maryland.

Bernadette Mayer is the author of *The Bernadette Mayer Reader* (1992) and *The Desires of Mothers to Please Others in Letters* (1994), among many other books. She lives in New York City.

Lyn Hejinian is the author of *My Life* (1980, 1987), *The Cell* (1992), and *The Cold of Poetry* (1994), among many other books. She is the co-editor, with Barrett Watten, of *Poetics Journal*. She teaches at New College in San Francisco.

Charles Bernstein is the author of *Rough Trades* (1991) and *Dark City* (1994), among many other books, as well as *Content's Dream: Essays 1975-1984* (1986) and *A Poetics* (1992). He is David Gray Professor of Poetry and Letters in the Poetics Program at the University of Buffalo, State University of New York.

Rosmarie Waldrop is the author of *A Form/ Of Taking/ It All* (1990) and *A Key Into the Language of America* (1995), among many other books. She lives in Providence and, with Keith Waldrop, edits Burning Deck Press.

Harry Mathews has been a member of OULIPO for twenty-four years. He is the author of *Armenian Papers: Selected Poems 1954-1984* (1987) and *A Mid-Season Sky: Poems 1954-1991* (1992), among many other books. He lives in Paris and Key West.

David Bergman is the author of *Cracking the Code* (1987) and *The Care and Treatment of Pain* (1994), as well as *Gaiety Transfigured: Gay Self-Representation in American Literature* (1991). He is Professor of English at Towson State University.

John Taggart is the author of *Loop* (1991) and *Standing Wave* (1993), as well as *Remaining in Light* (on Edward Hopper, 1993) and

Songs of Degrees: Essays on Contemporary Poetry and Poetics (1994). He is Professor of English at Shippensburg University in Pennsylvania.

Rachel Blau DuPlessis is the author of *Tabula Rosa* (1987) and *Drafts 3-14* (1991), as well as *H. D.: The Career of That Struggle* (1986) and *The Pink Guitar: Writing as Feminist Practice* (1990). She is Professor of English at Temple University.

C. D. Wright is the author of *Further Adventures With You* (1986), *String Light* (1991), and *Just Whistle* (1993), among other books. She teaches in the Writing Program at Brown University and, with Forrest Gander, edits Lost Roads Publishers.

Albert Cook is the author of more than twenty books, including, most recently, *Canons and Wisdoms* (1993) and *The Reach of Poetry* (1995). His recent books of poetry include *Affability Blues* (1993) and *Modes* (1993). He is Ford Foundation Professor (Emeritus) of Comparative Literature, English, and Classics at Brown University.

Robert Creeley's *Collected Poems*, *Selected Poems, Collected Prose* and *Collected Essays* are published by University of California Press. His recent books include *Windows* (1990) and *Echoes* (1994). He is Samuel P. Capen Professor of Poetry and Humanities at the University of Buffalo, State University of New York.

Stephen Rodefer is the author of *Four Lectures* (1982), *Emergency Measures* (1987), *Passing Duration* (1991) and *Erasers* (1994), among many other books. He lives in Paris.

Clark Coolidge is the author of more than twenty books of poetry, including, recently, *The Crystal Text* (1986), *At Egypt* (1988), *The Book of During* (1991), *Odes of Roba* (1991) and *The Rova Improvisations* (1994). He lives in the Berkshires.

Michael Palmer is the author of many books of poetry, including *First Figure* (1984), *Sun* (1988) and *At Passages* (1995). He is also the editor of *Code of Signals: Recent Writings in Poetics* (1983). He lives in San Francisco.

Joan Retallack is the author of *Circumstantial Evidence* (1985), *Errata 5uite* (1993), and *Afterrimages* (1995), as well as *Musicage: Cage Muses on Words, Art and Music (John Cage in Conversation with Joan Retallack)* (1996). She teaches in the Honors Program at the University of Maryland.

Nicole Brossard has published over twenty books of poetry, including, recently, *A Tout regard* (1989) and *Langues obscures* (1992). She has also published several novels, most recently *Le Désert mauve* (1987) and *Baroque d'aube* (1995). Many of these works are available in English translation, including *Mauve Desert* (1990) and *Picture Theory* (1991). She lives near Montréal.

Carolyn Forché is the author of several books of poetry, including most recently, *The Angel of History* (1994). She is also the editor of *Against Forgetting: Twentieth-Century Poetry of Witness* (1993). She lives in Maryland and is the director of the Poetry Program at George Mason University.

Bob Perelman is the author of many books of poetry, including *The First World* (1986), *Face Value* (1988), *Virtual Reality* (1993), as well as *The Trouble with Genius: Reading Pound, Joyce, Stein and Zukofsky* (1994). He teaches in the English Department at the University of Pennsylvania.

Barrett Watten is the author of many books of poetry, including *Progress* (1985), *Conduit* (1988) and *Under Erasure* (1991), as well as *Total Syntax* (1985). He teaches American Studies at Wayne State University in Detroit.

John Ashbery is the author of numerous books of poetry, including, most recently, *Flow Chart* (1991), *Hotel Lautréamont* (1992), *And the Stars Were Shining* (1994) and *Can You Hear, Bird* (1995). He is Charles P. Stevenson Professor of Languages and Literature at Bard College.